Our Twentieth Century Wilderness Adventure

A color-photo essay about pioneering on the Last Frontier just before cell-phones were invented.

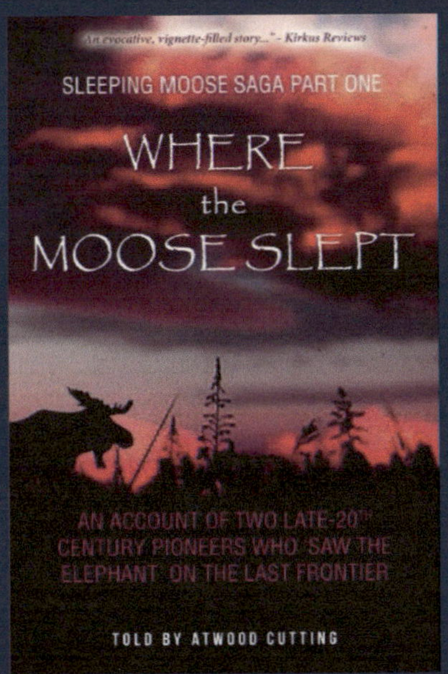

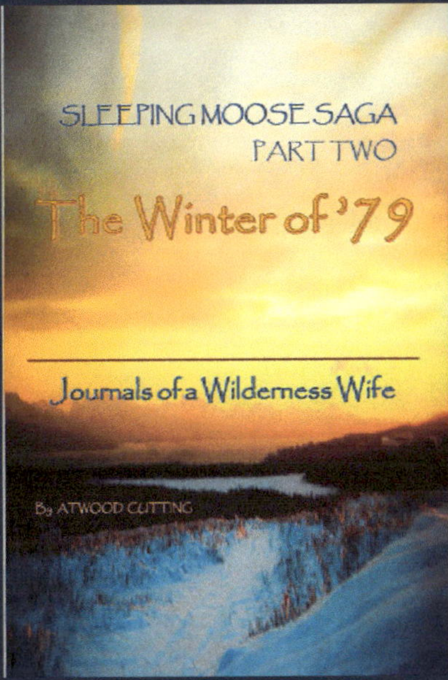

Bringing to life parts one and two of
"Sleeping Moose Saga"

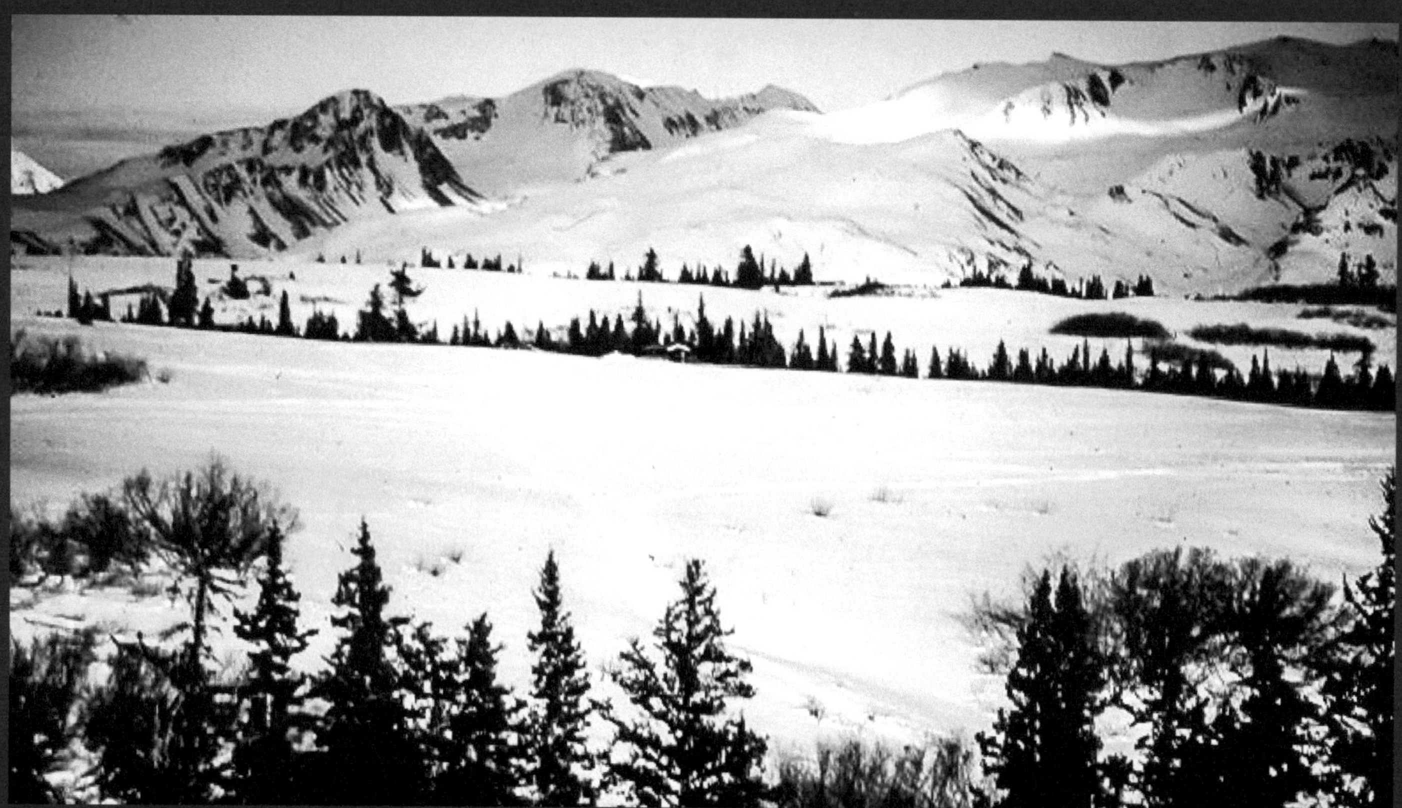

Our Twentieth Century Wilderness Adventure

by Atwood Cutting

—with first person commentary by Kate Peters—

Copyright 2018 by Echo Hill Arts Press
ISBN 13: 978-0999561-7-2

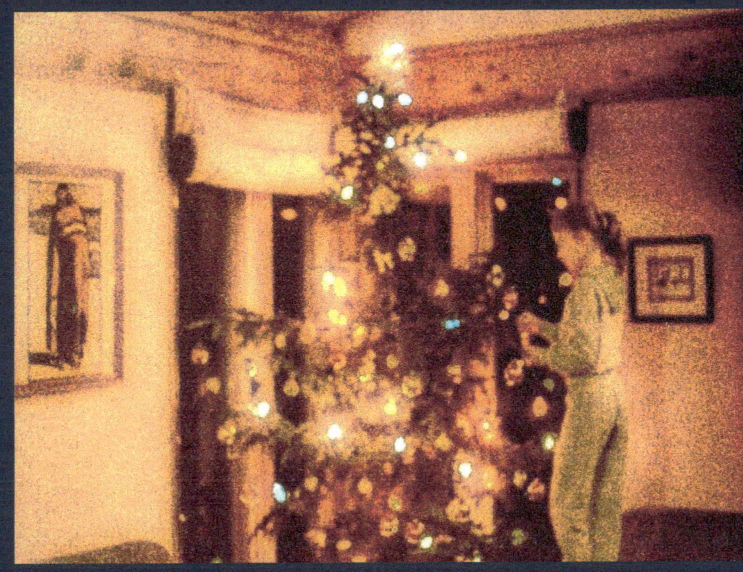
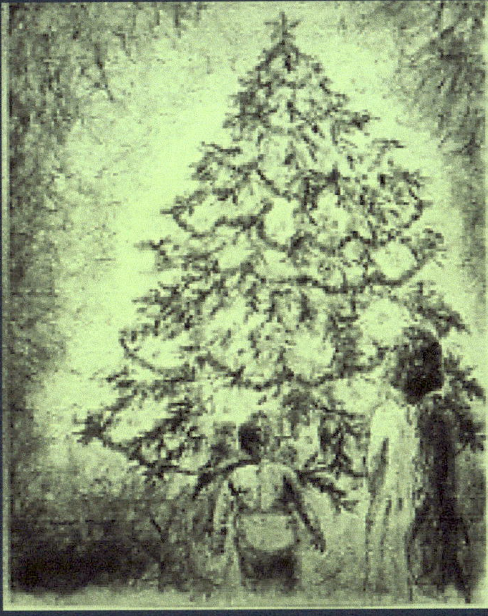
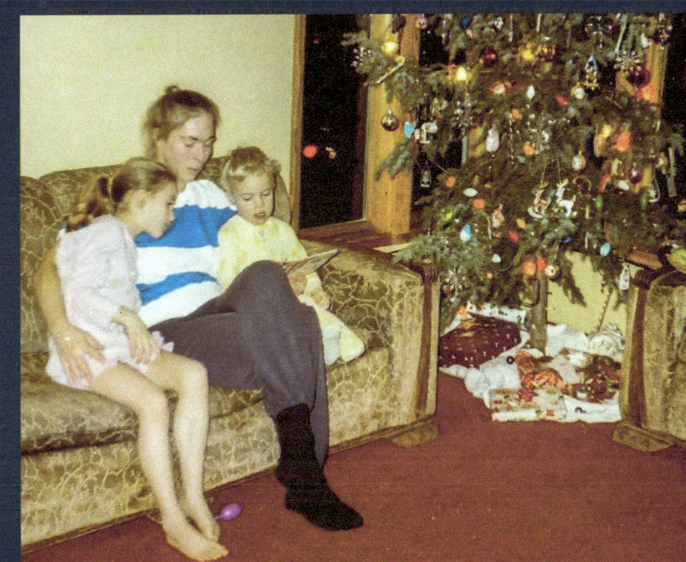
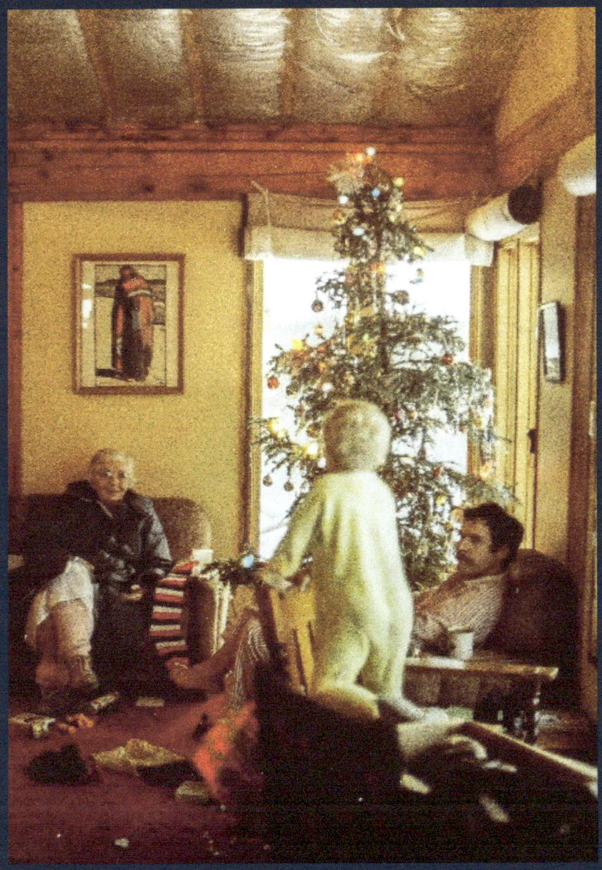
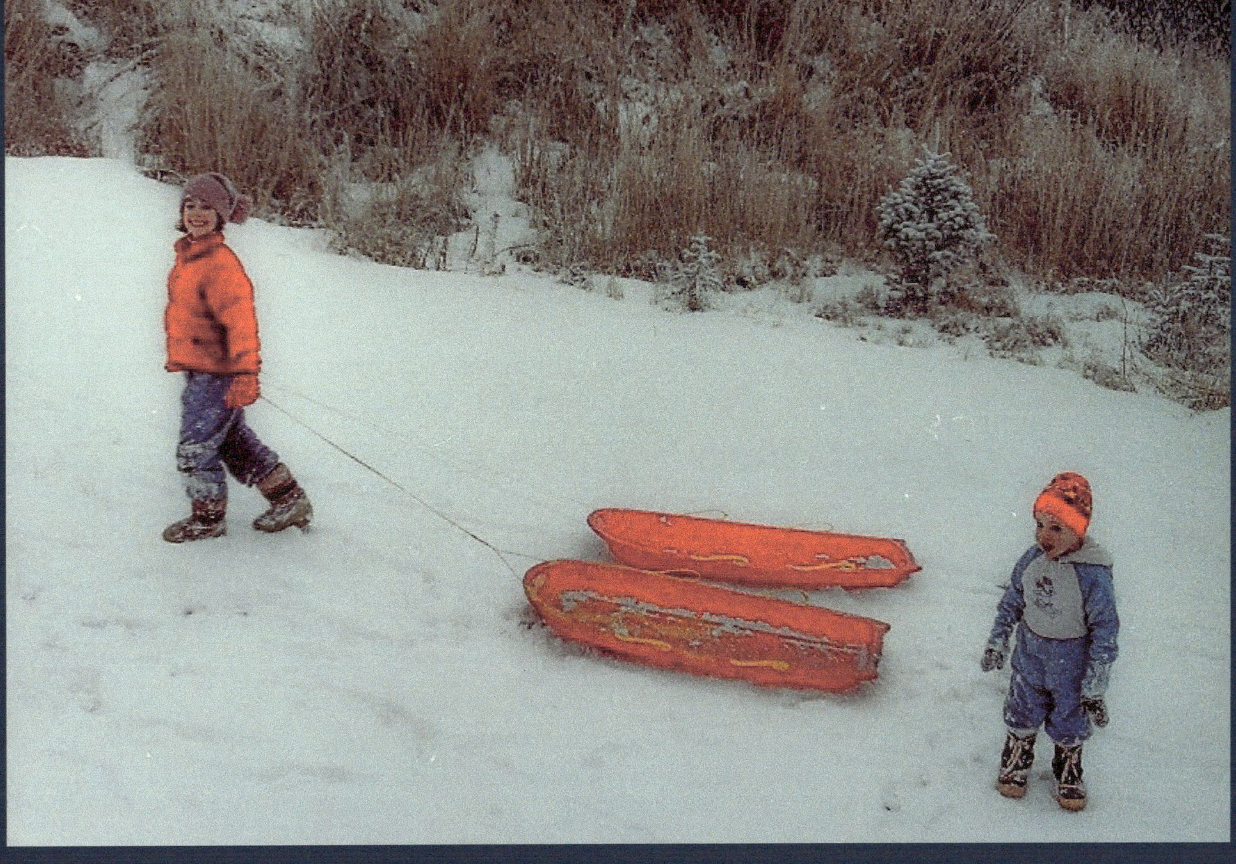

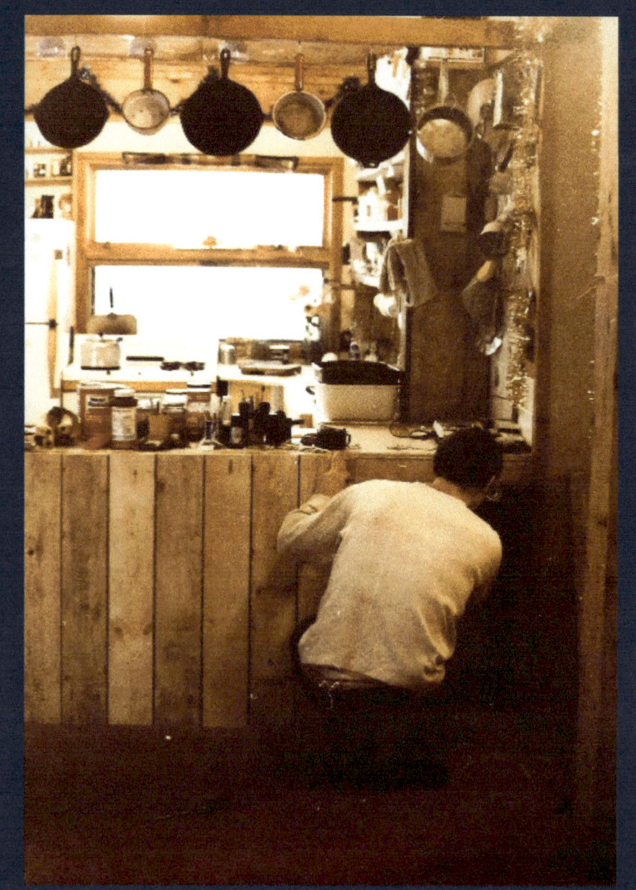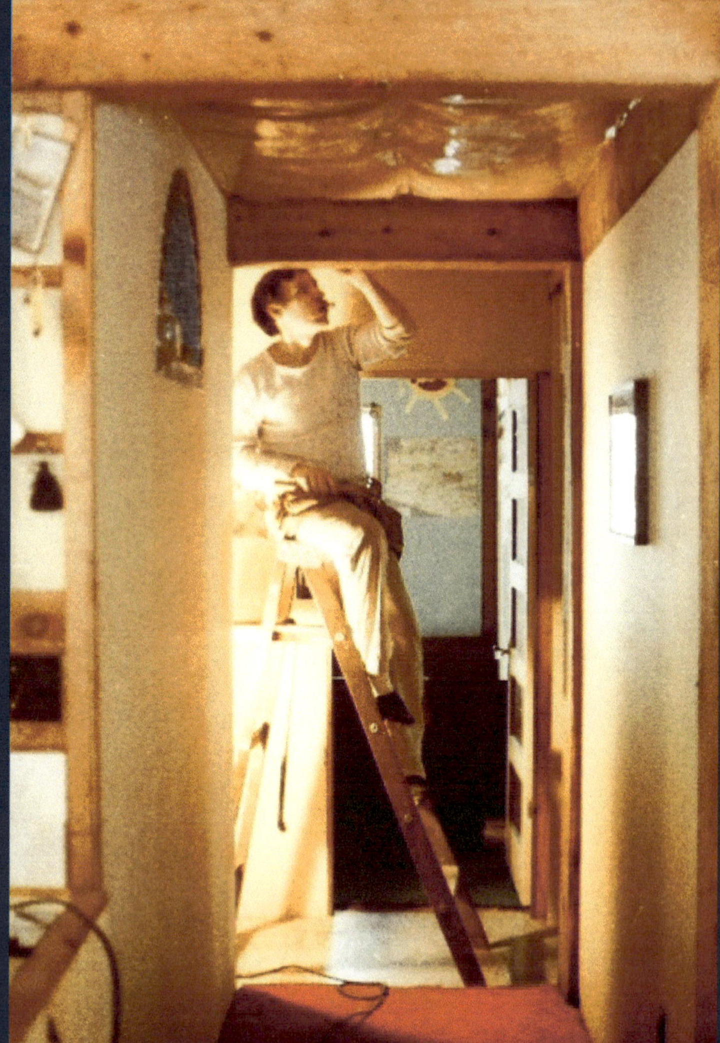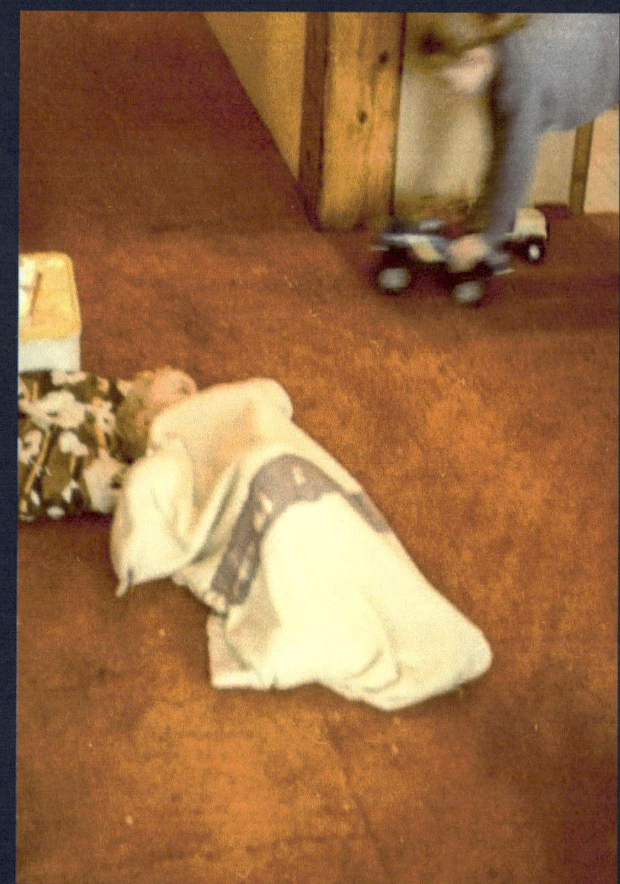

How came we to this **mountain peak** moment?

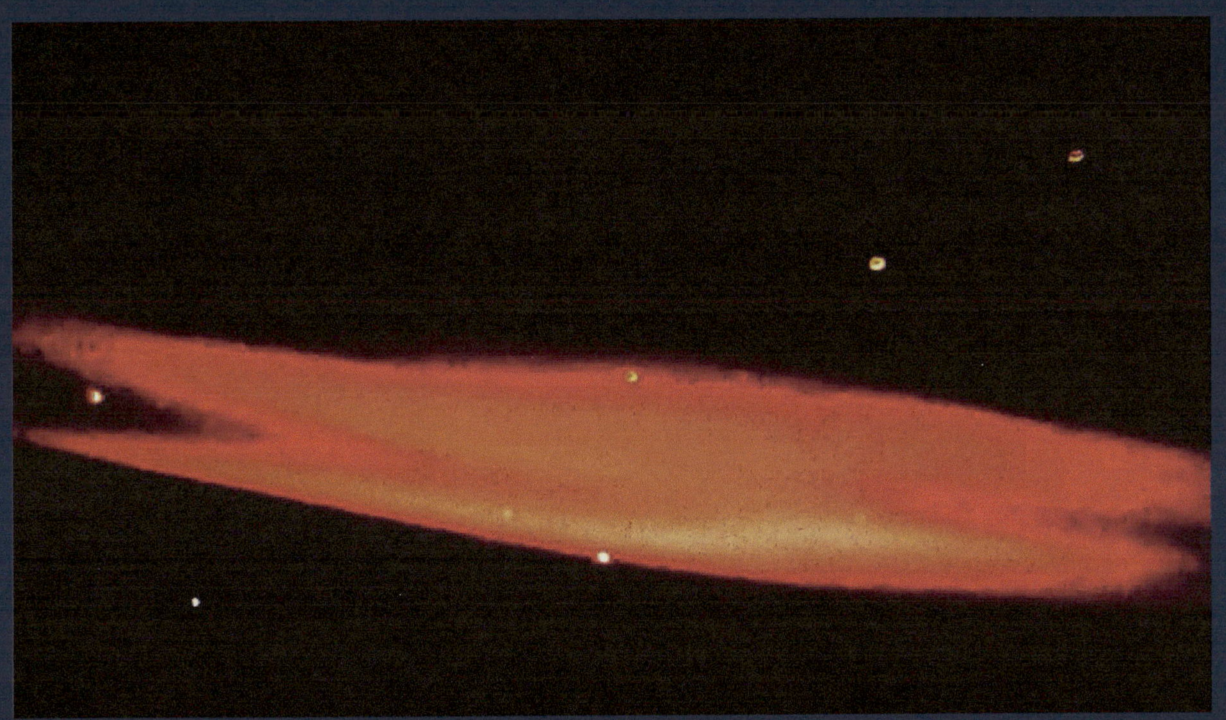

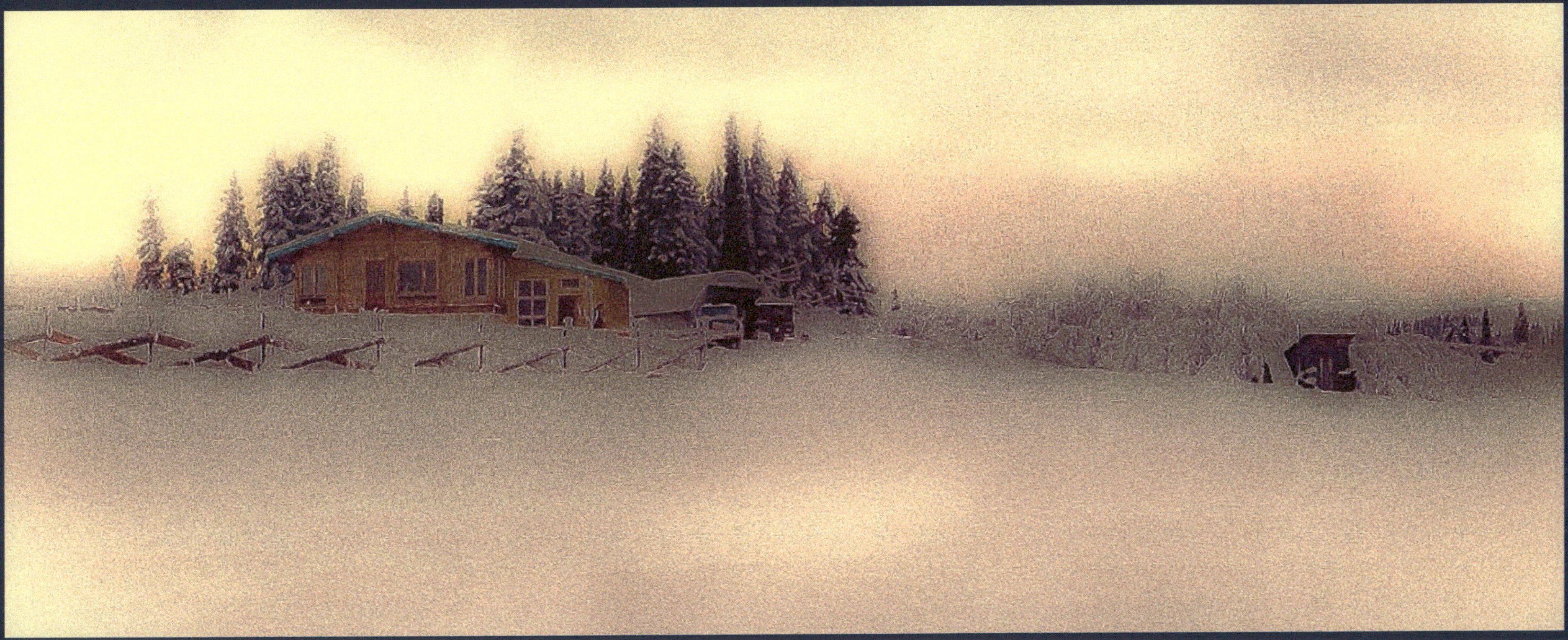

Where in this world can one find Camelot?

We met in Fairbanks, Alaska.
I had come to see snow.

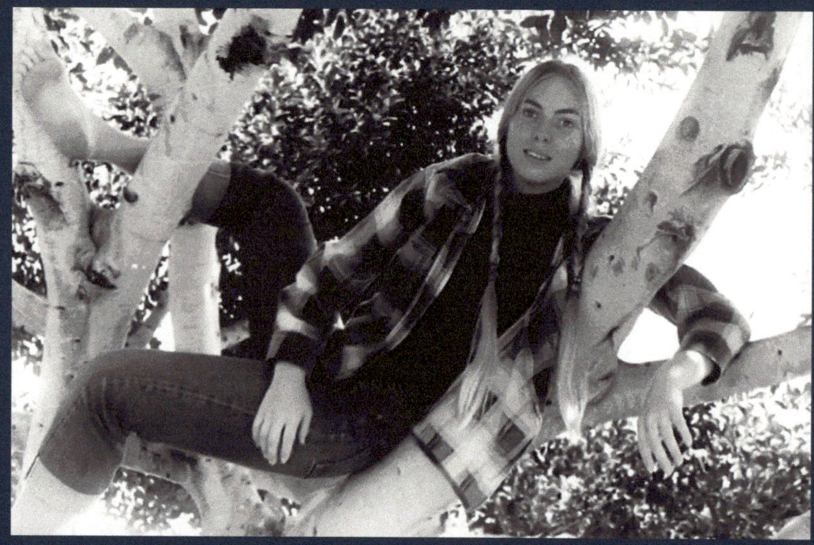

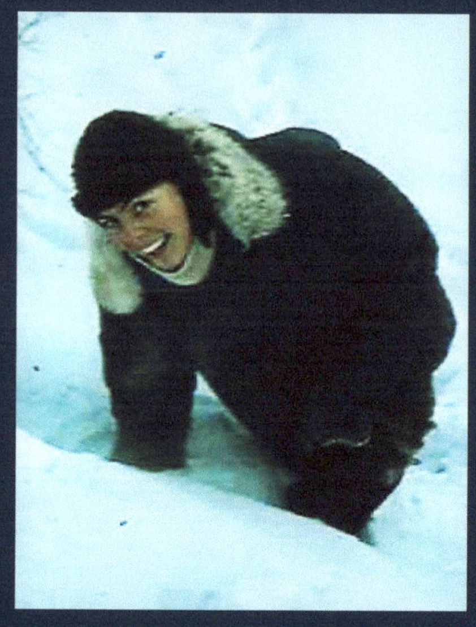

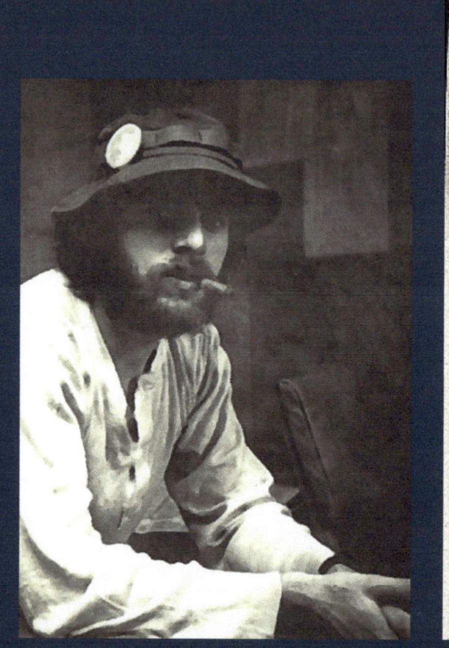

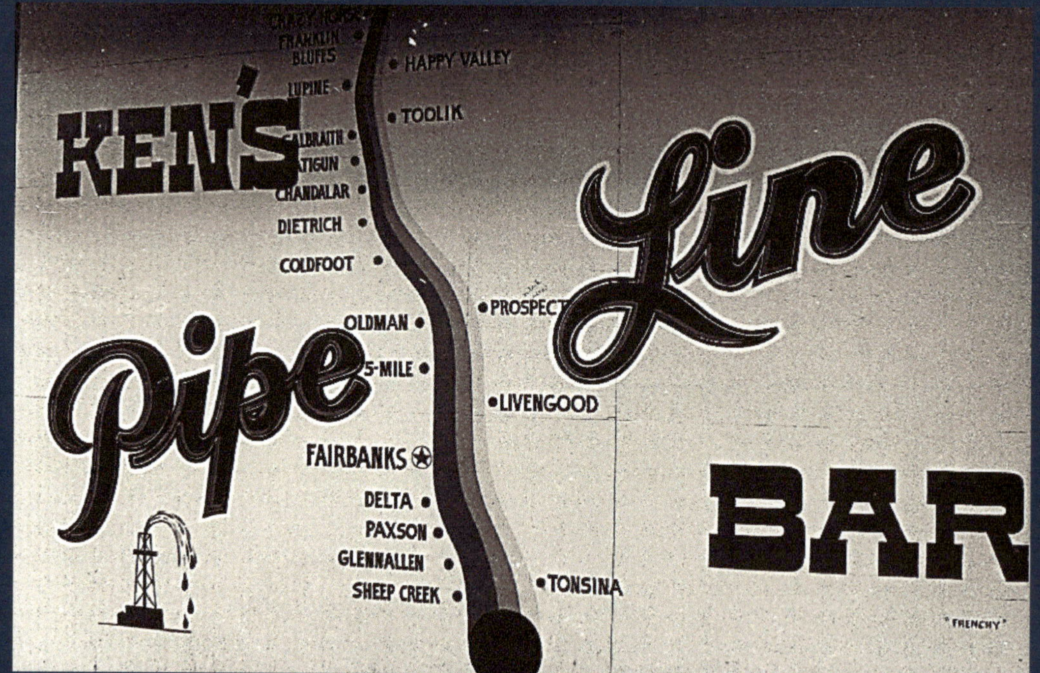

Tim was answering the "call of the wild."

As two young, strong adventurers
we built up a "nest egg" working on the Trans-Alaska Pipeline.
It was the "Gold Rush" of our time.

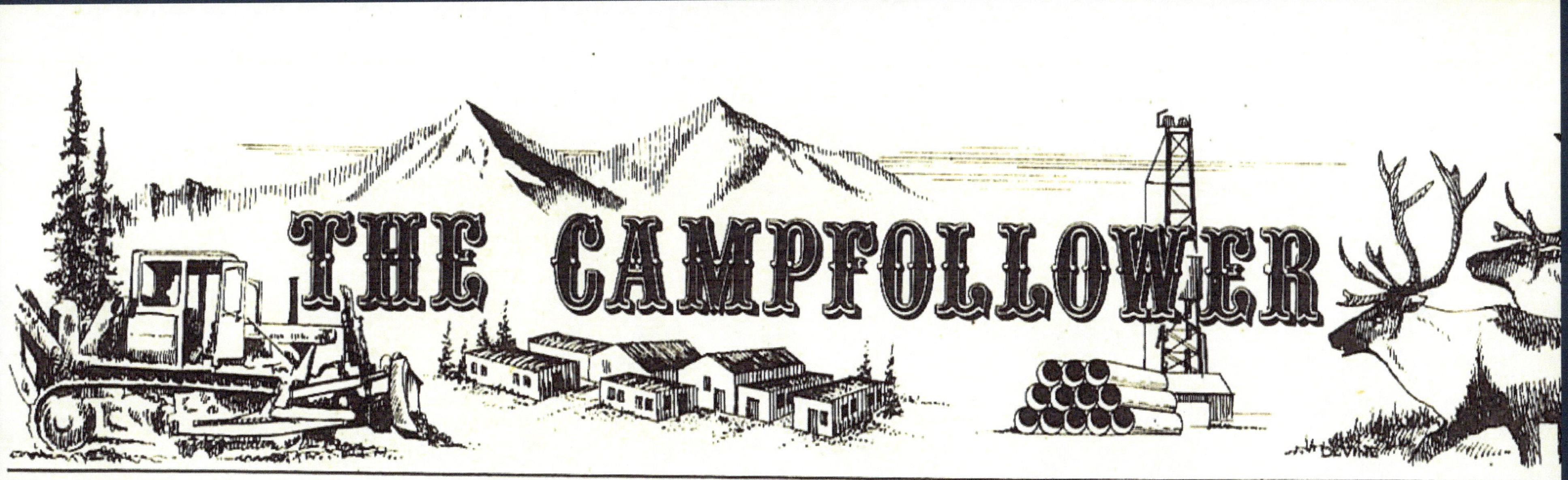

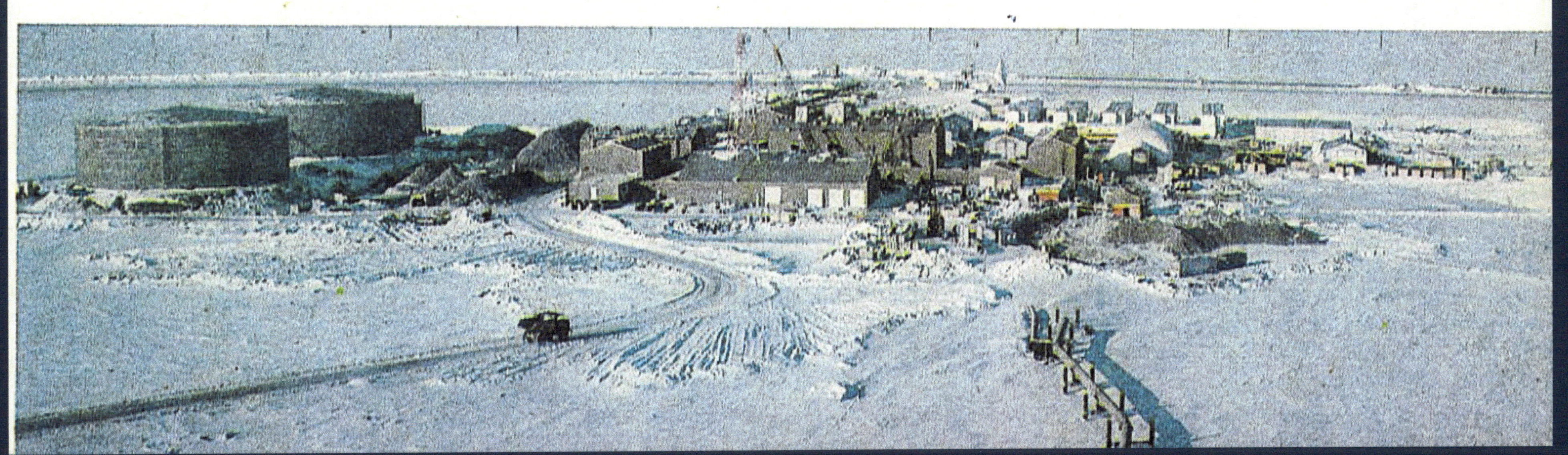

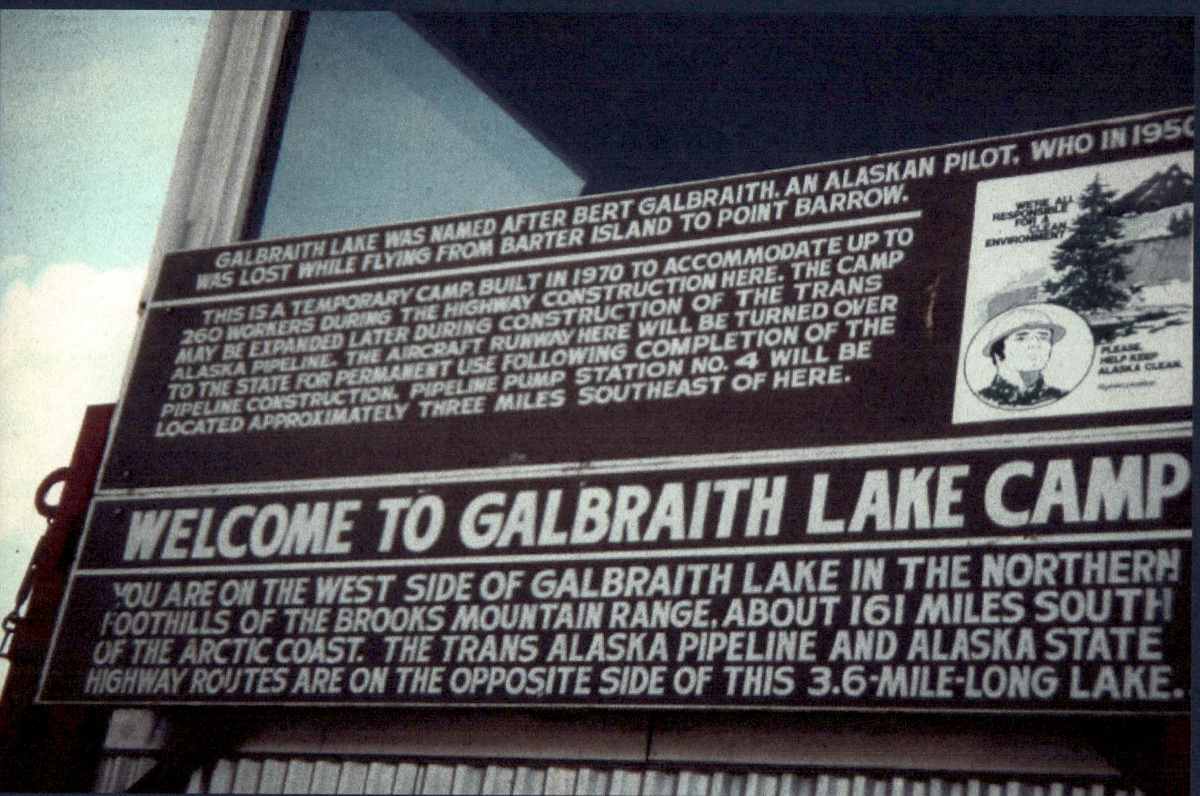

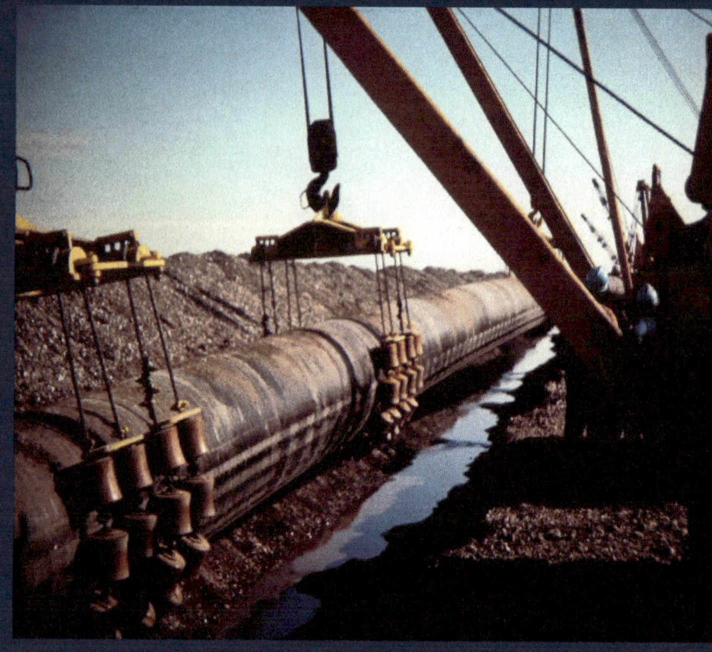

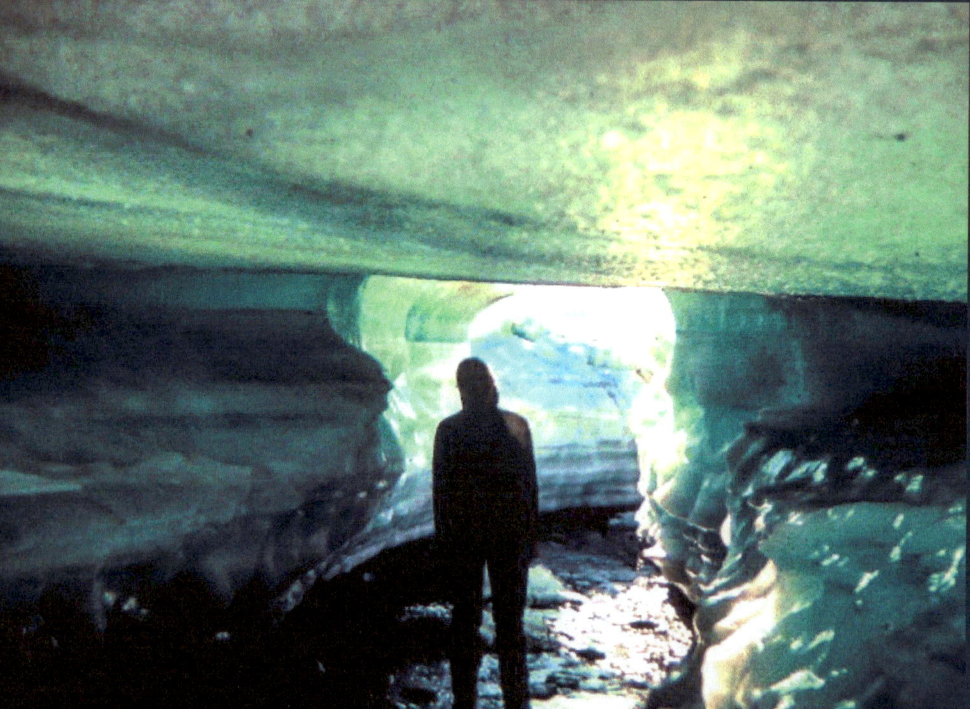

Classified   Classified

"Boob" HAPPY VALLEY: Happy 8th, Babe, as of June 29, 1976. Thanks for those joyful years. See 'ya in July.

Love 'ya till then,
Nancy &   Pet

VALDEZ TERMINAL: Please call Don in Anchorage. He needs to speak with you.

Susan

ISABEL PASS CAMP: Happy Birthday June 29. Hoping we can be with you soon "if!?" Please don't forget what we really want **together**! We love and miss you greatly!

Love always,
Your Greenweenies

MIDNIGHT MOVER: Thank you for all the beautiful memories. You're Dynomite and I love you.

Tu Esposa y Amour,
Nancy

TO THE LADIES FORMERLY RESIDING AT THE PINK PALACE—YOU ARE NOW FOUR! Do you miss Chez Sue? Loyat Caribou and Mary at Five Mile. Congrats, and persevere! Now when will I ever run into you again? Ren at Franklin: I thought you were gonna work at FMH? What's the buzz? Nan: where are you? After 17 weeks I feel "bushy" and am taking my R & R end-June, then it's Galbraith. Love-hugs from Chan-Chandalar Candy.

We united as a team.

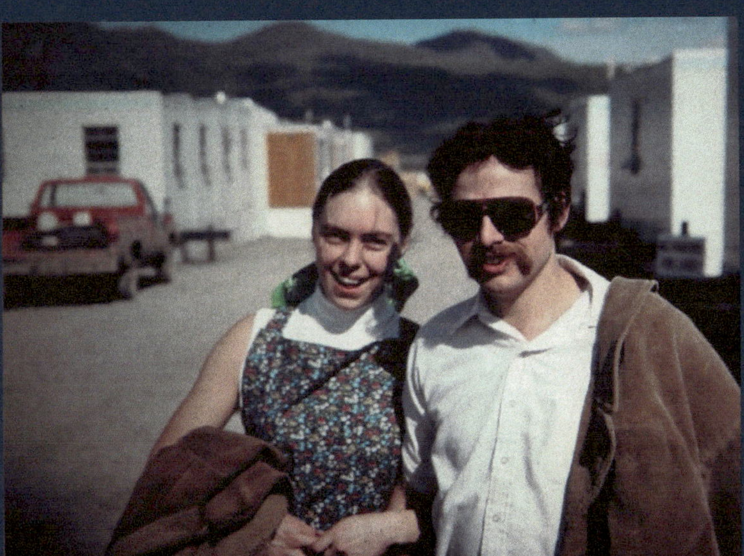
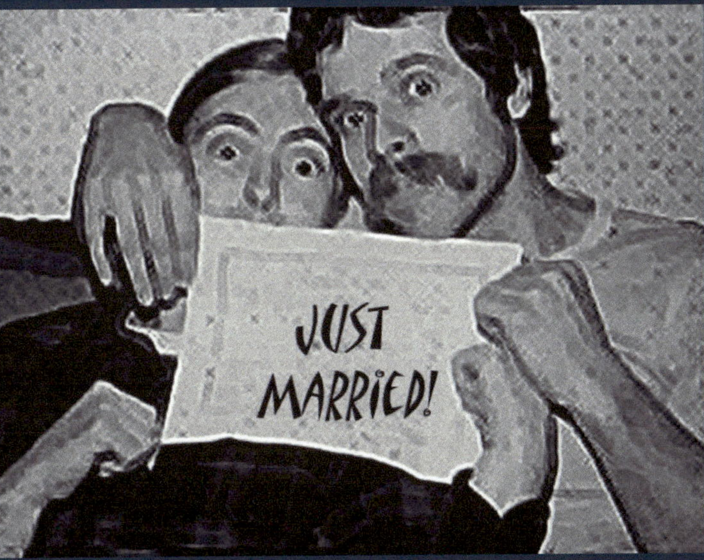

Tim's mother said I was lucky because Tim was handy.

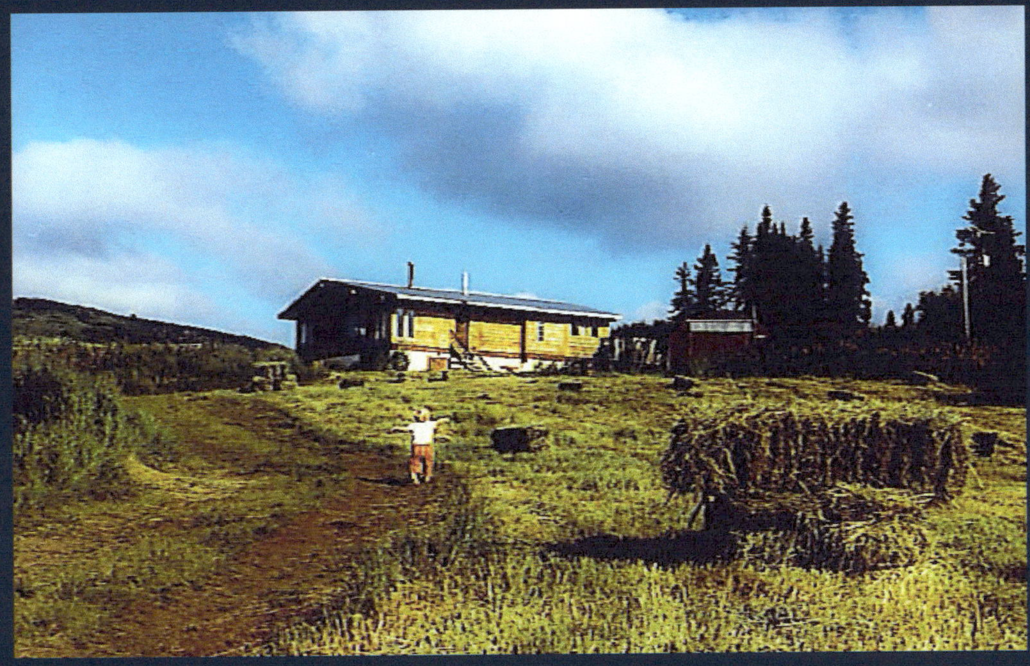

After "dragging up" from the Pipeline, we went off in search of a perfect world.

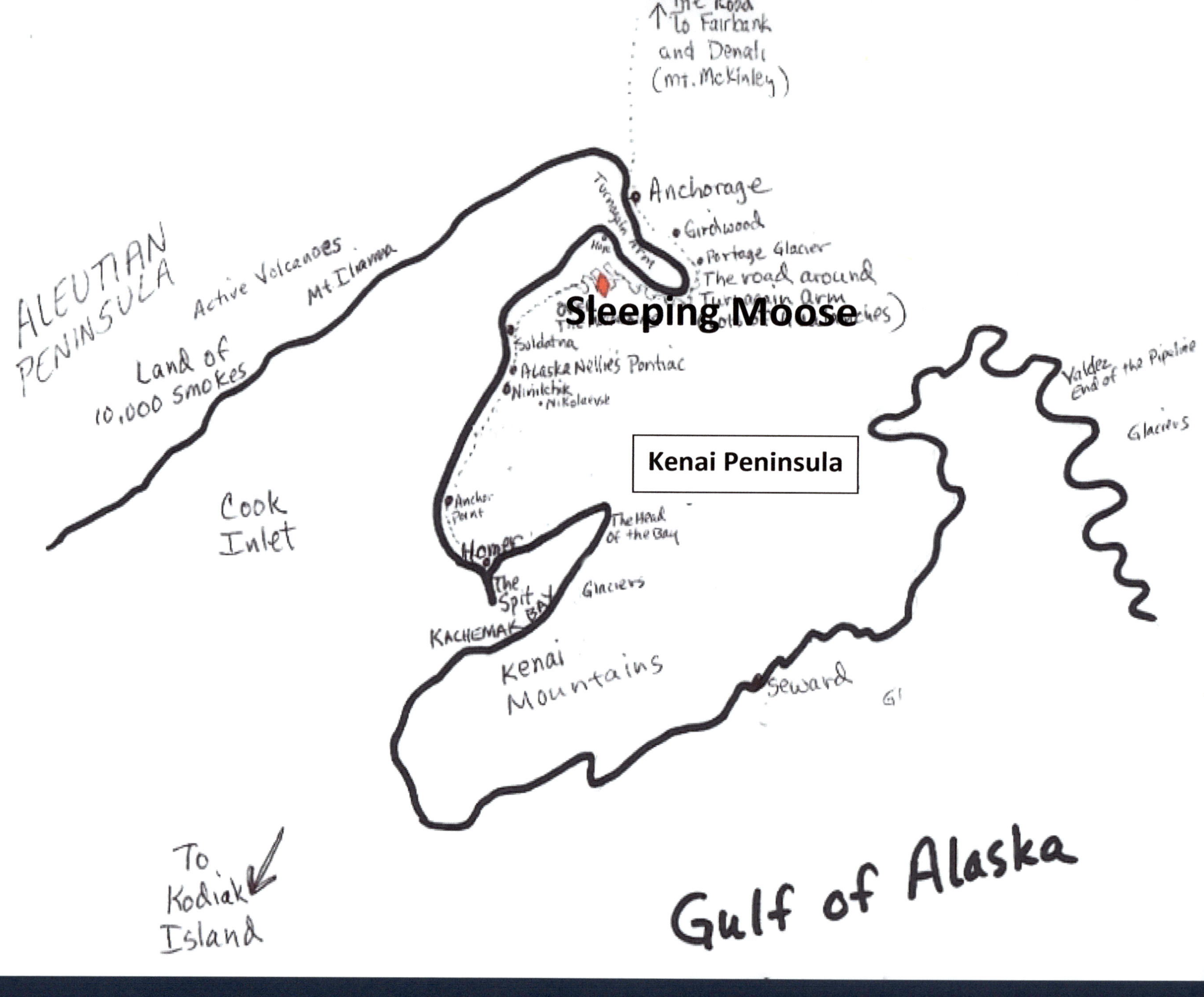
The Road To Fairbank and Denali (Mt. McKinley)
ALEUTIAN PENINSULA
Active Volcanoes
Mt Iliamna
Turnagain Arm
Anchorage
Girdwood
Portage Glacier
The road around Turnagain Arm
Land of 10,000 Smokes
Hope
Sleeping Moose
Soldotna
Alaska Nellie's Pontiac
Ninilchik
Nikolaevsk
Kenai Peninsula
Valdez End of the Pipeline
Glaciers
Cook Inlet
Anchor Point
The Head of the Bay
Homer
The Spit
KACHEMAK BAY
Glaciers
Kenai Mountains
Seward
To Kodiak Island
Gulf of Alaska

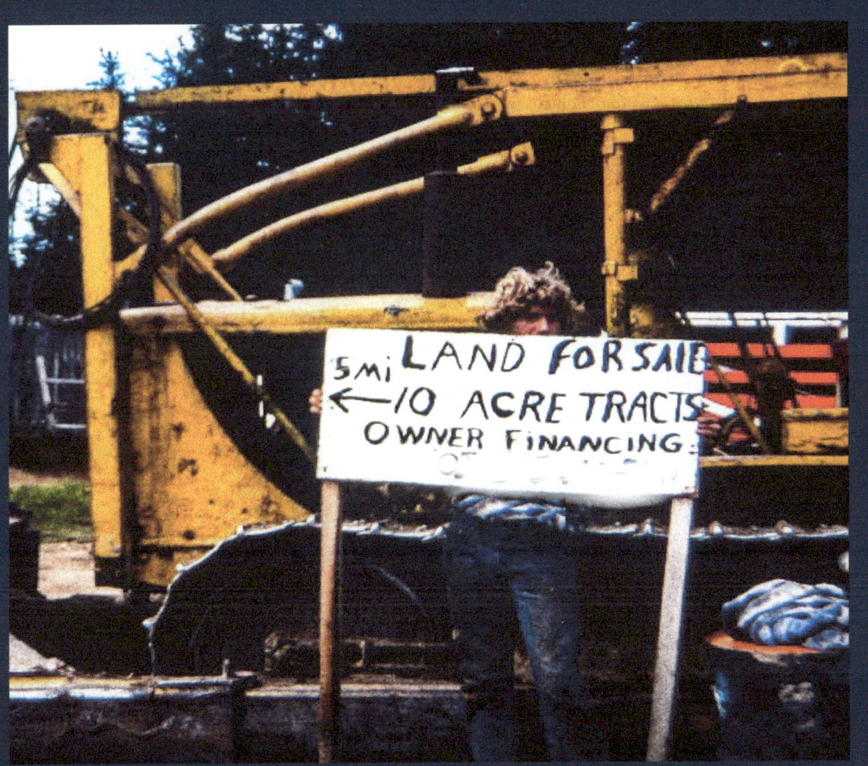

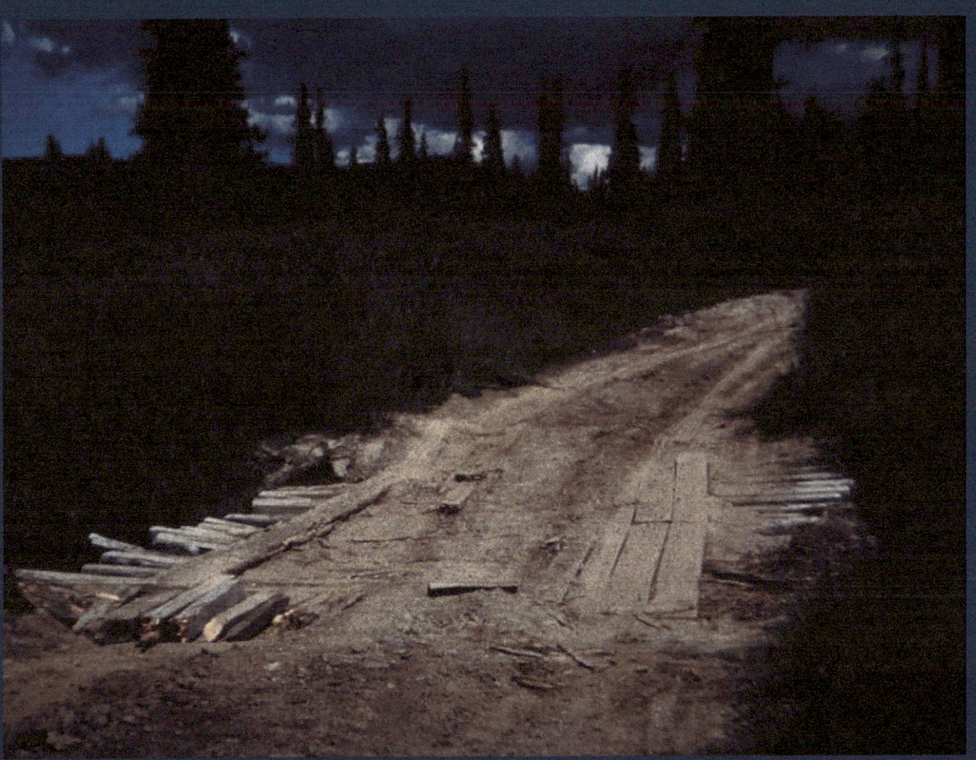

A dusty dirt road led over this bridge and ended
at an old homestead. Beyond that was the land that was for sale.

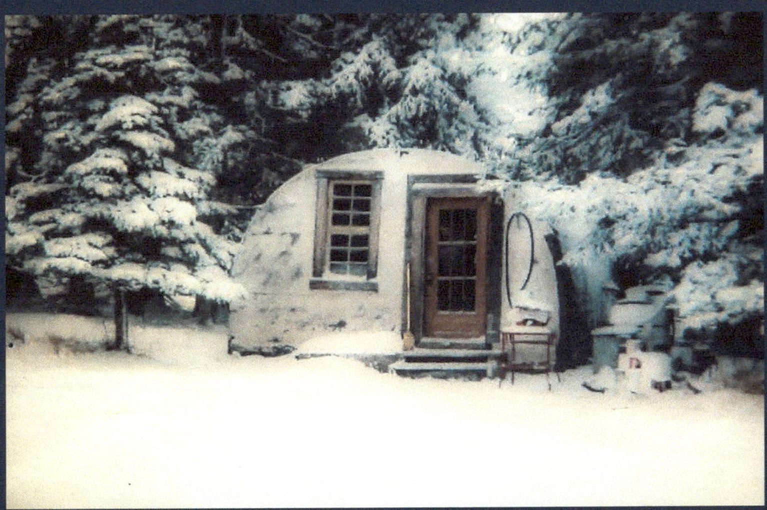

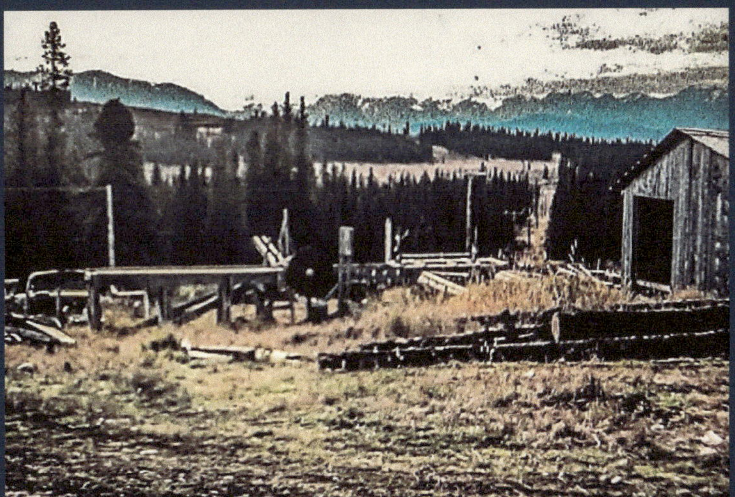

The remoteness was very appealing,
and a woman wouldn't have to wear a dress very often.

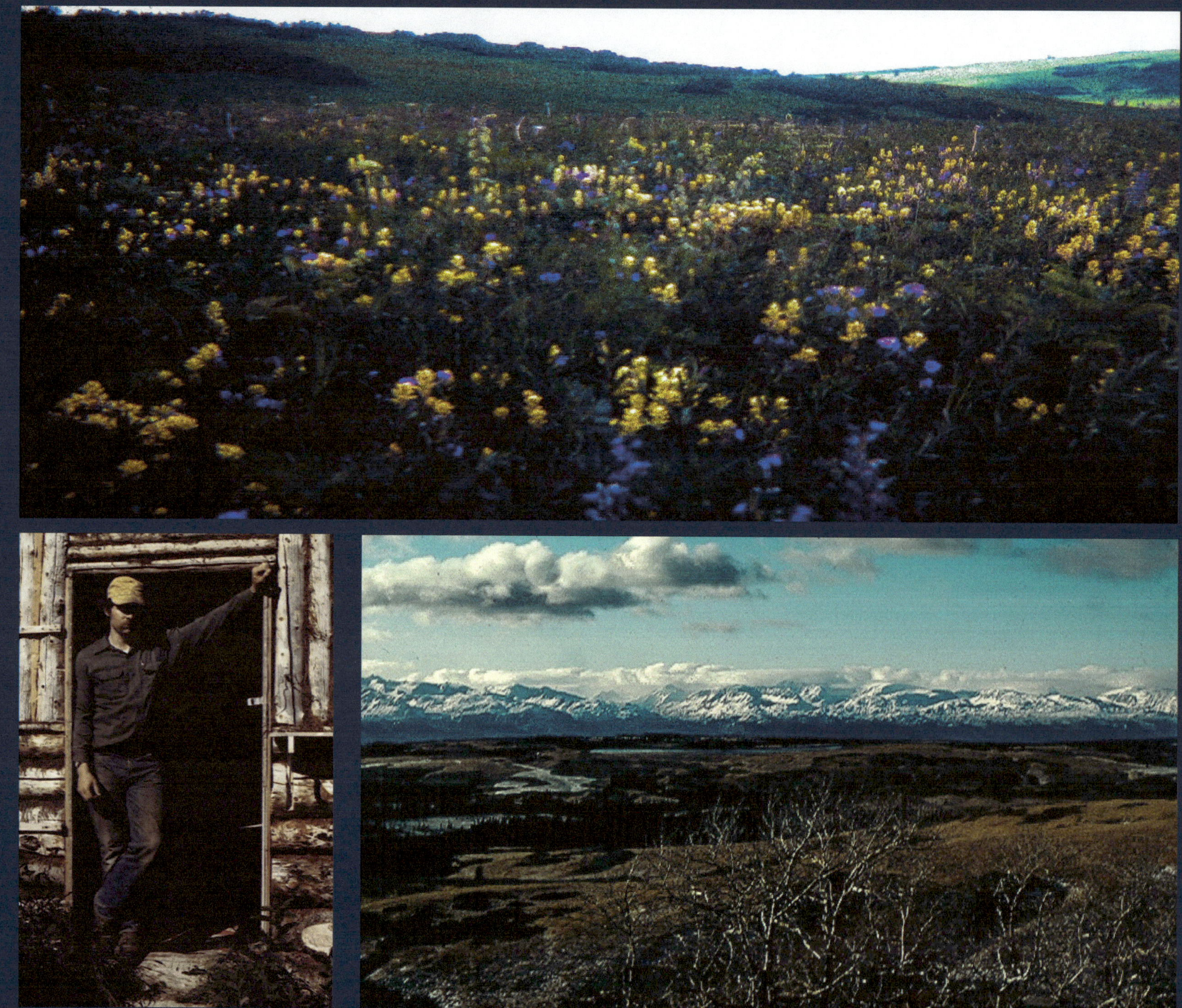

The privacy, plus the stunning beauty

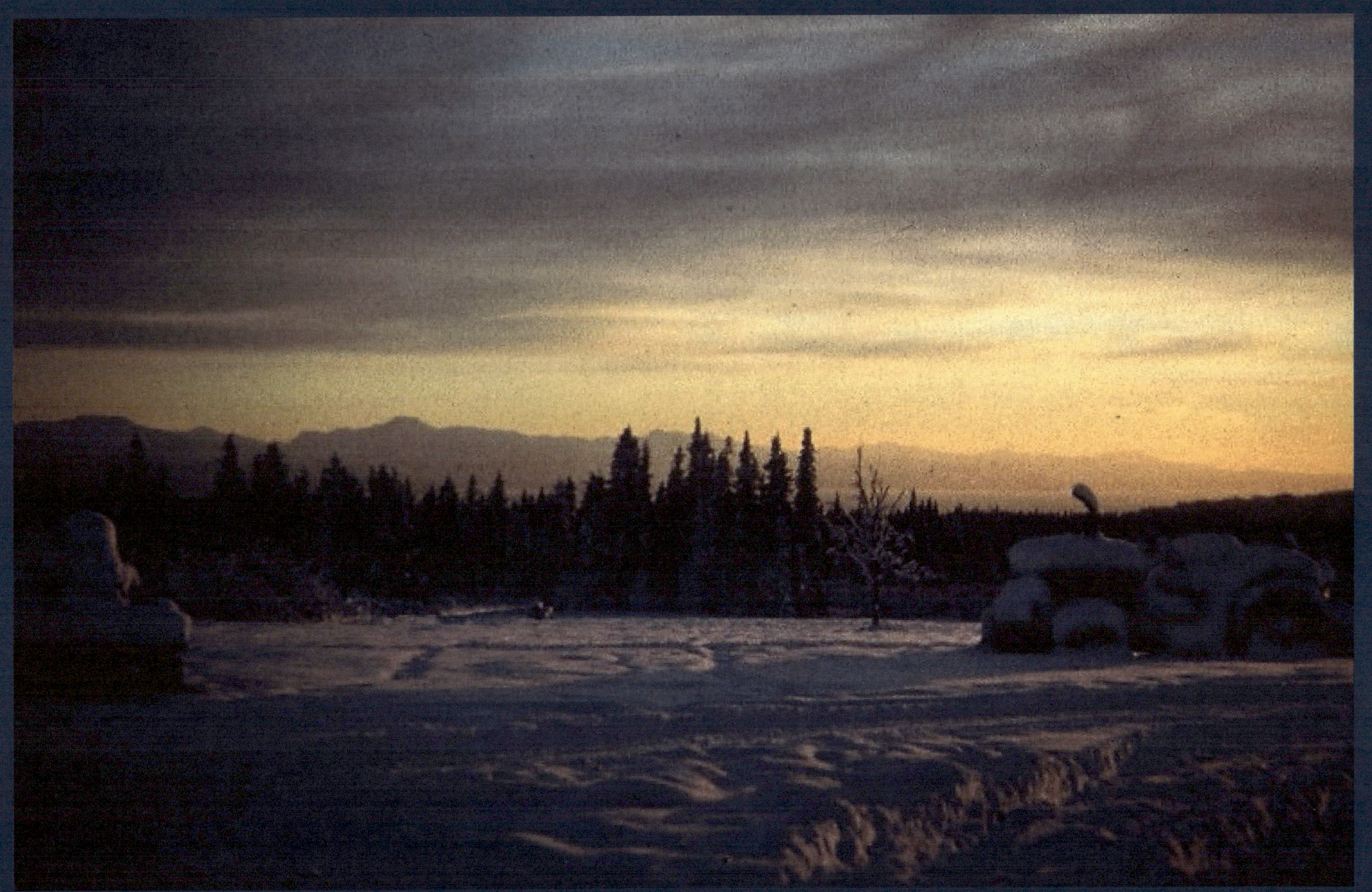

prompted us to take a *spontaneous* leap.

We bought the back forty of that homestead on-the-spot.

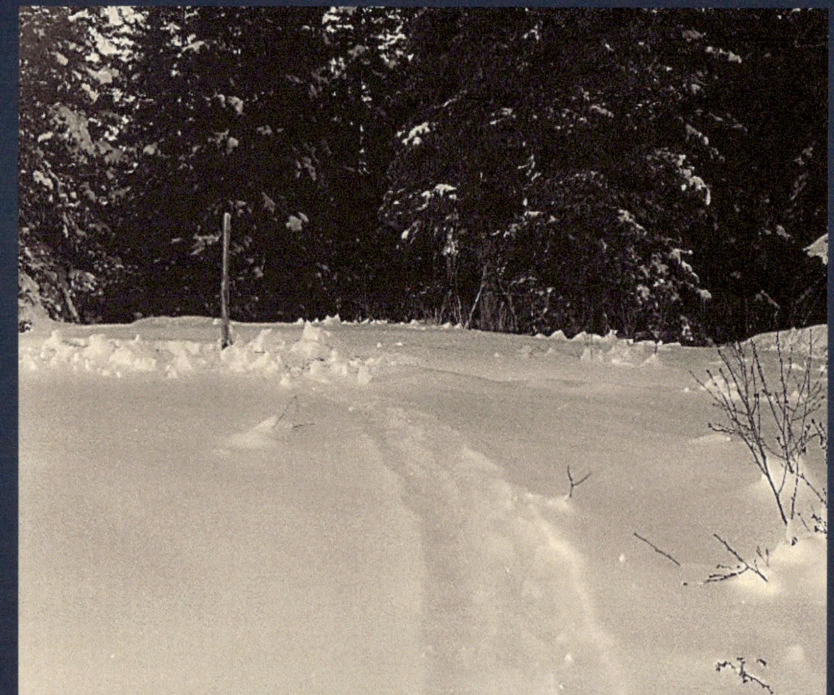
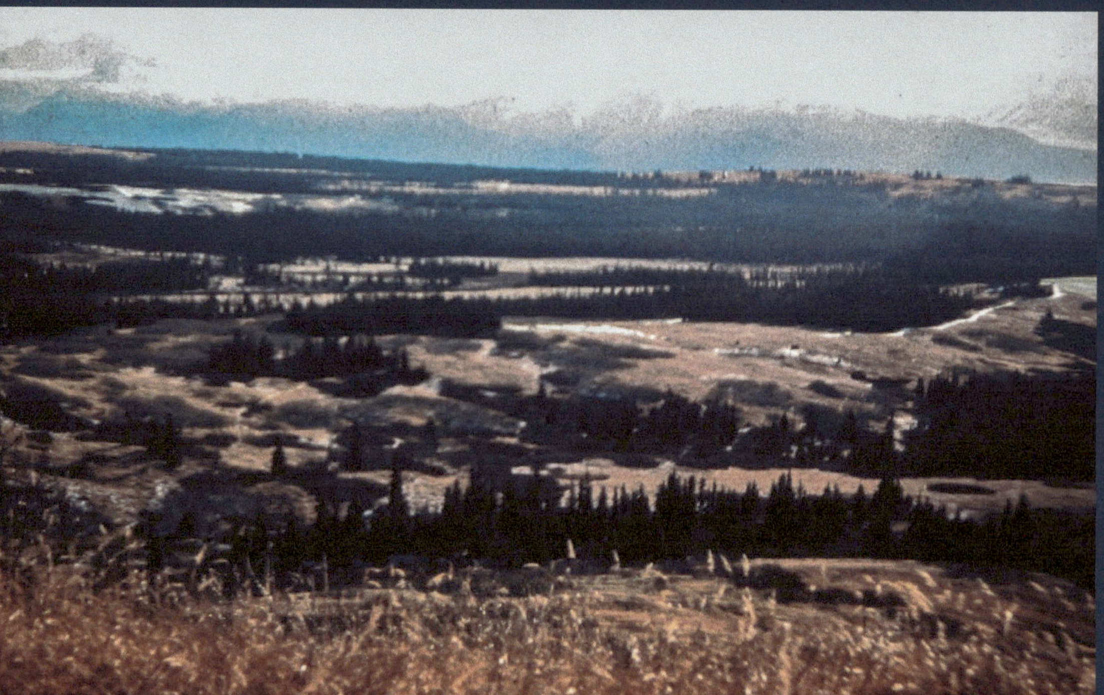

Total wilderness lay behind our new piece of heaven.
We would build our life together right there, where a moose had slept!

All around us lived moose, bear, and wolf.

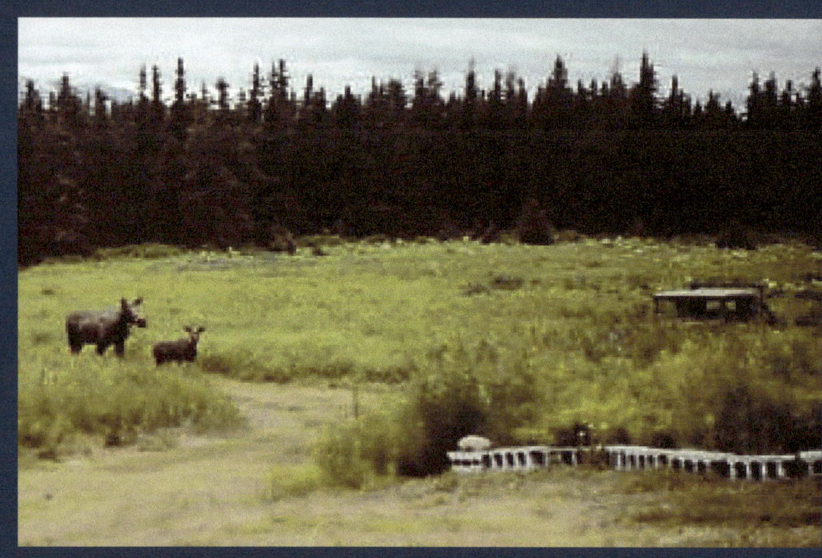
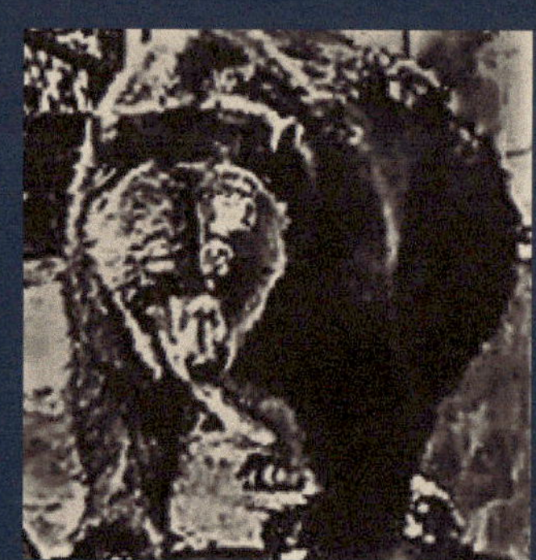
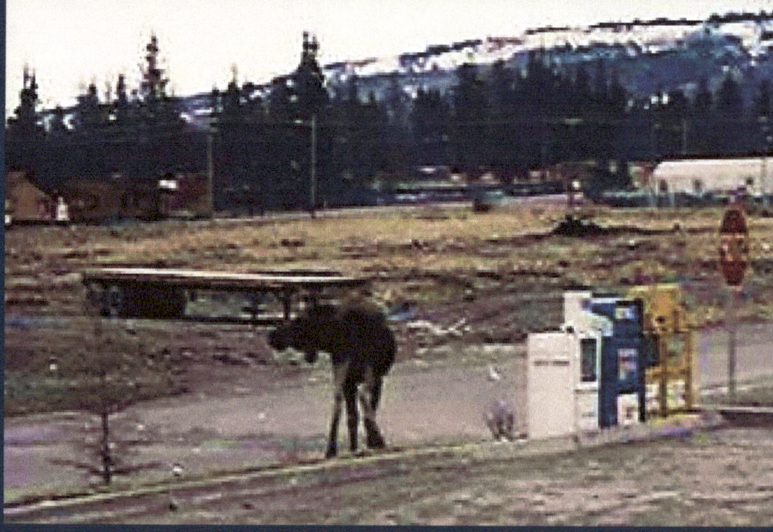

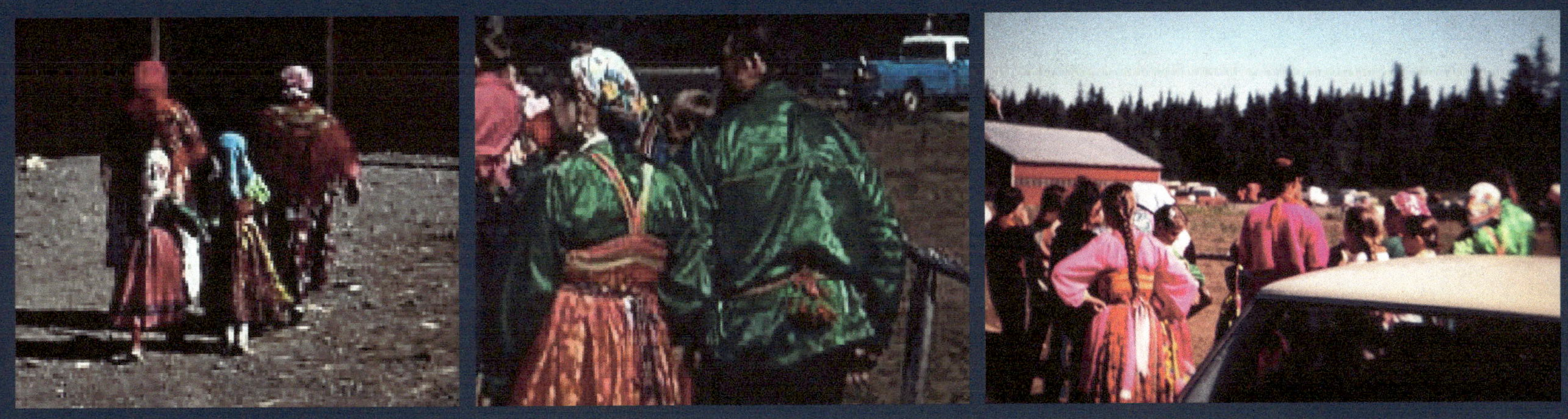

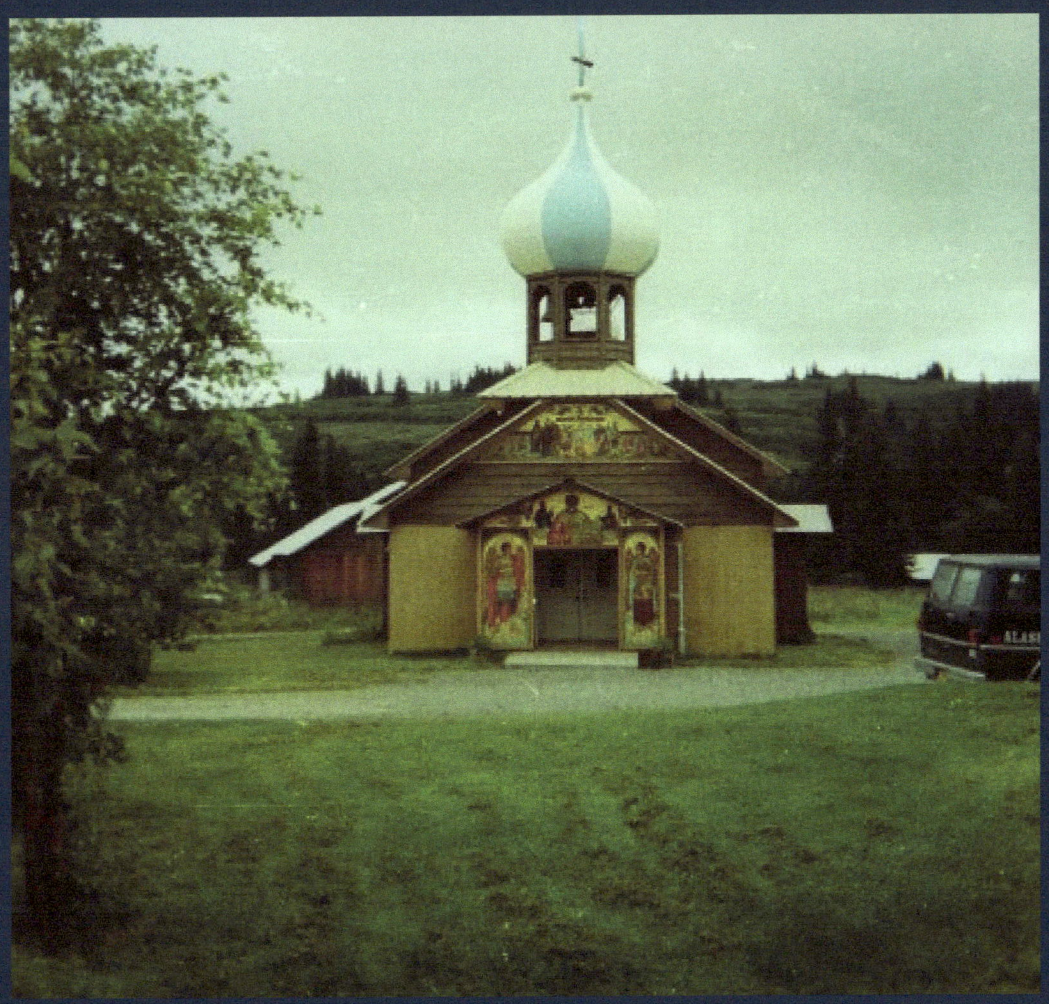

And there was a colorful community of Russian emigrants fairly near, as well.

We built our starter home. "Honeymoon Cottage" was
nestled into an alder grove, near the top of the highest mountain around.

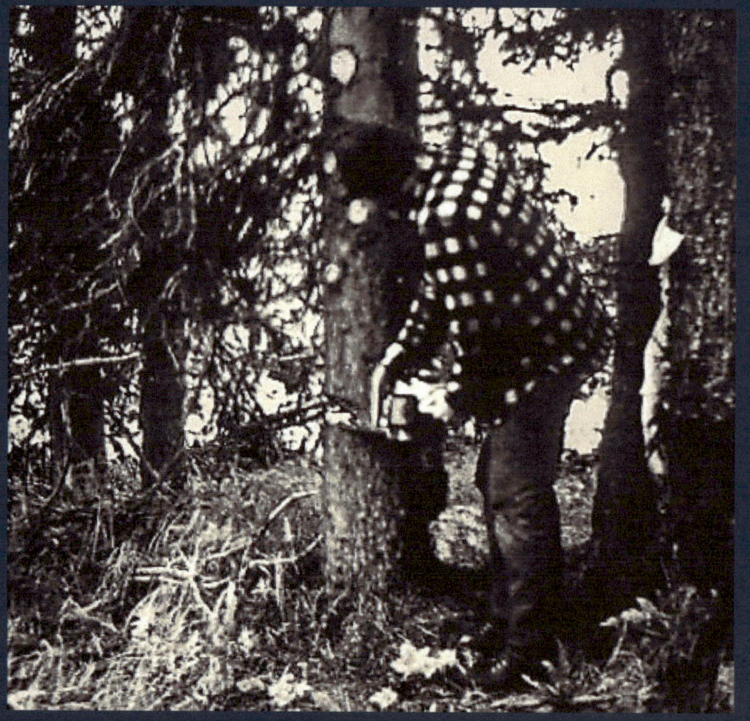

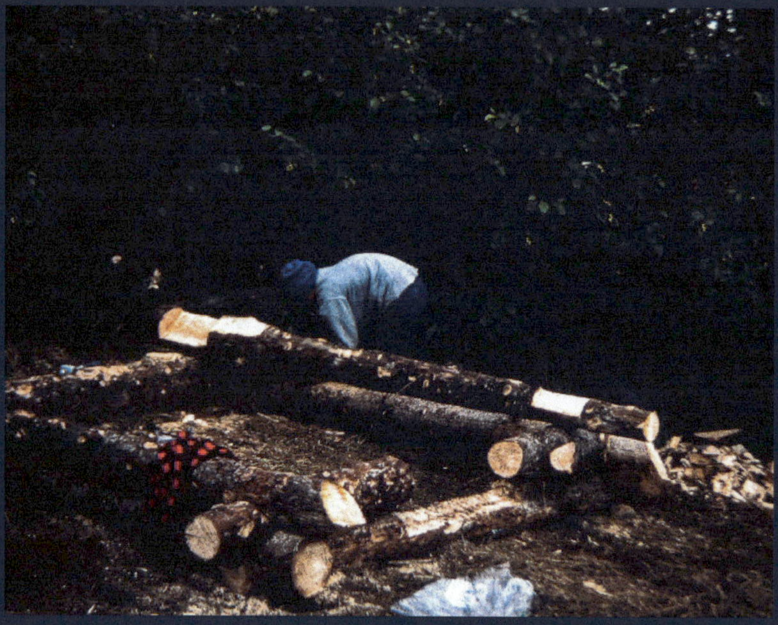

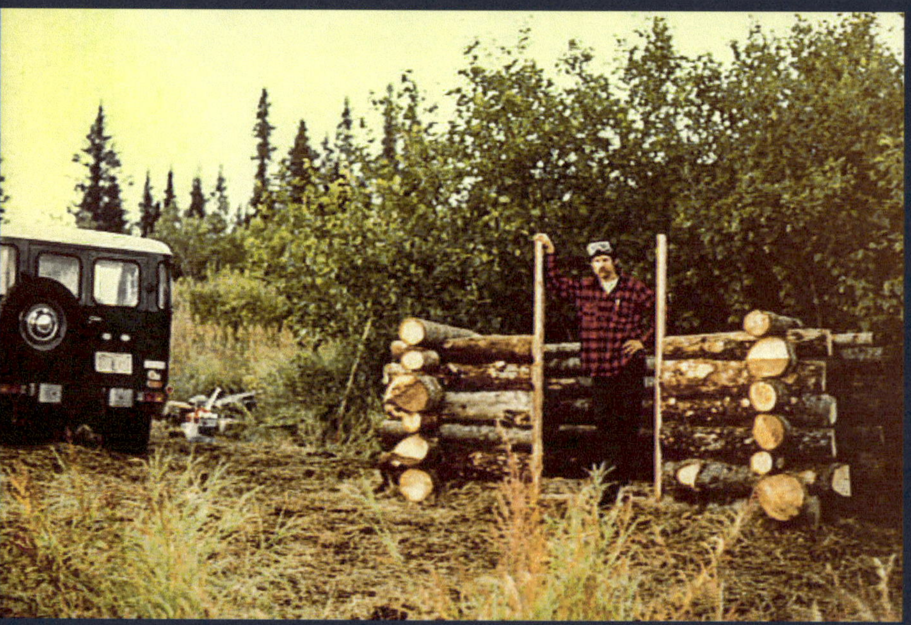

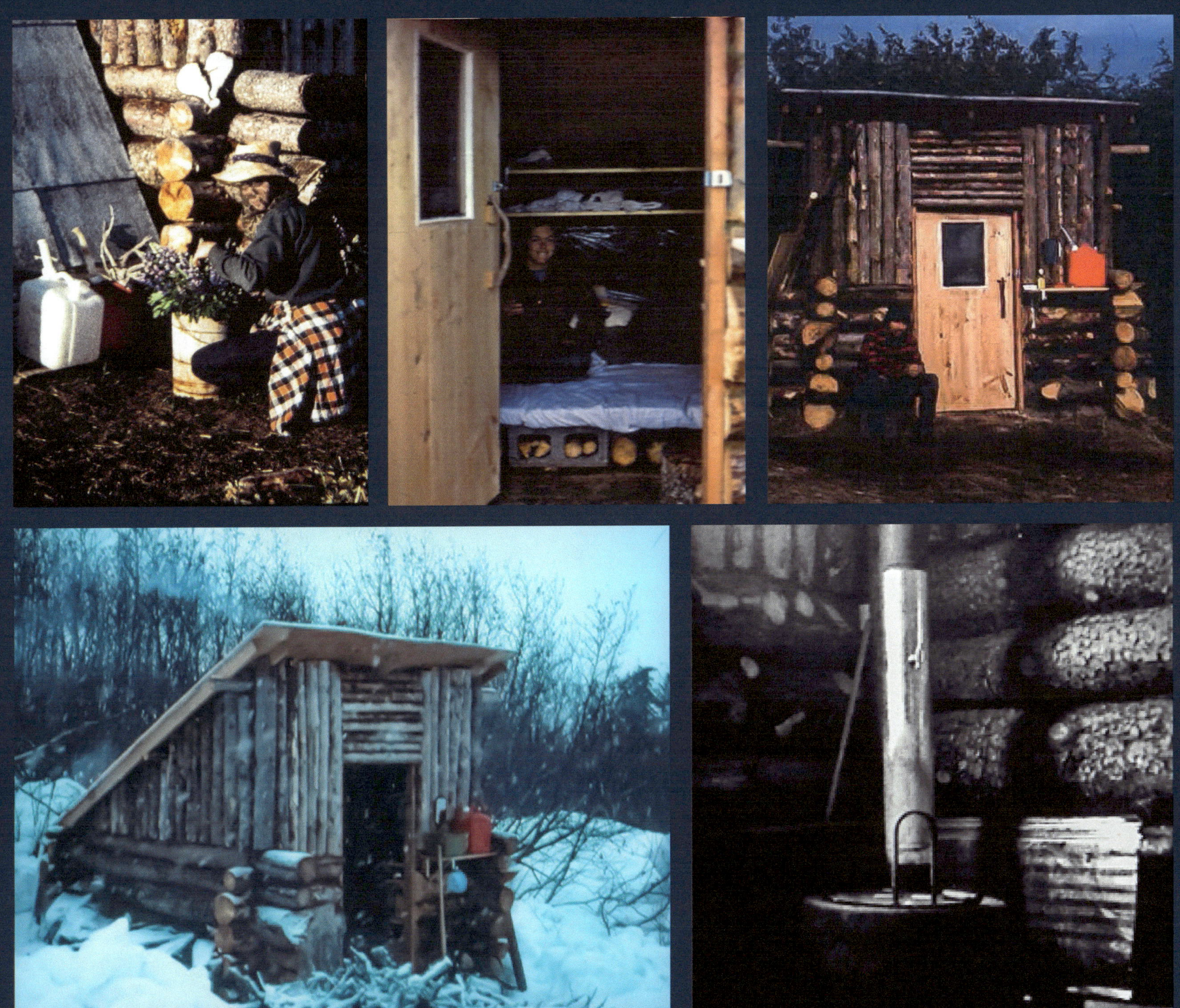

Living six miles off the edge of civilization meant many long, arduous trips home.

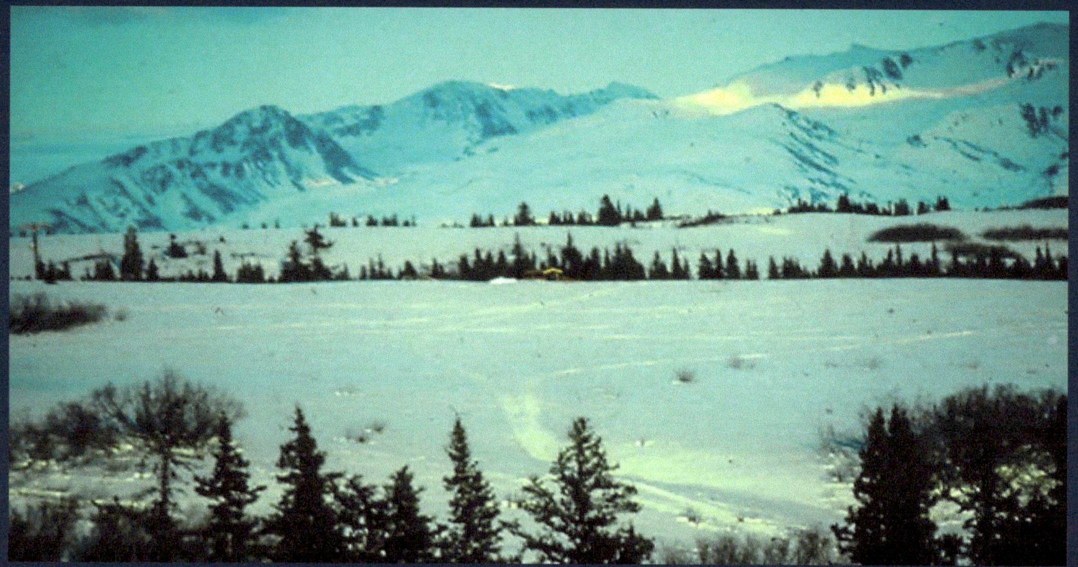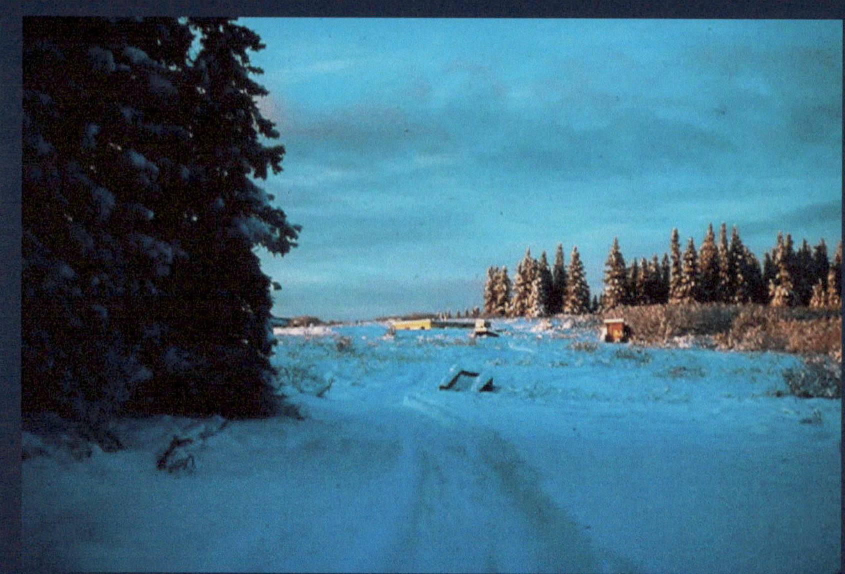

But upon clearing those last woods,
there stood our little kingdom, glittering in the alpenglow.

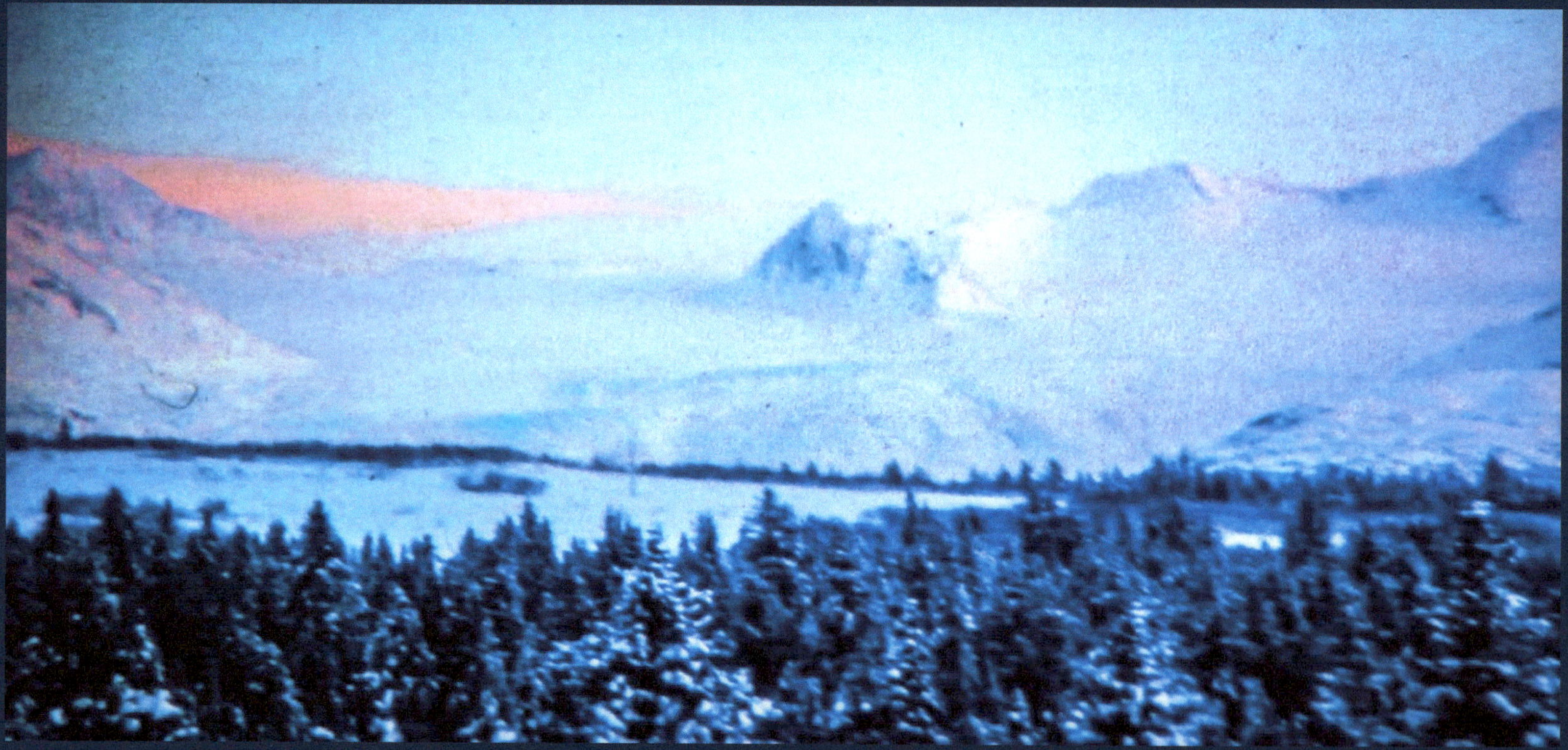

"Tim Peak."

We were living the dream.

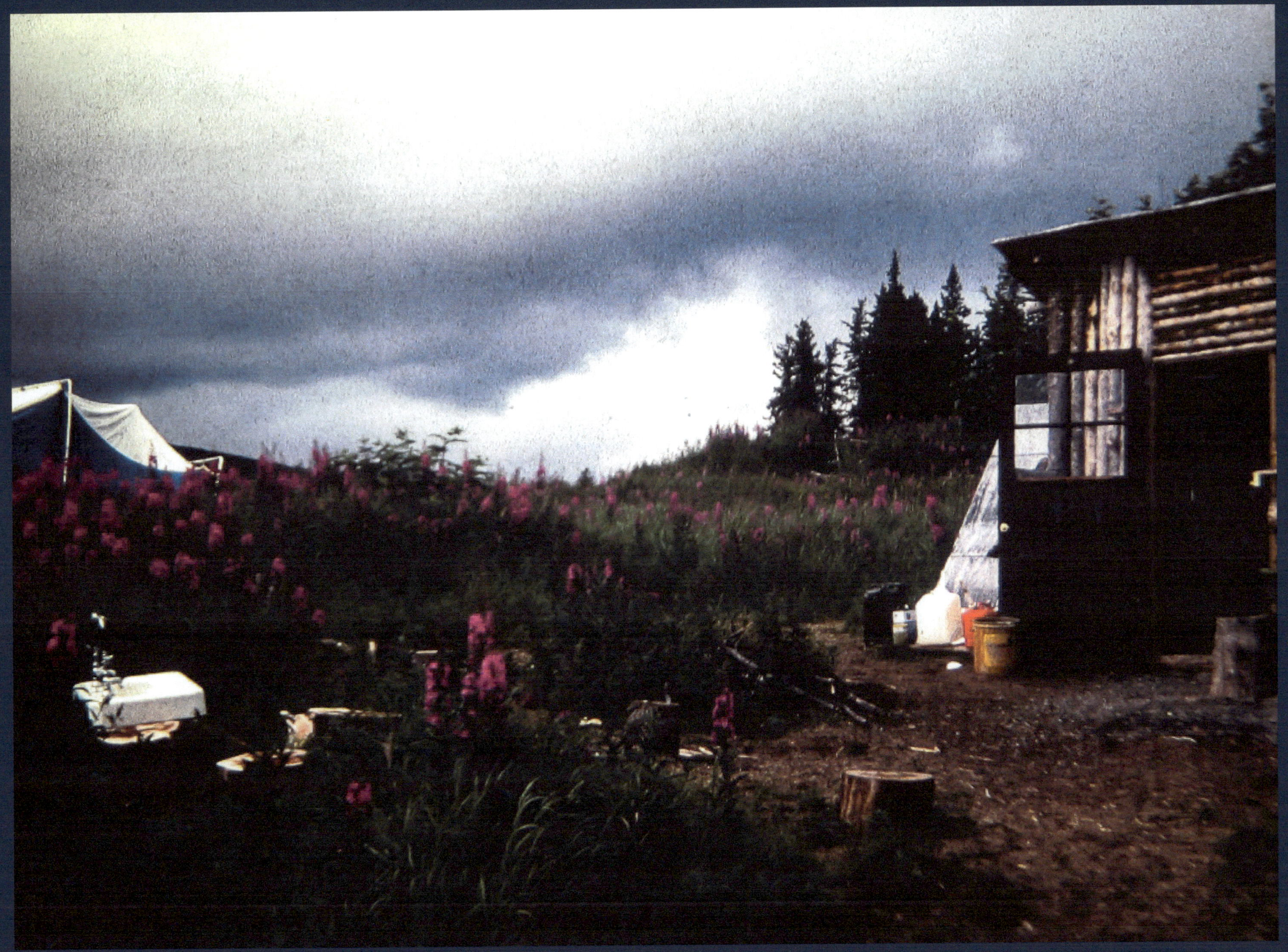

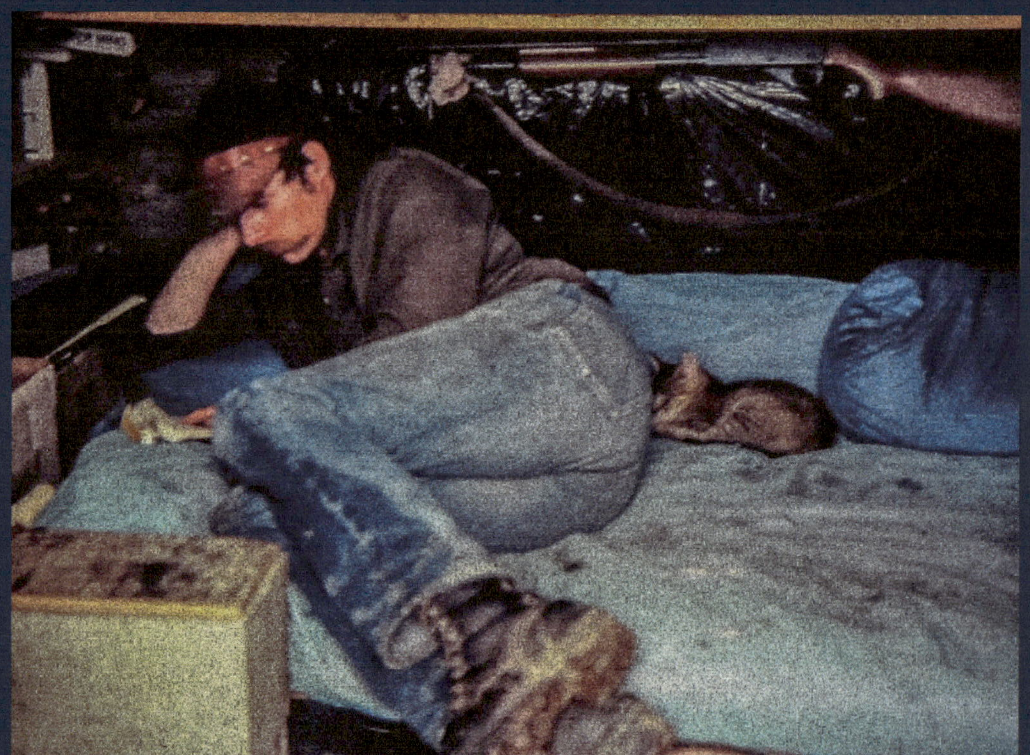

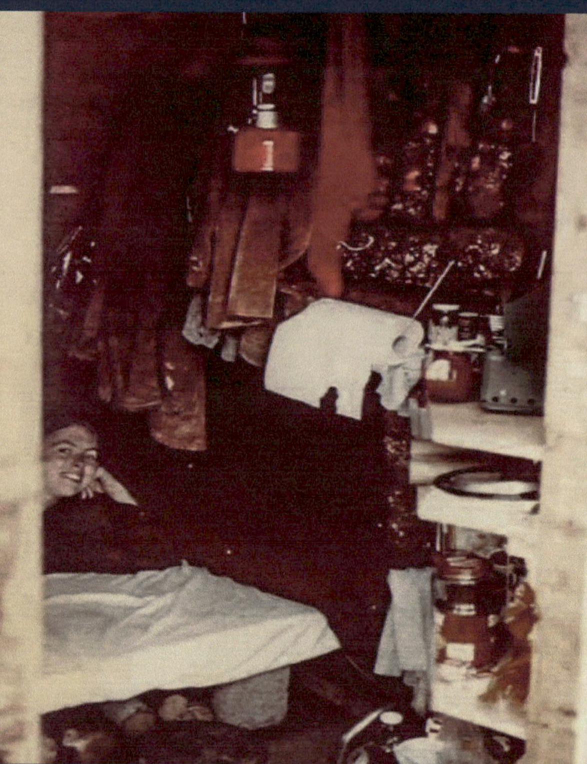

Two newlywed "cheechakos" blazing a trail to Camelot.

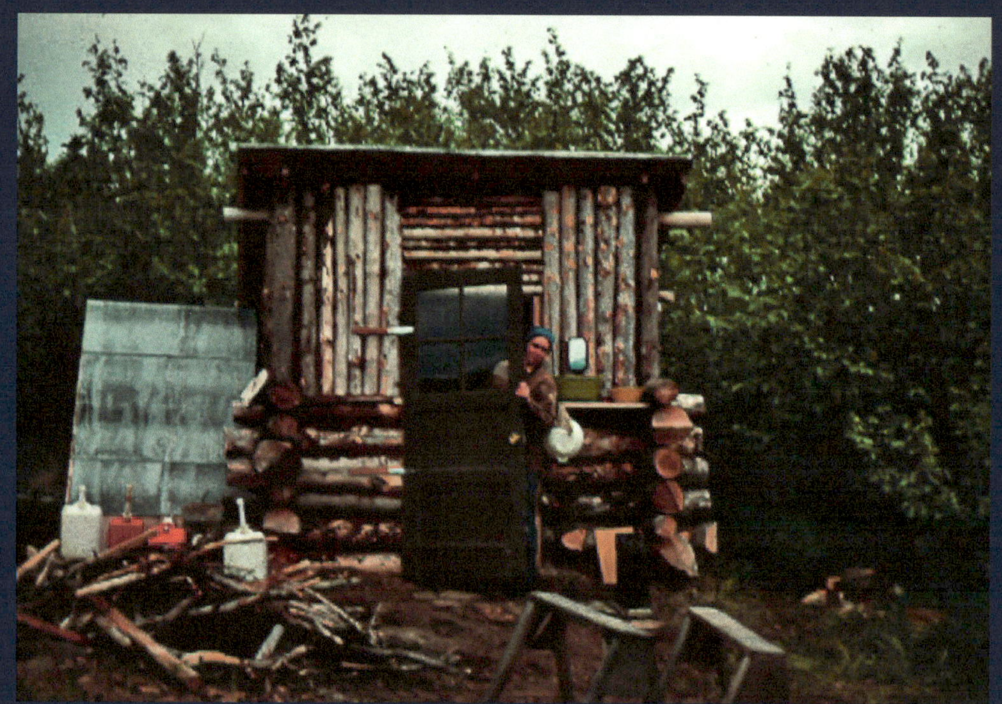

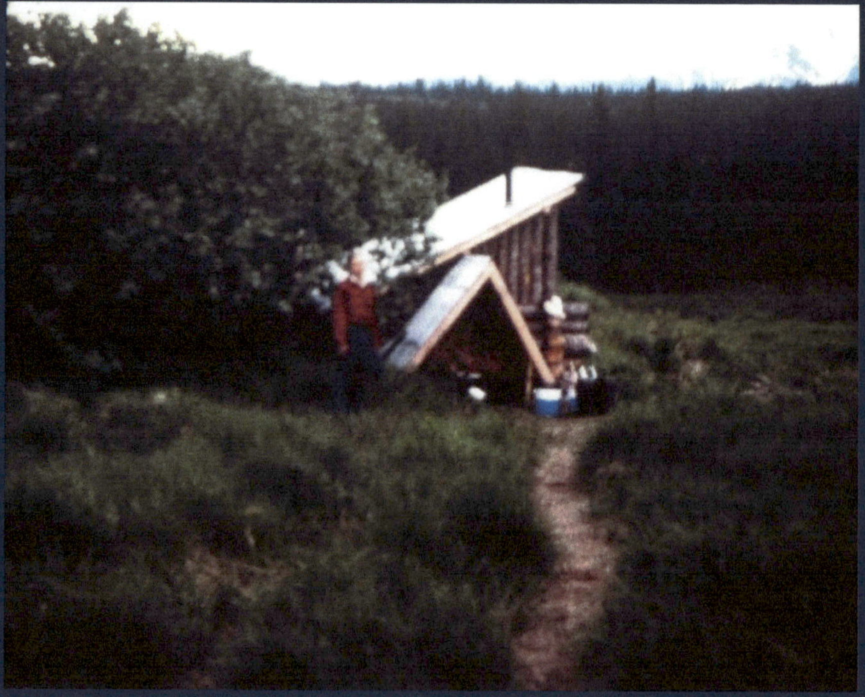

Sometimes we repurposed
the remnants of other folks' abruptly-ended dreams,

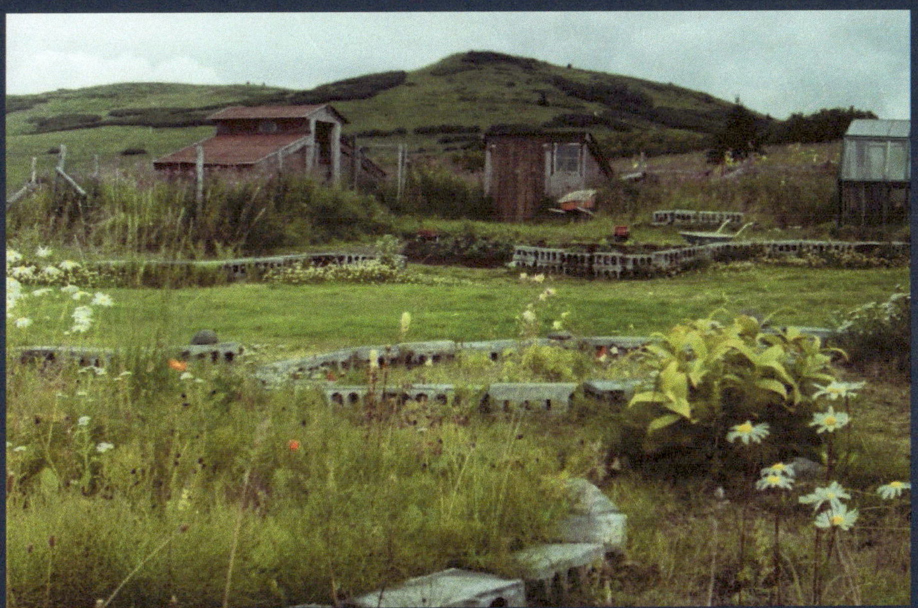

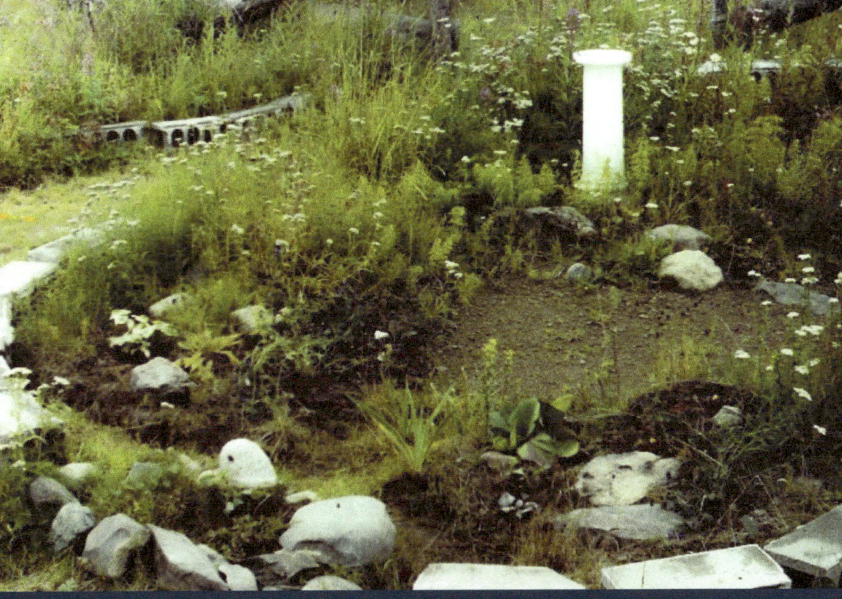

—such as hog sheds, Quonset huts, and unusual three-holed cinderblocks—

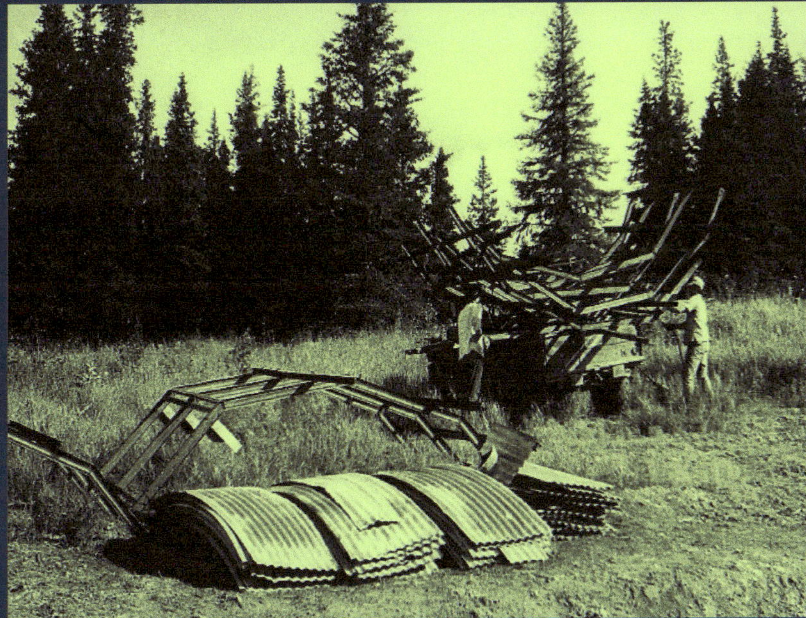

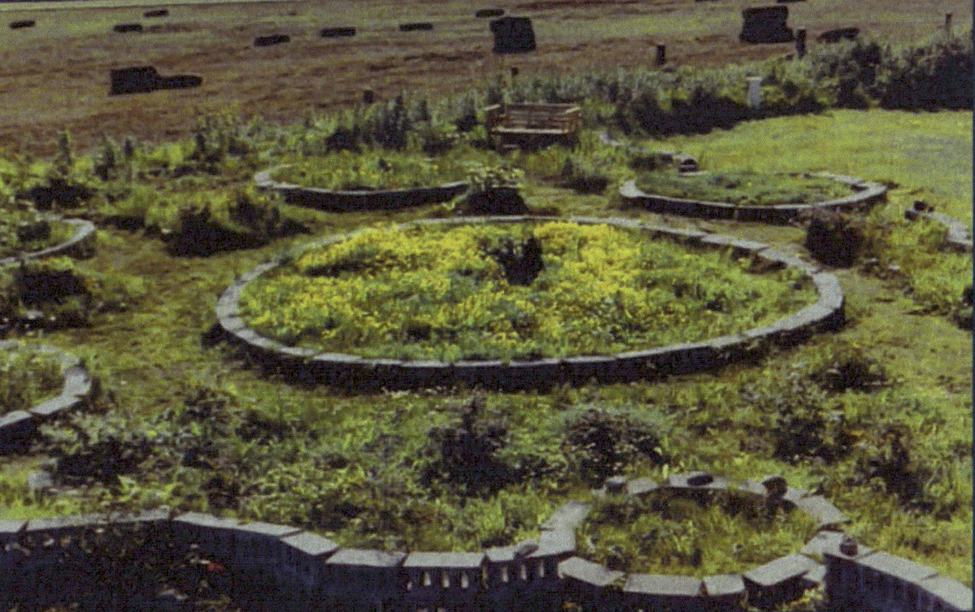

Incorporating them into our own "Victory Garden of Delights."

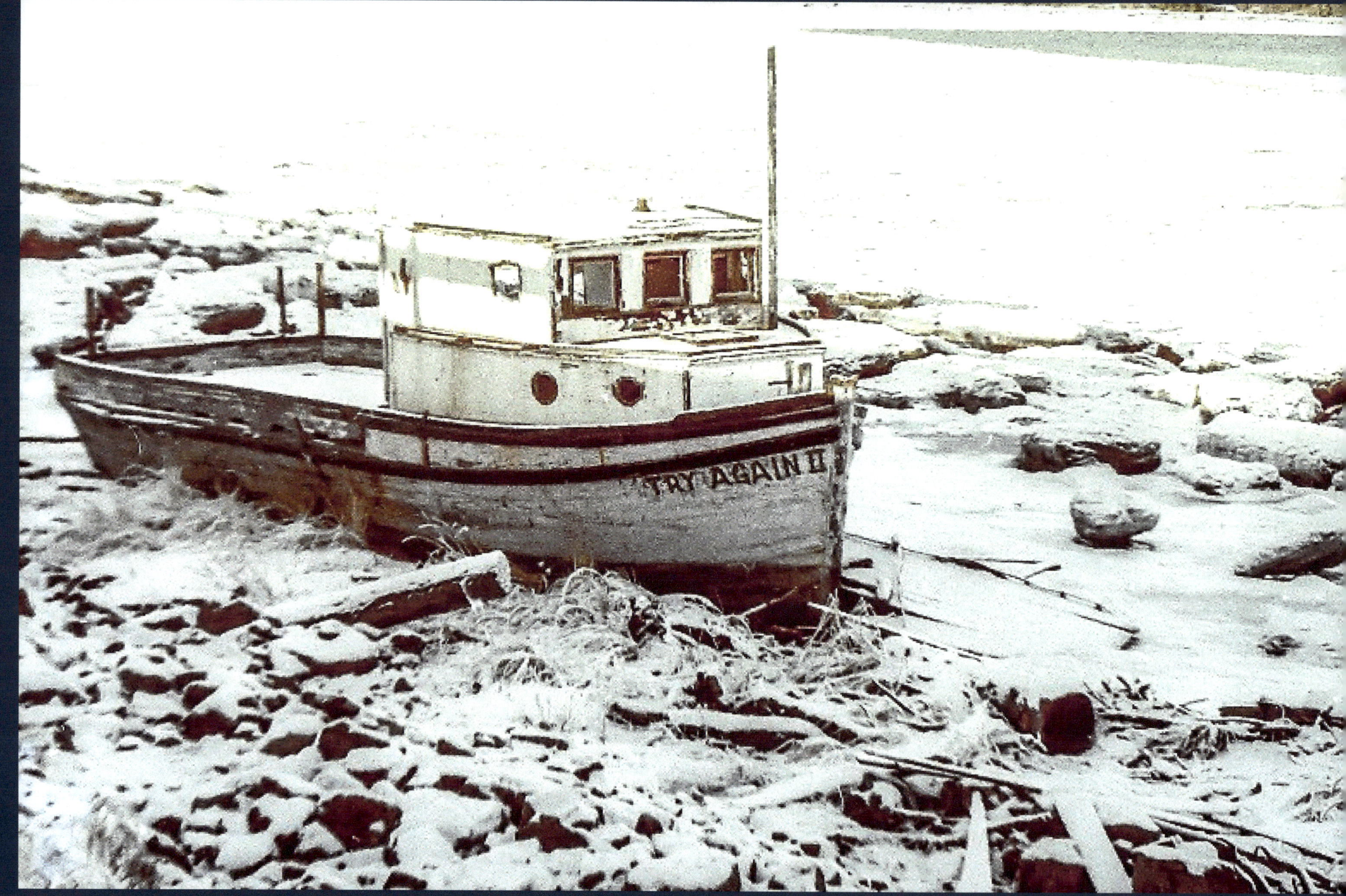

What happened to the "Try Again?" And to that first "Try?"
Reaching for a dream is risky, I guess.

Here are mason and hod carrier fashioning cinderblock masonry
using wheel barrows and water in cans.

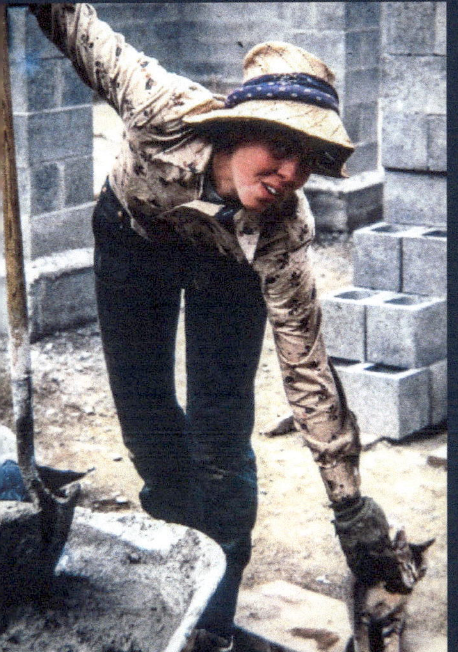

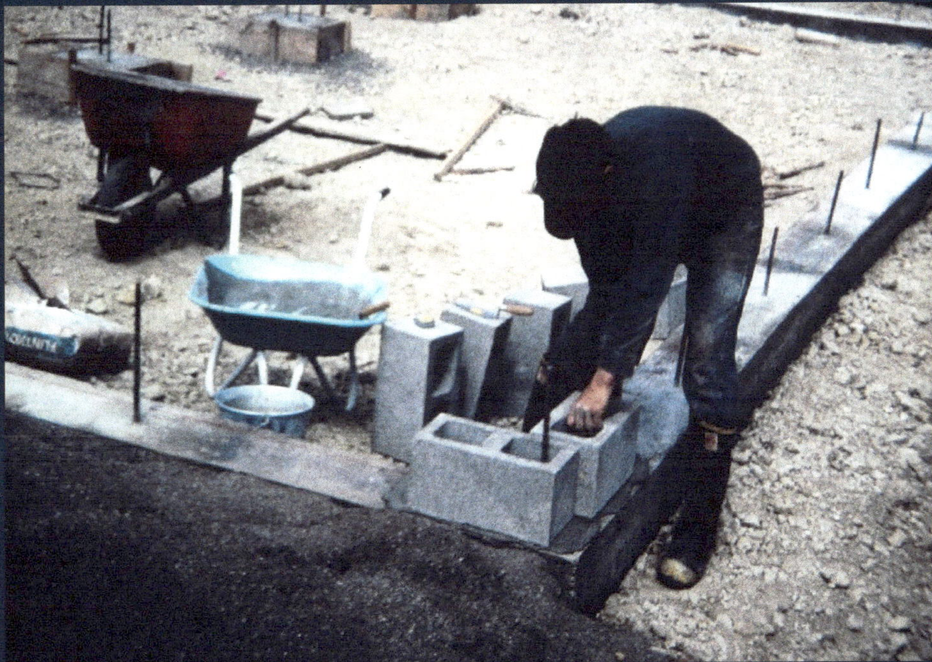

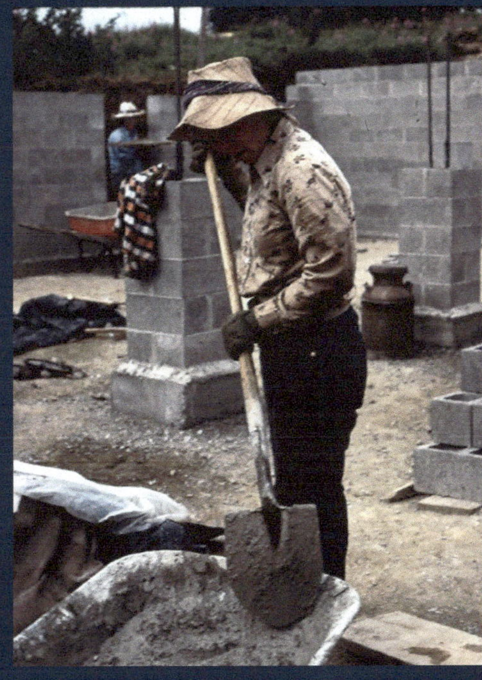

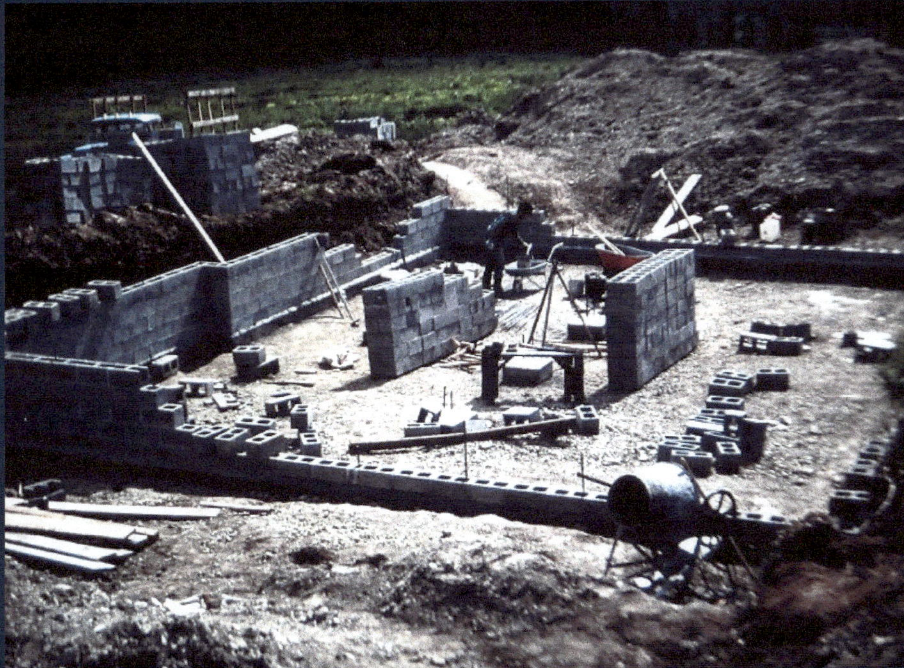

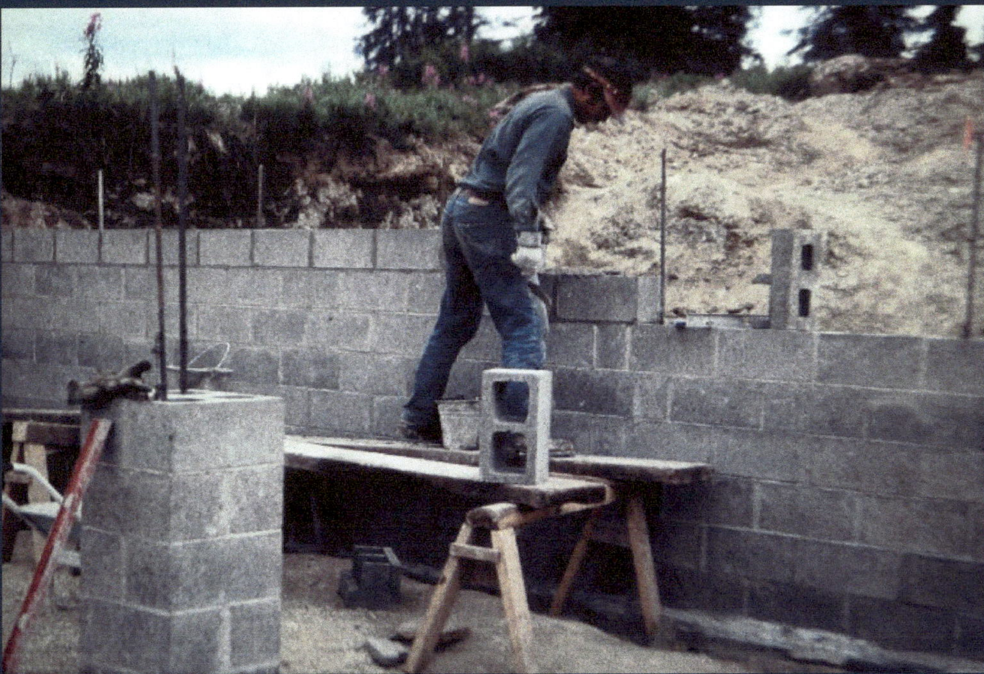

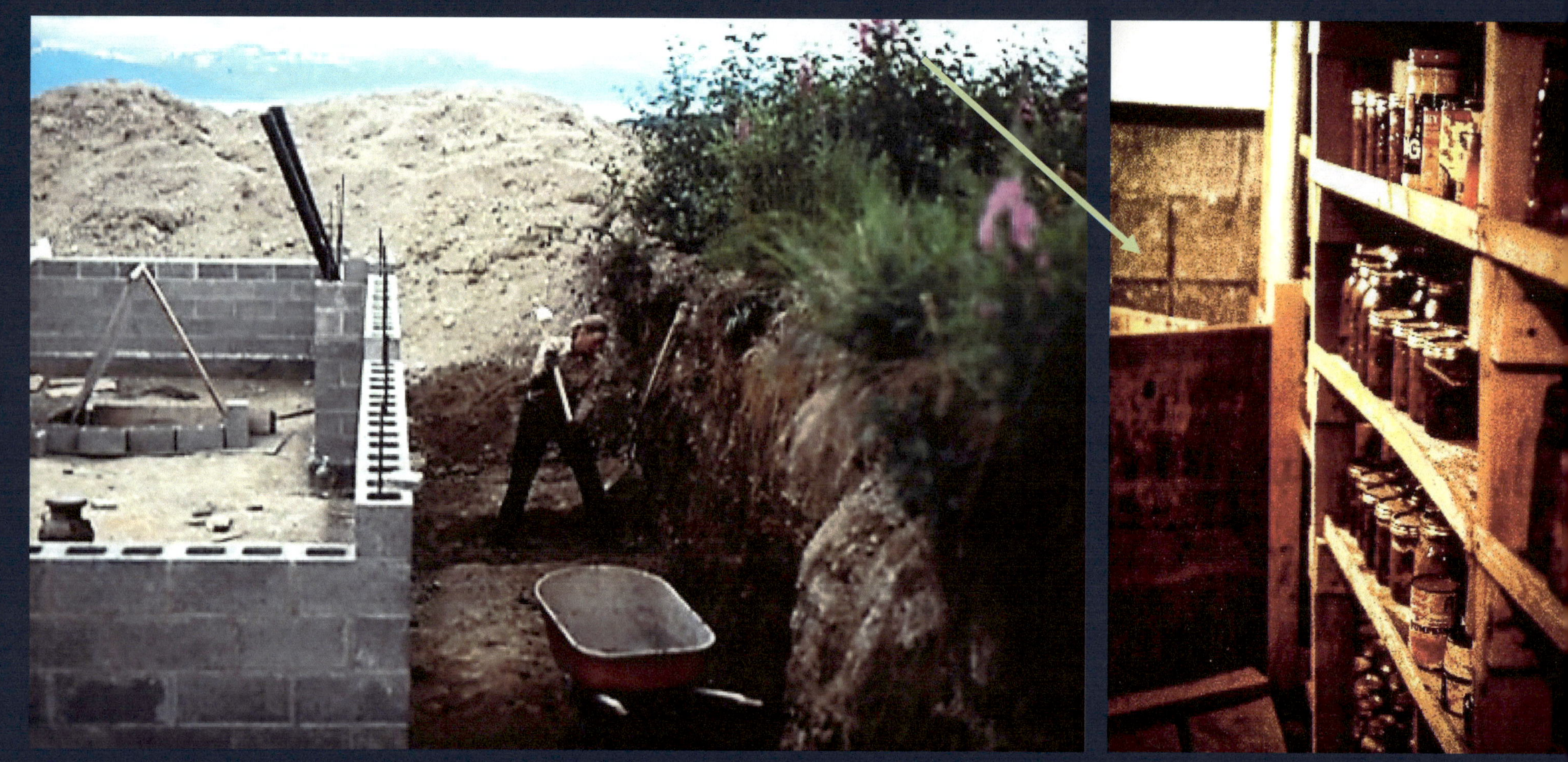

My own illogical contribution to the root cellar wall
was the only flaw in
Tim's mathematically-precise walls.

This snug basement was our home for over two years,
as we prepared parts for a palace above.

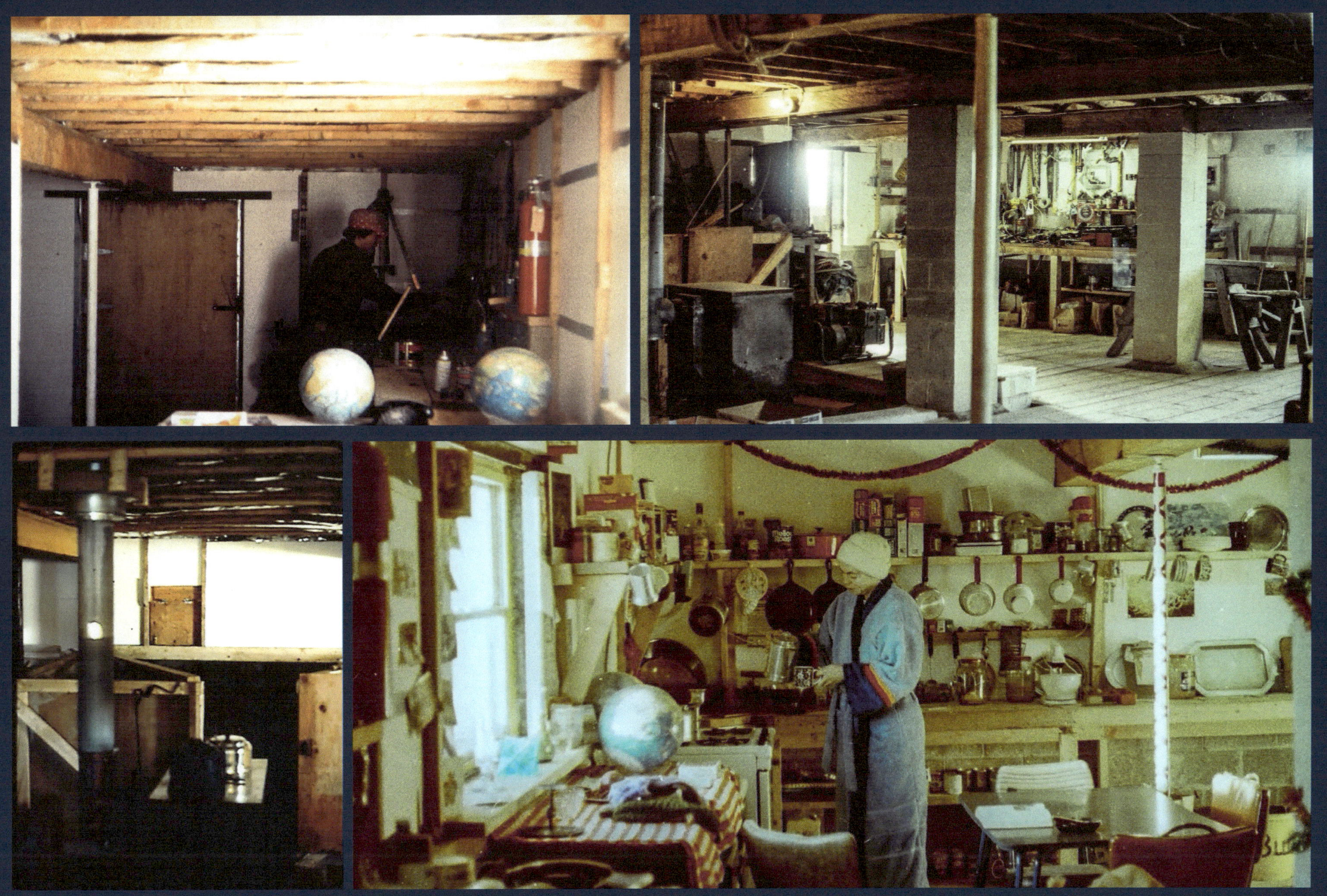

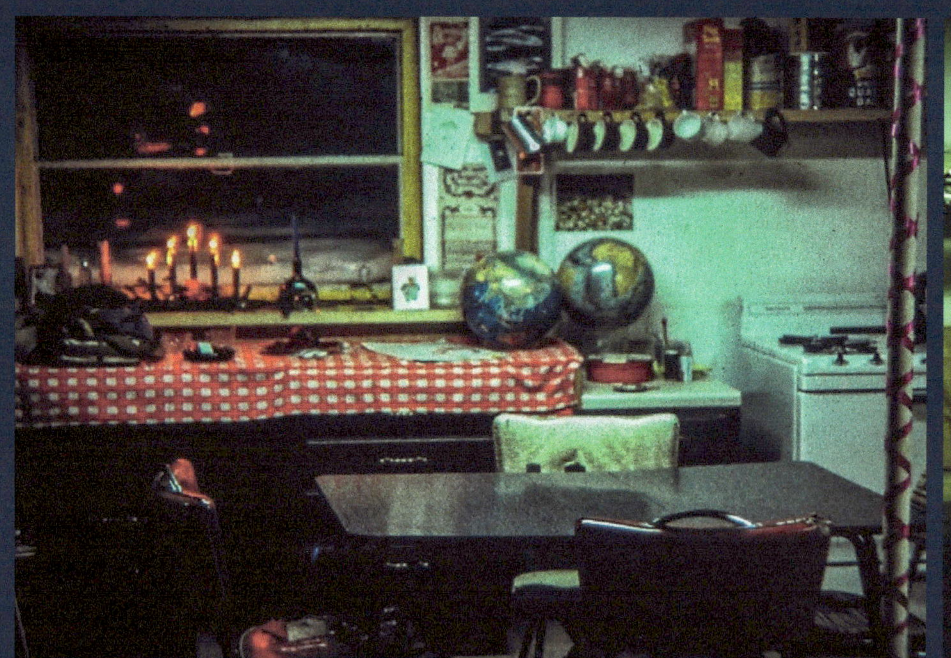
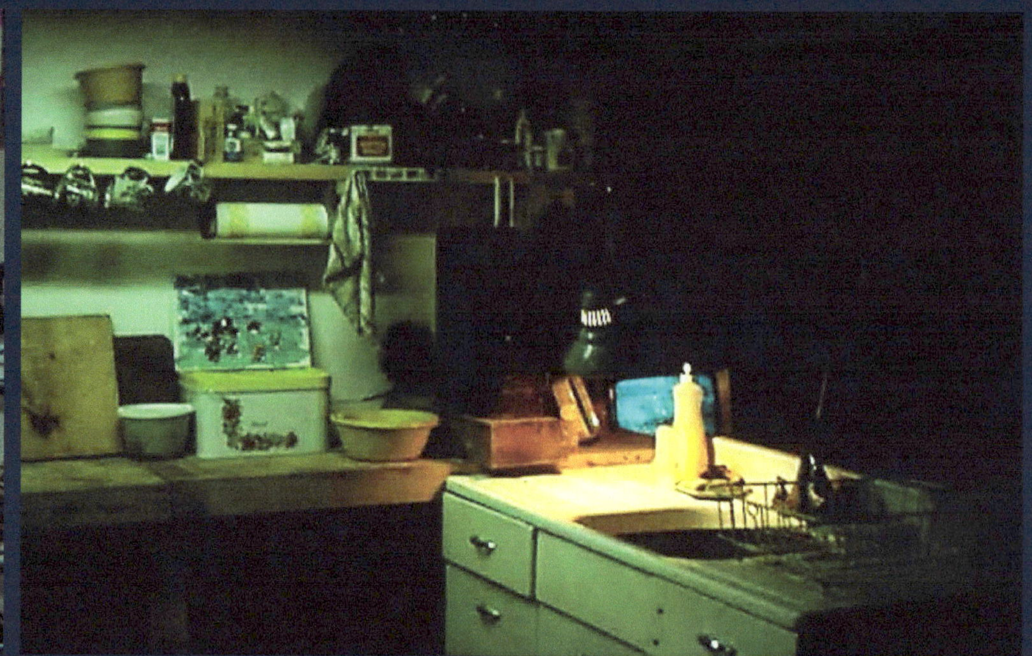
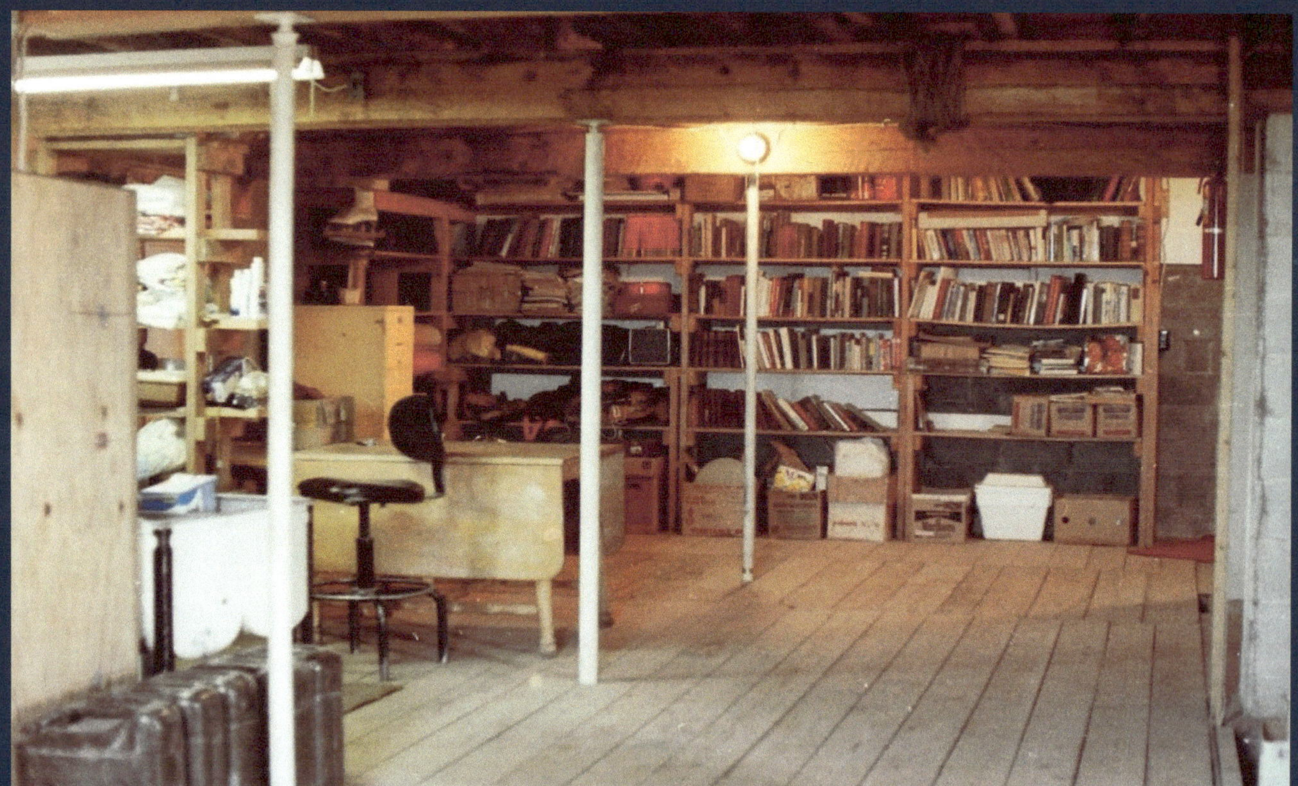
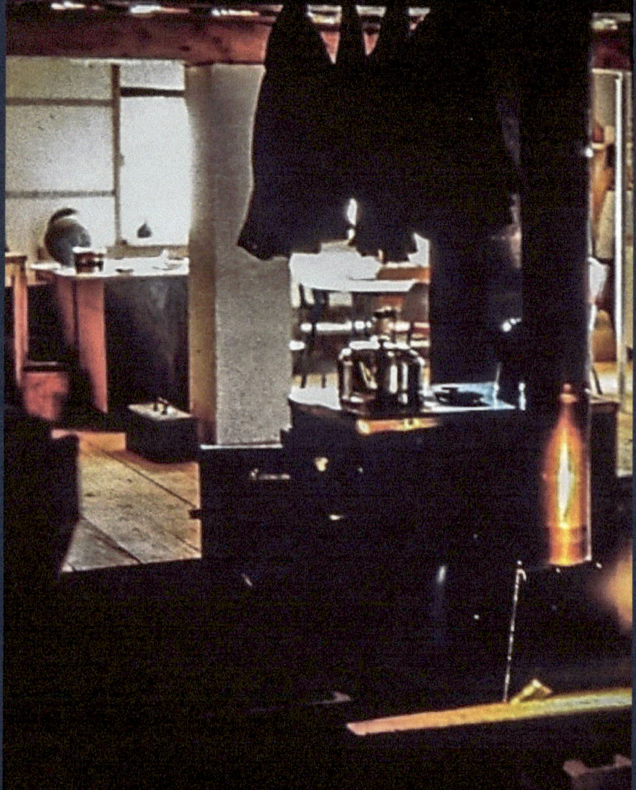

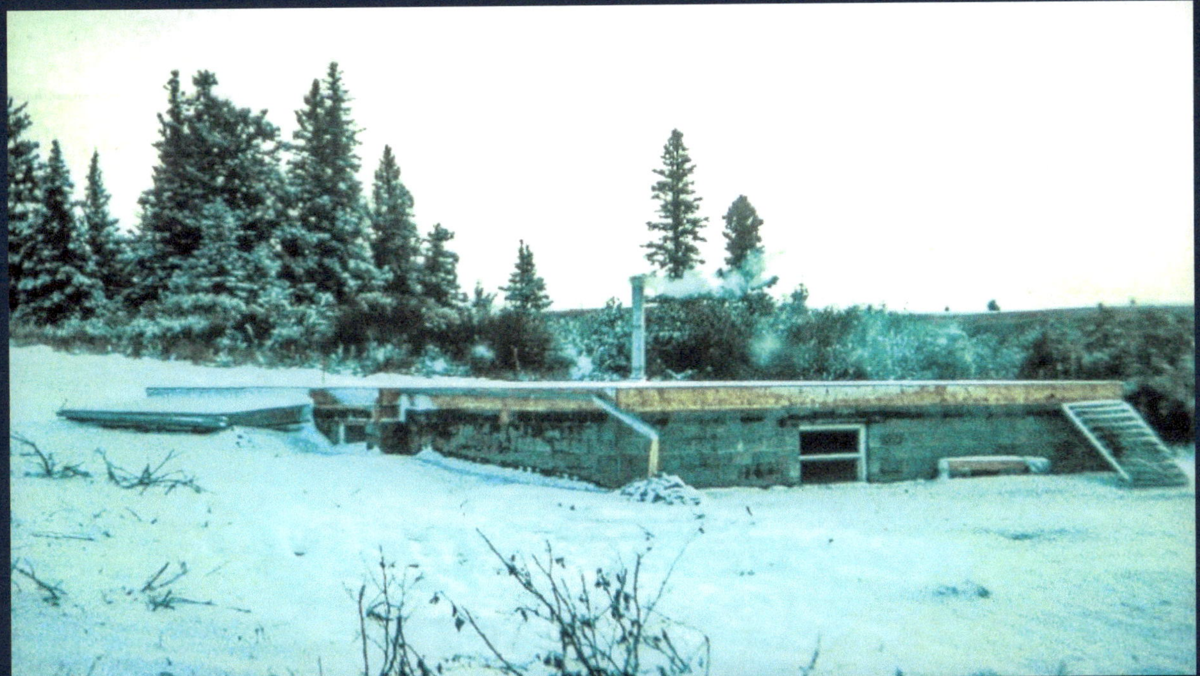

Painting the new underground fortress a light yellow
presented a friendly smile shining out of the snow.

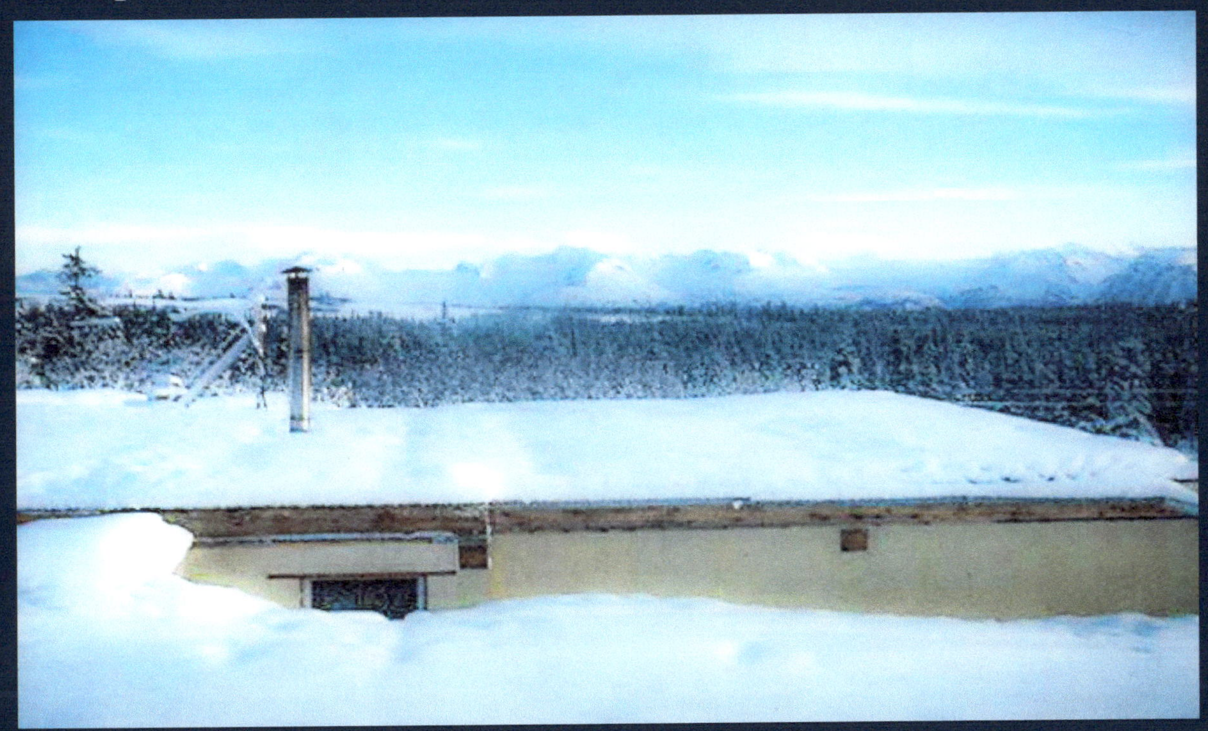

That glowing smile would be a welcome sight to anyone
riding through a storm.

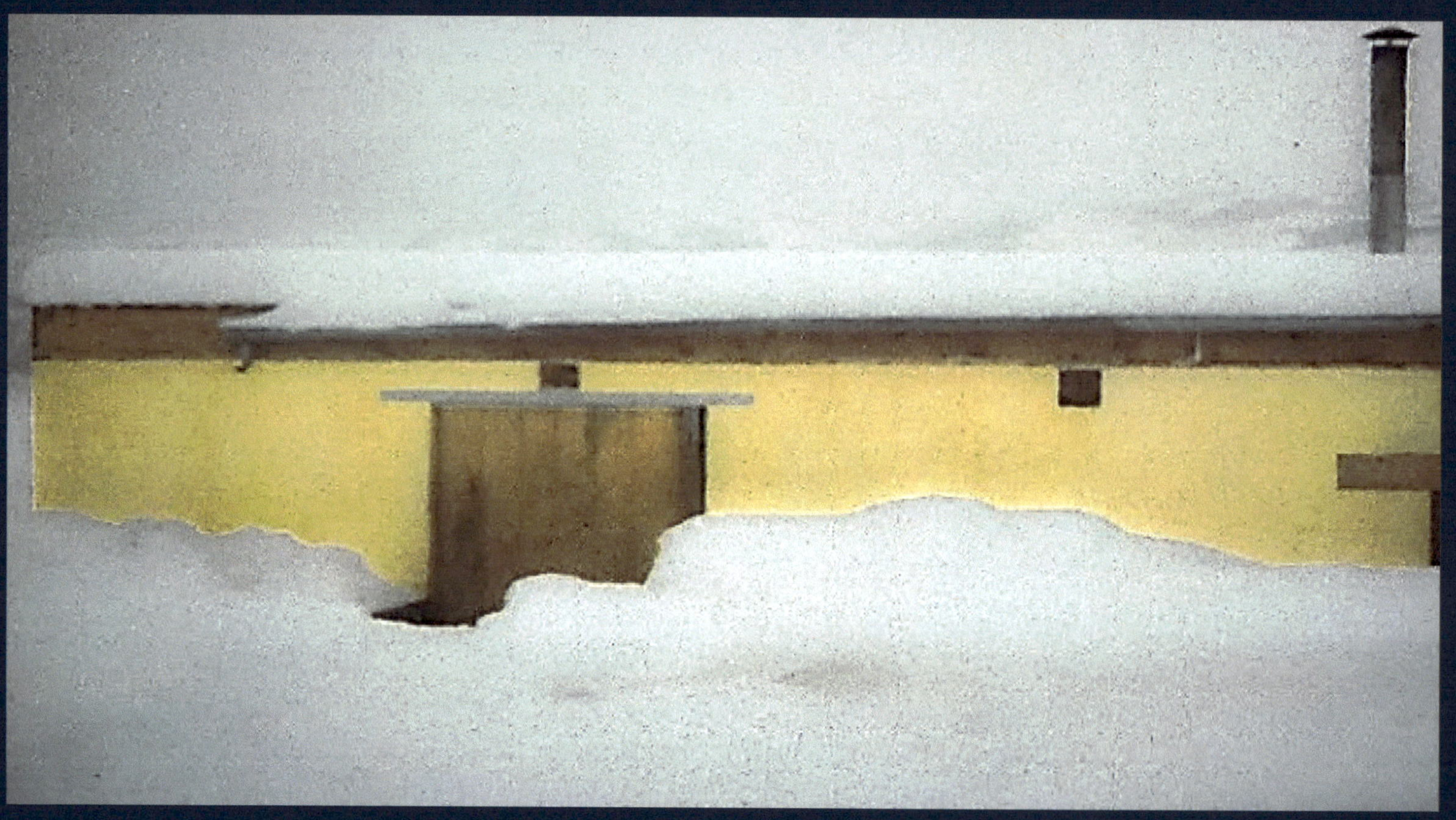

It was always a good feeling to make it home, *especially* in a storm.

A Christmas gift to us from Rural Electric came just in time.

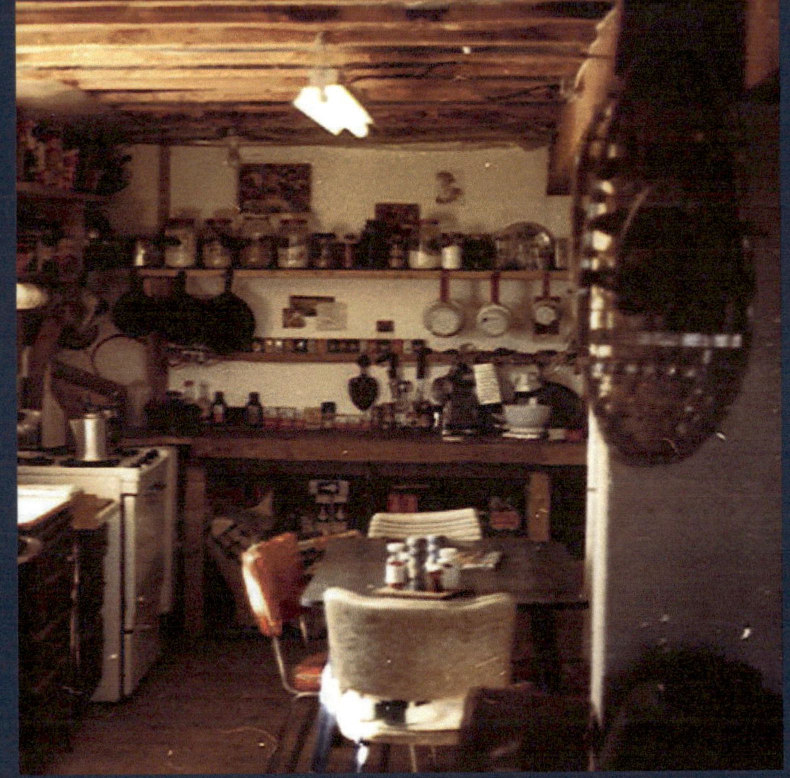

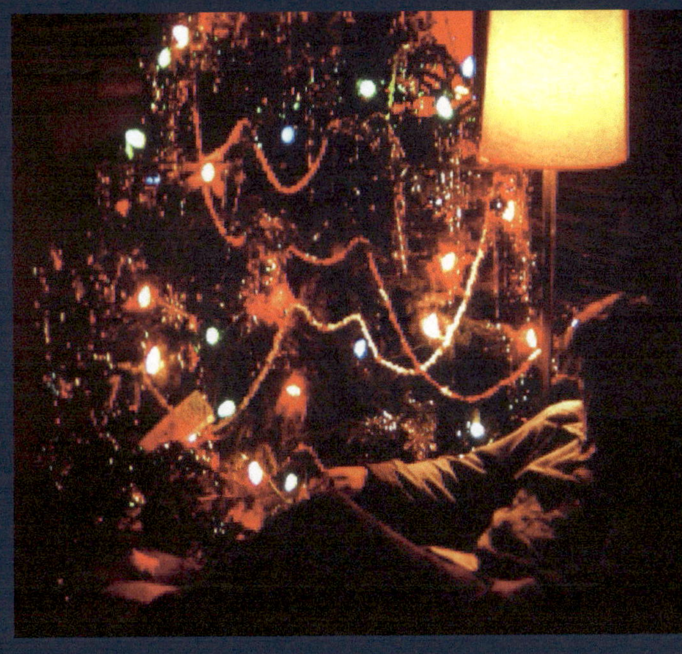

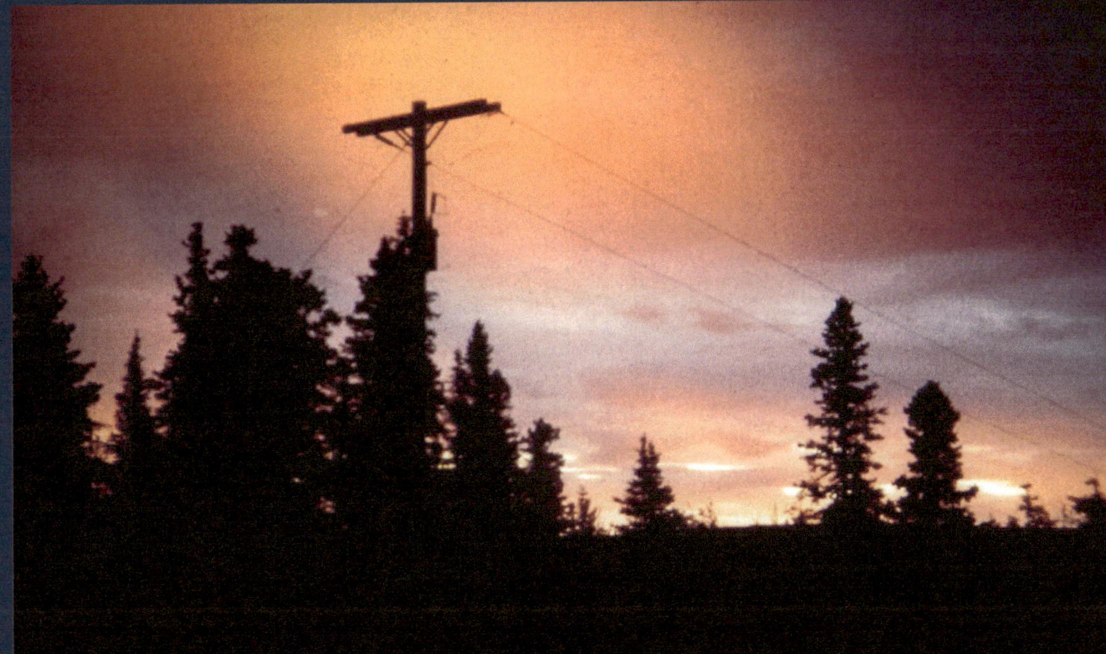

Tim was ready to establish a family.

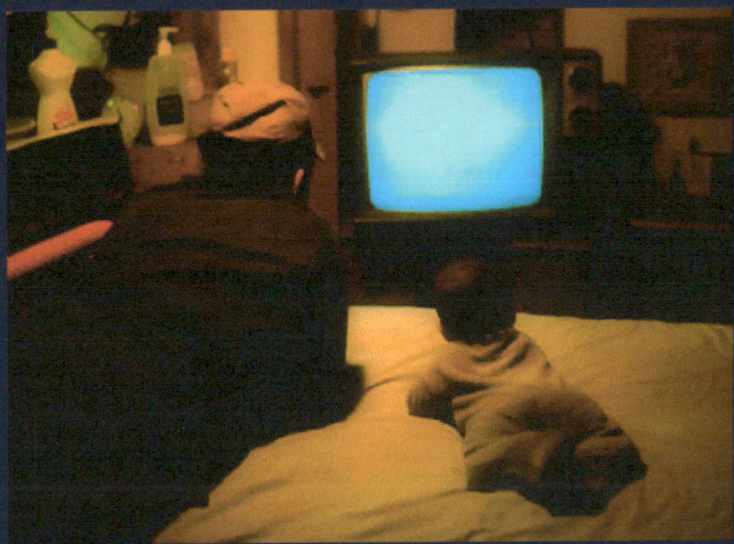

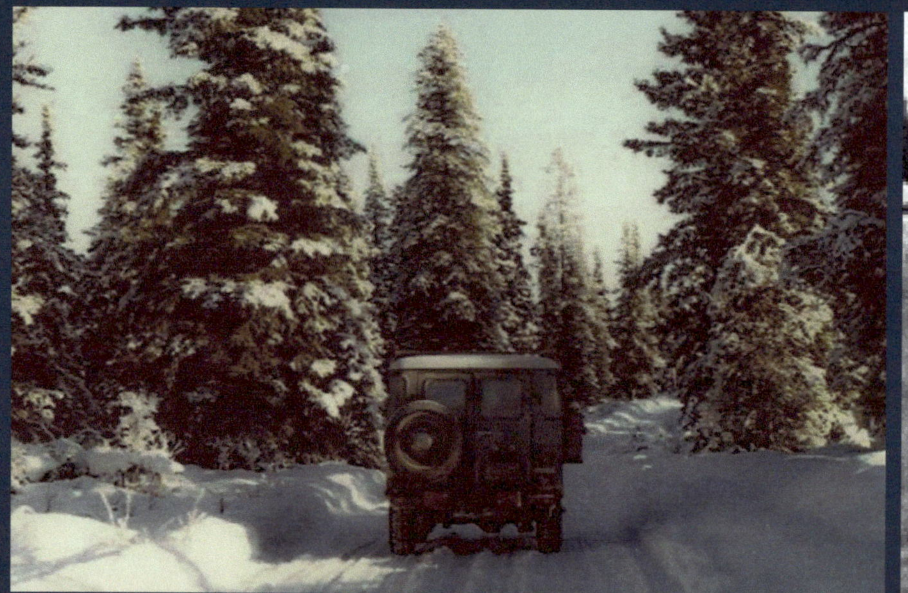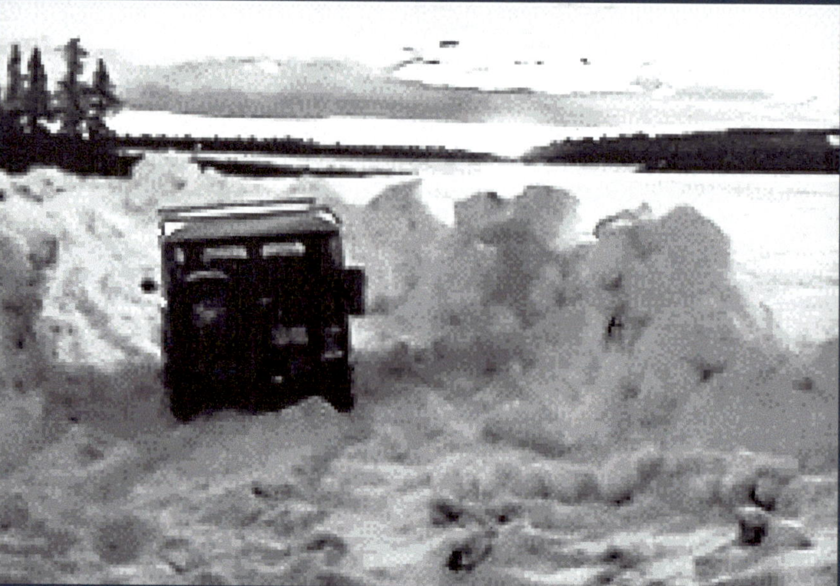

What we had thought would be a perfect road
turned out to be driveable only 20% of the year.

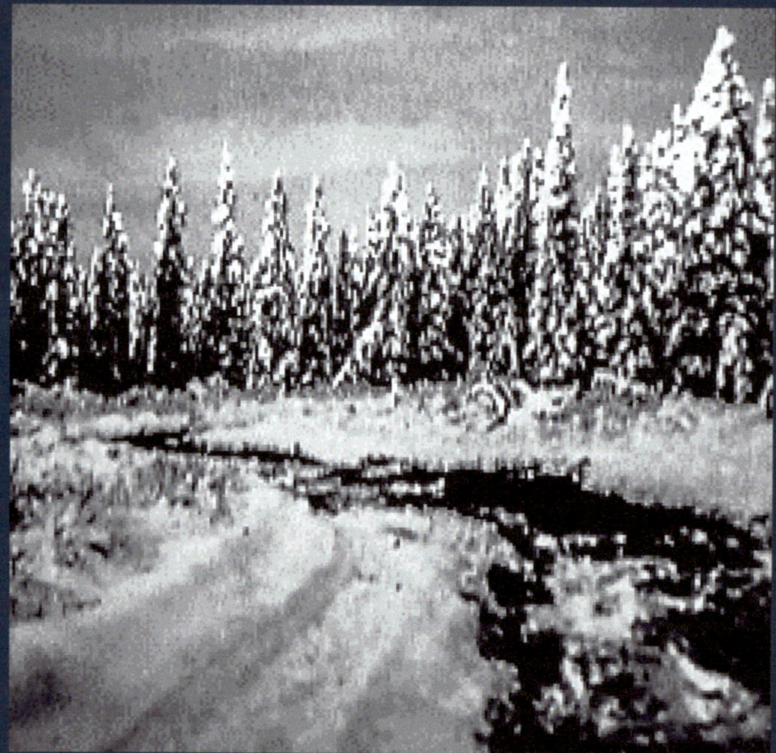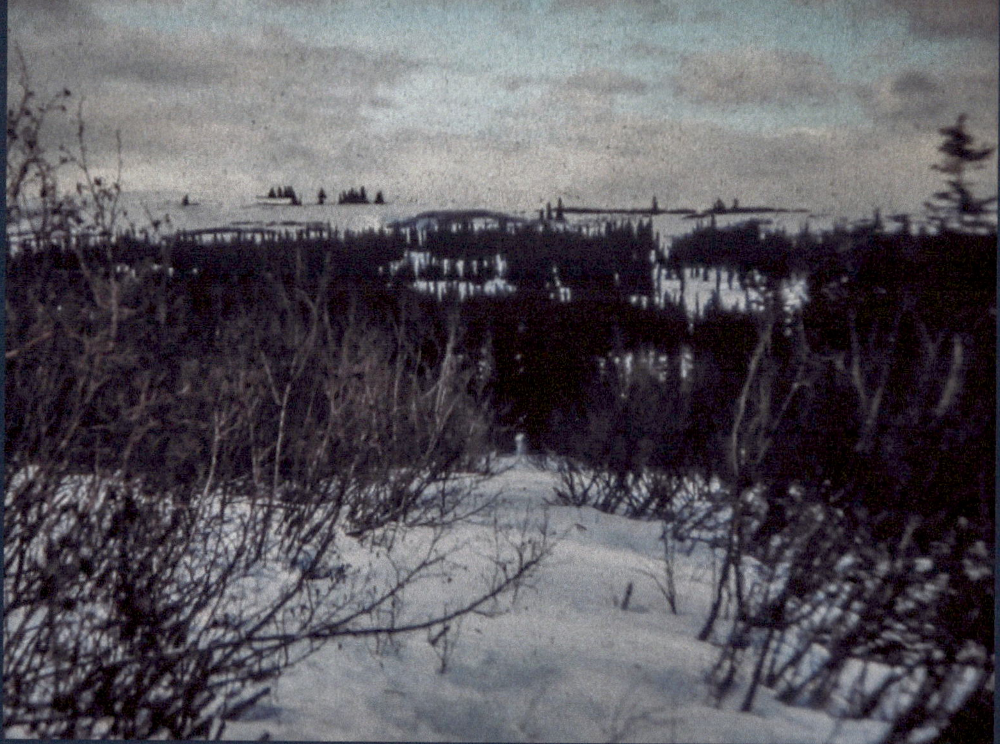

We used different rigs to get home, depending upon the season.
Most of the year we used snow-machines to get in and out.

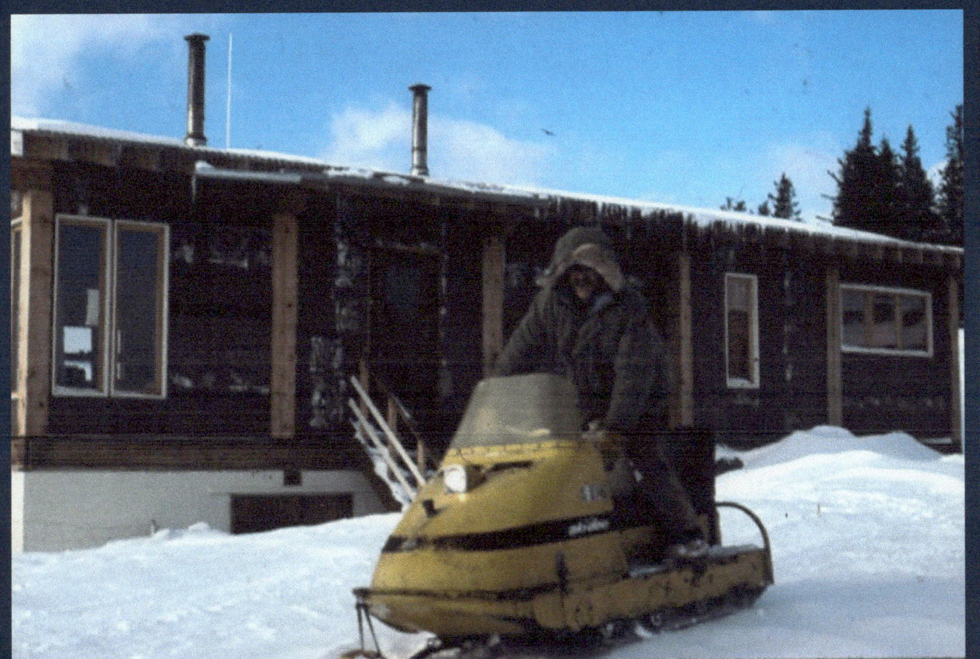

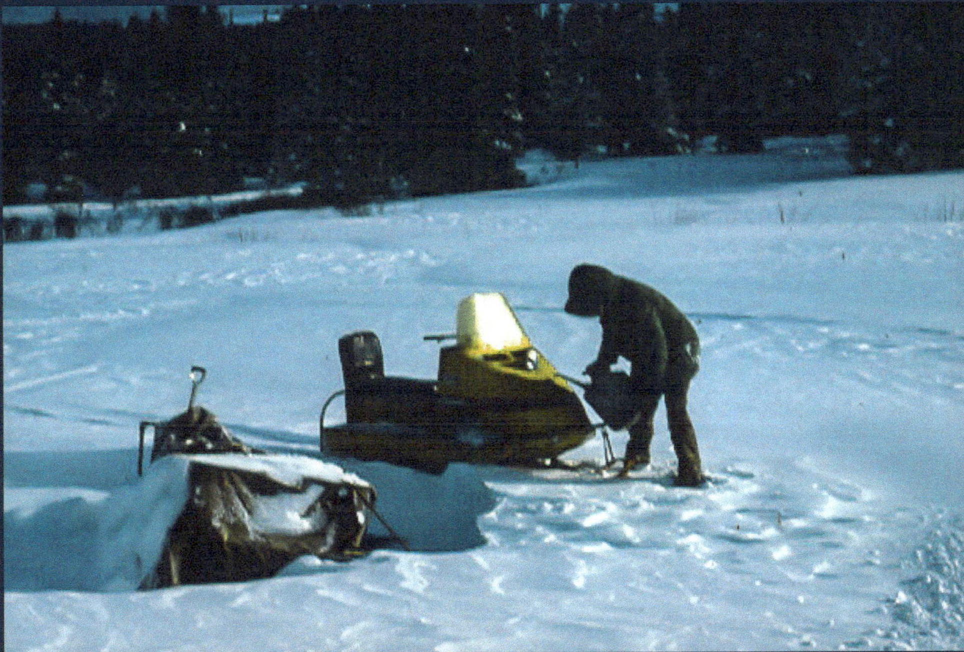

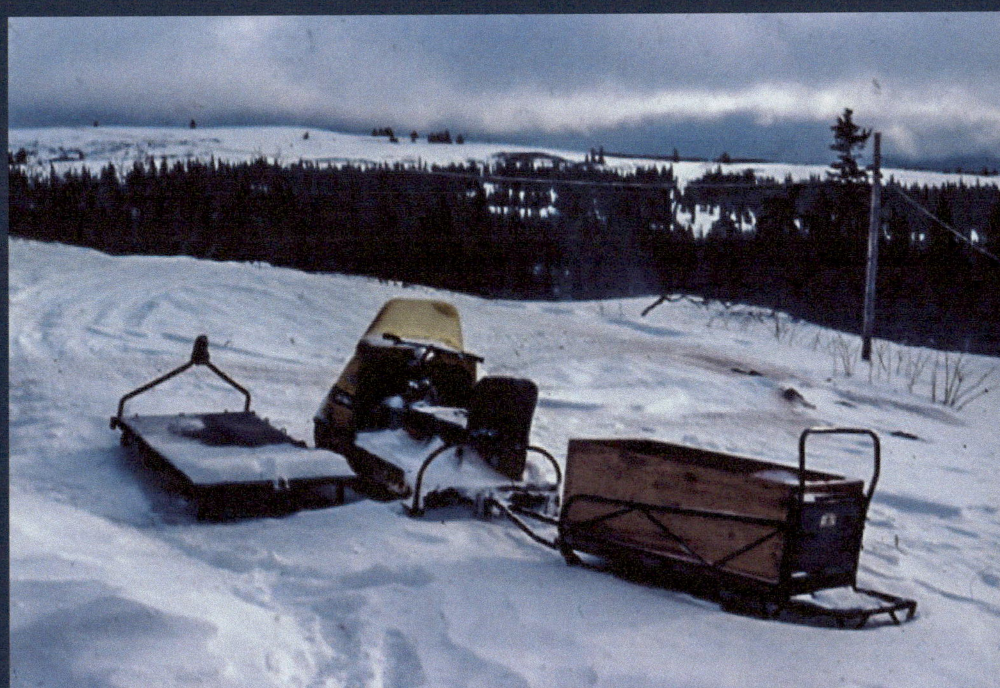

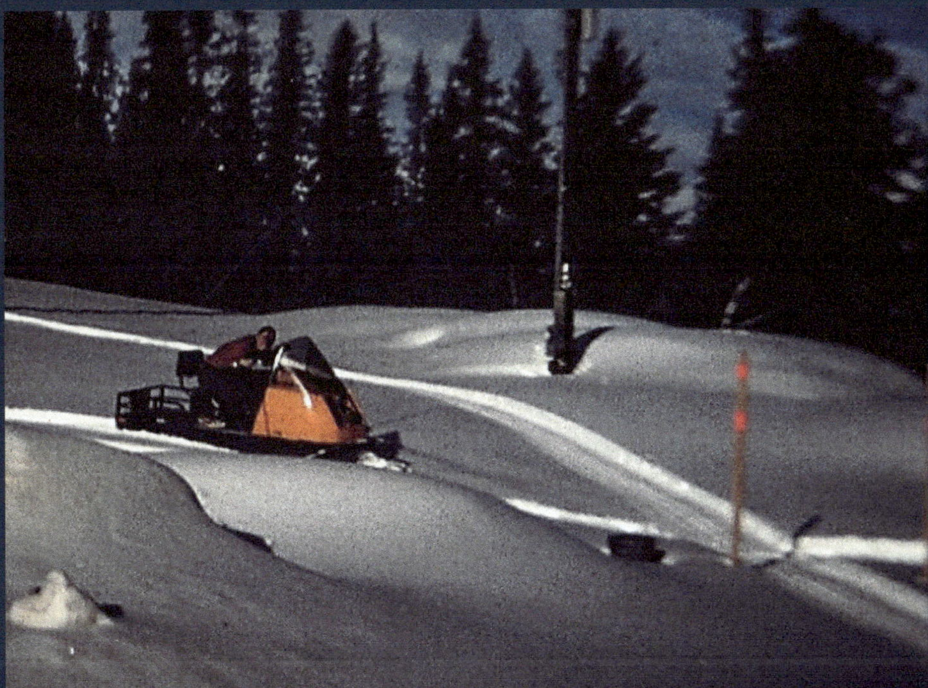

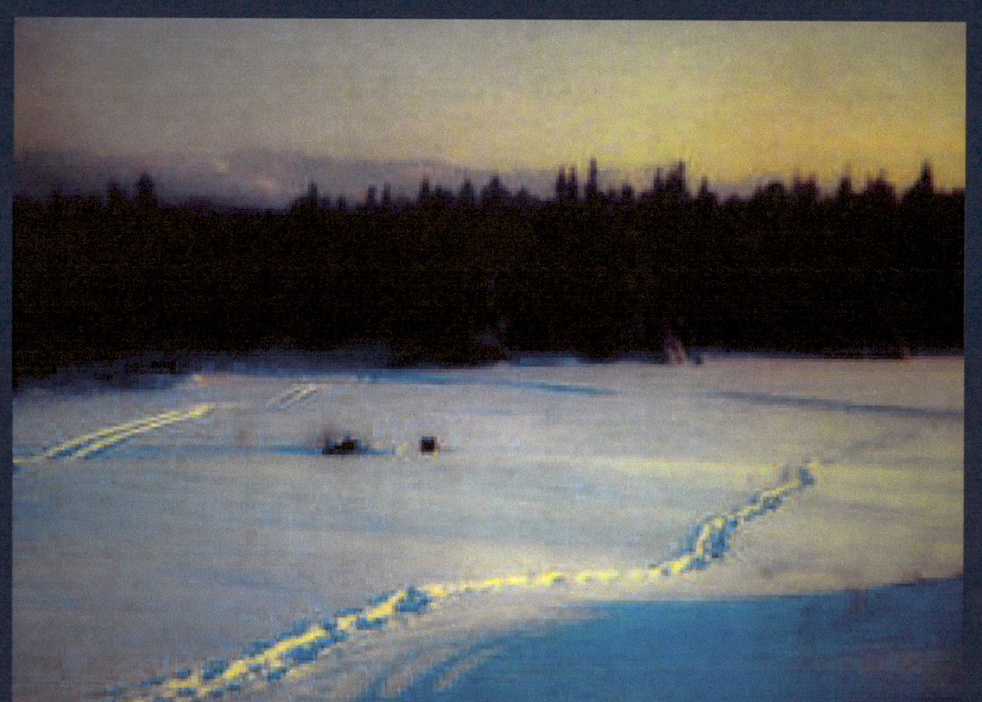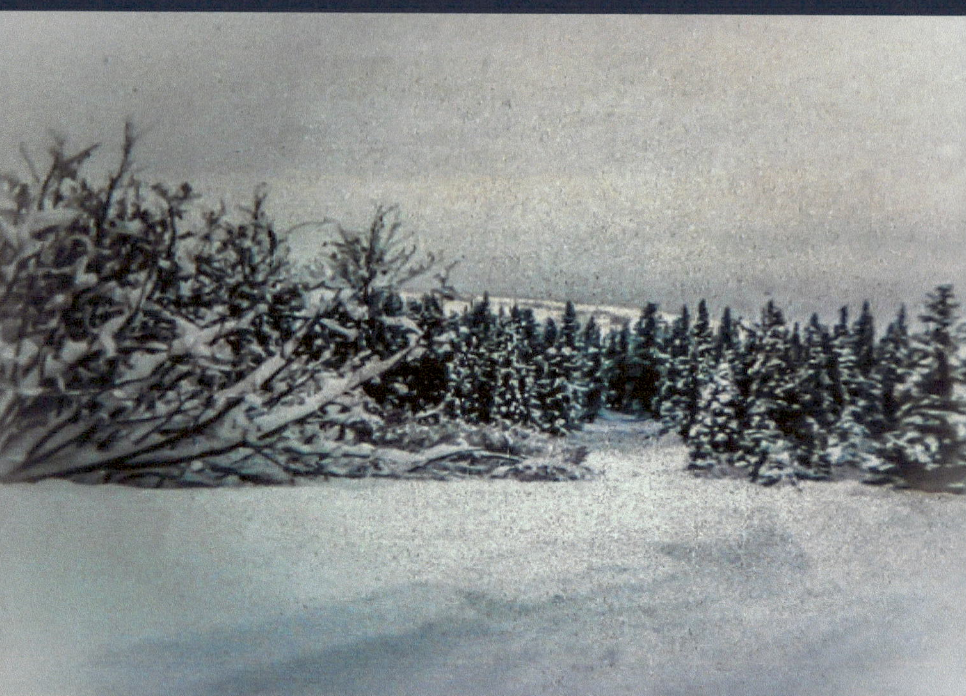

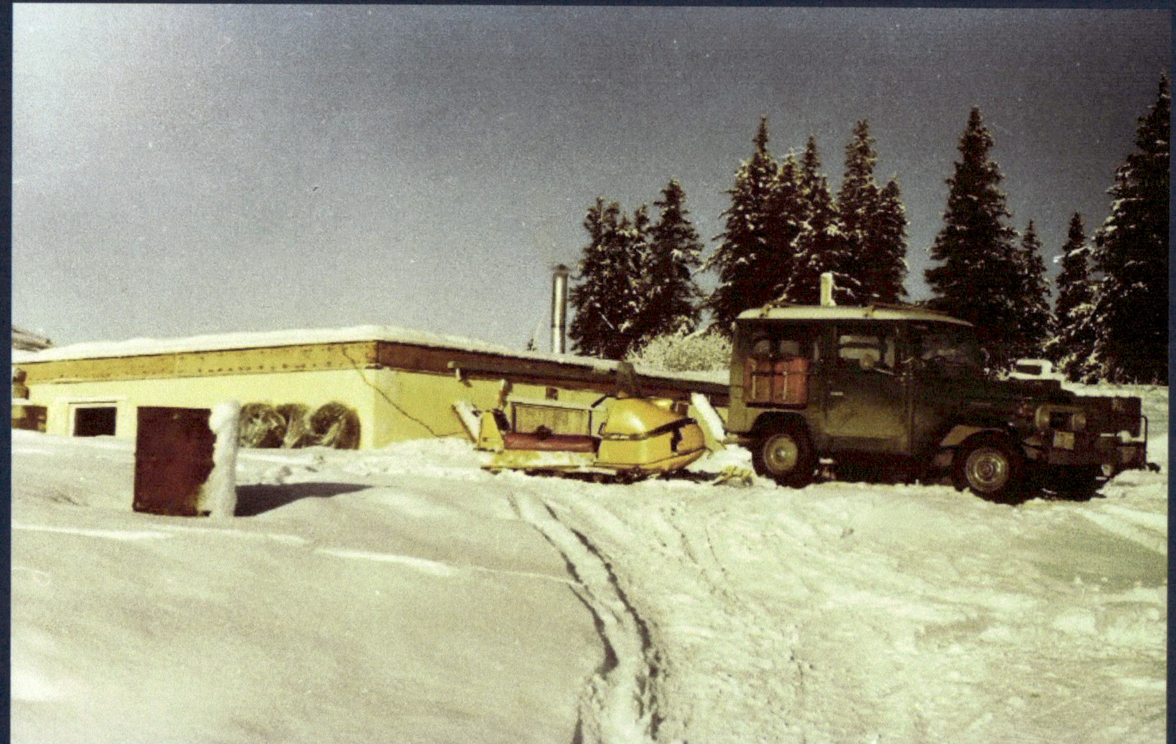

Any day that you could park by the front door was a good day.

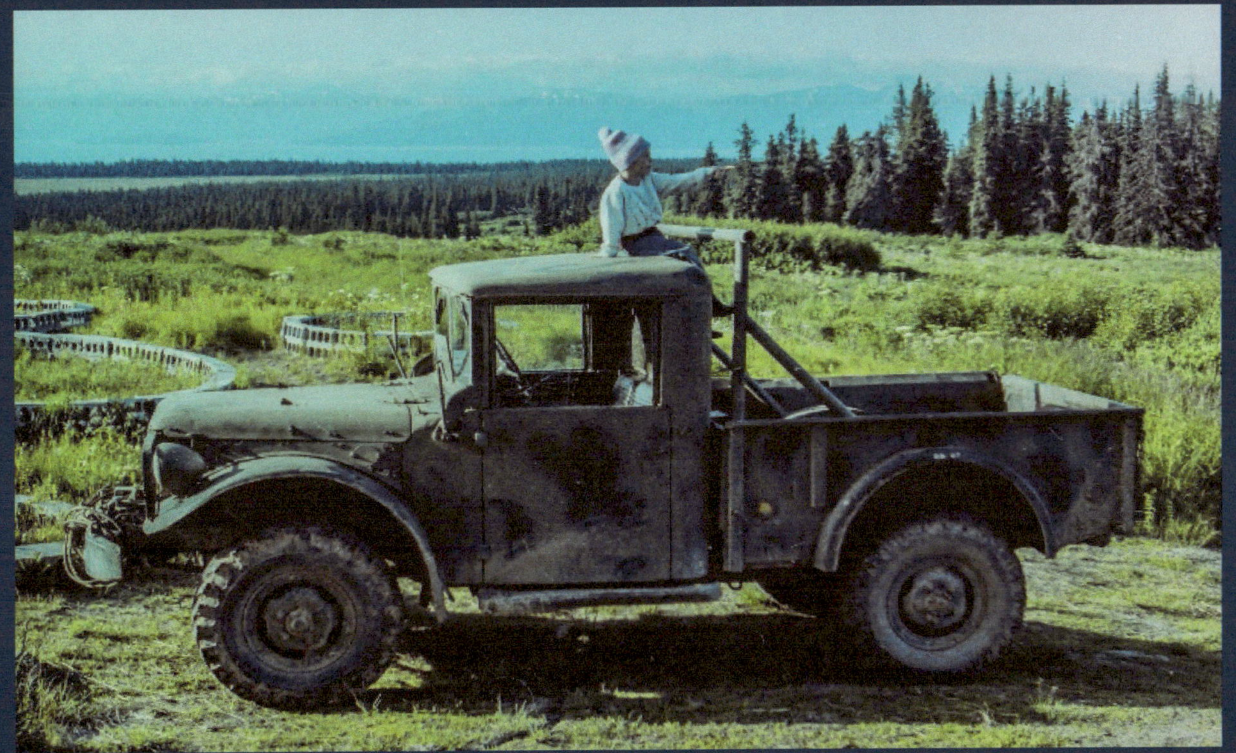

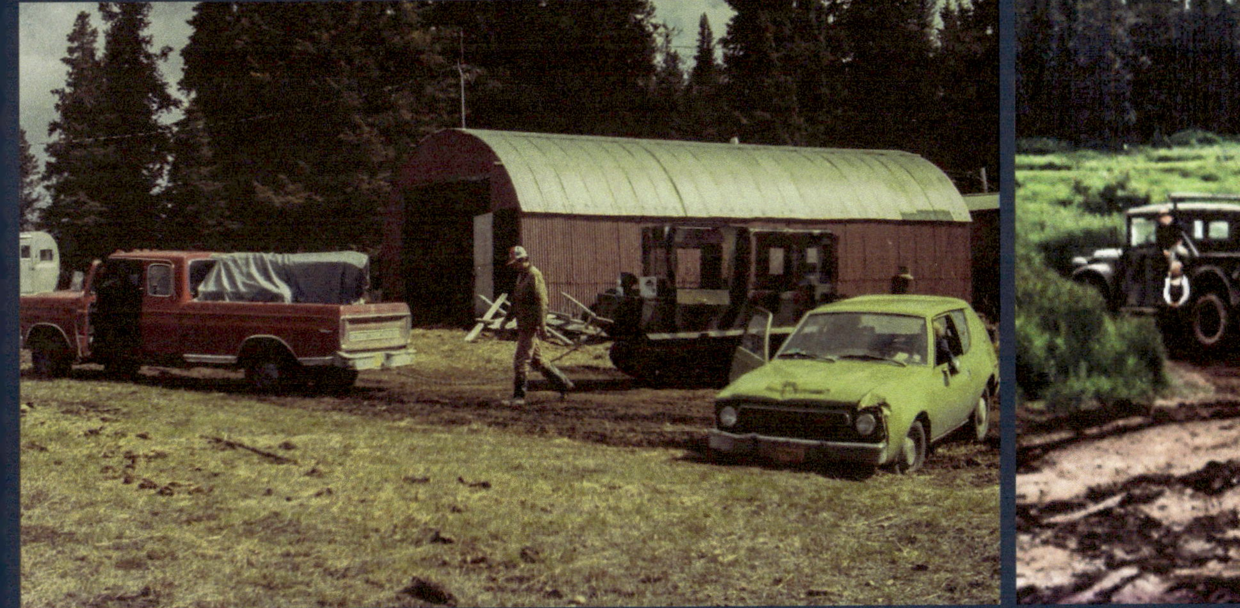

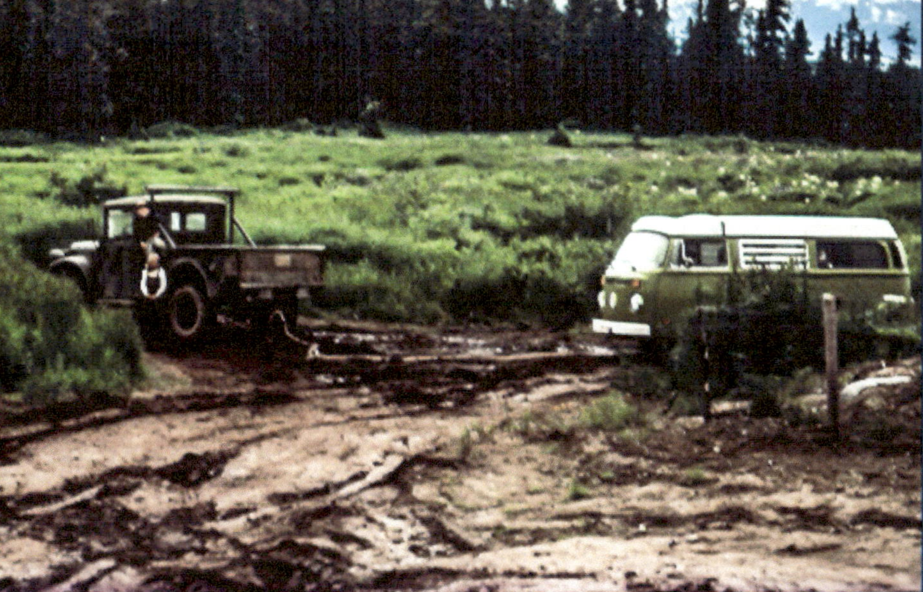

We rarely had visitors—except Grandma Tutu, who came up several times.
To board our "new" military Weasel she climbed in through the window.

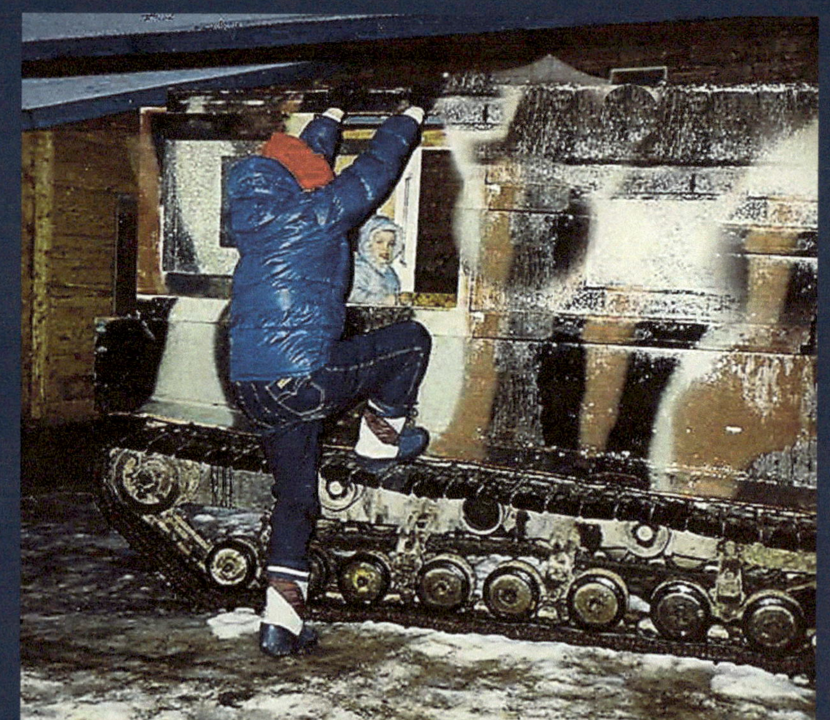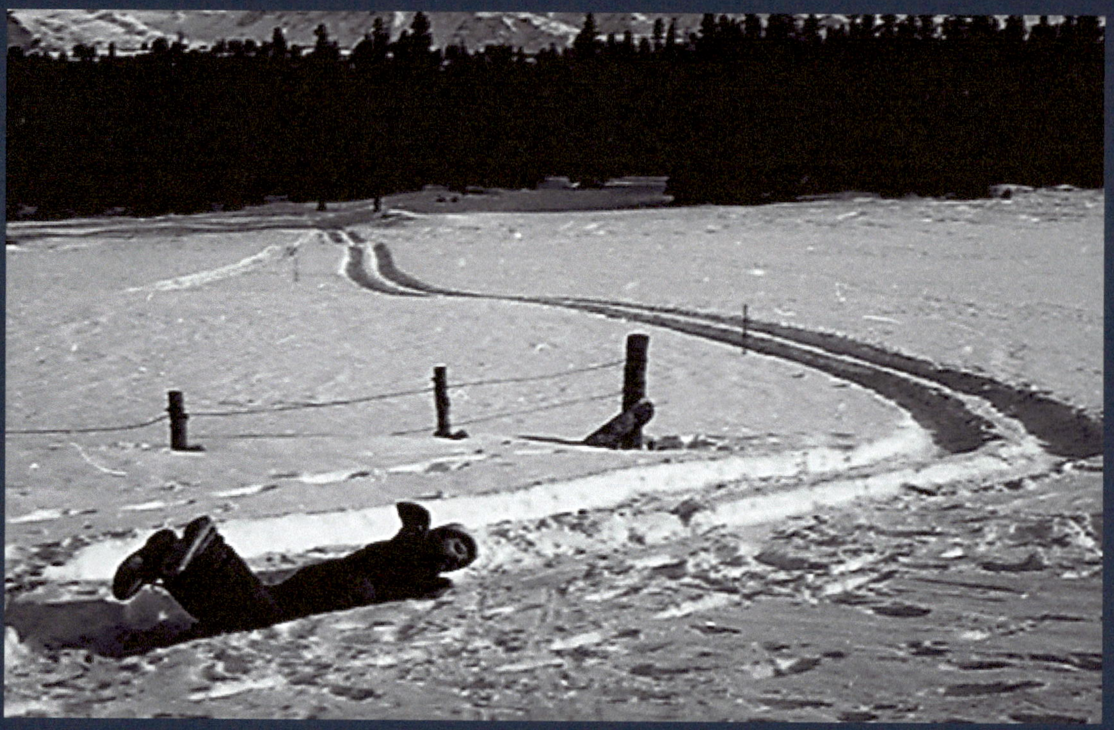

That 1943 M-29 etched a perfect pair of sledding tracks down into the woods,
but I really preferred snowshoeing.

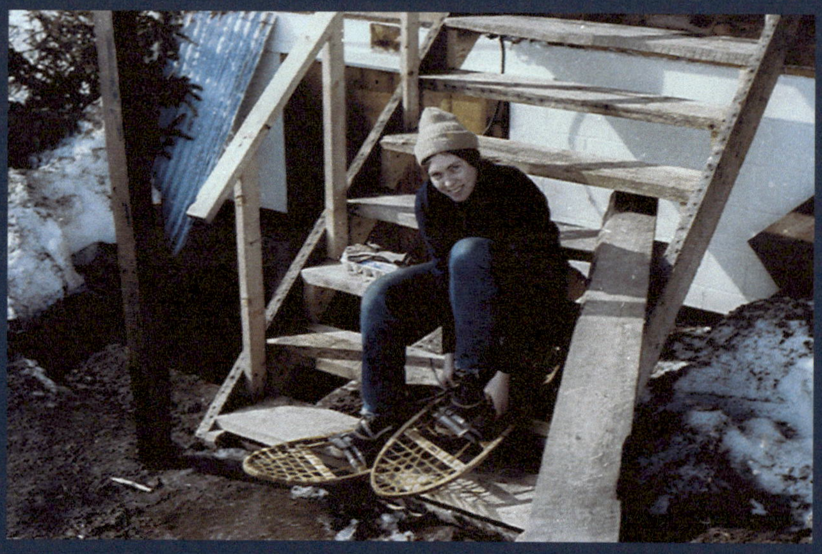

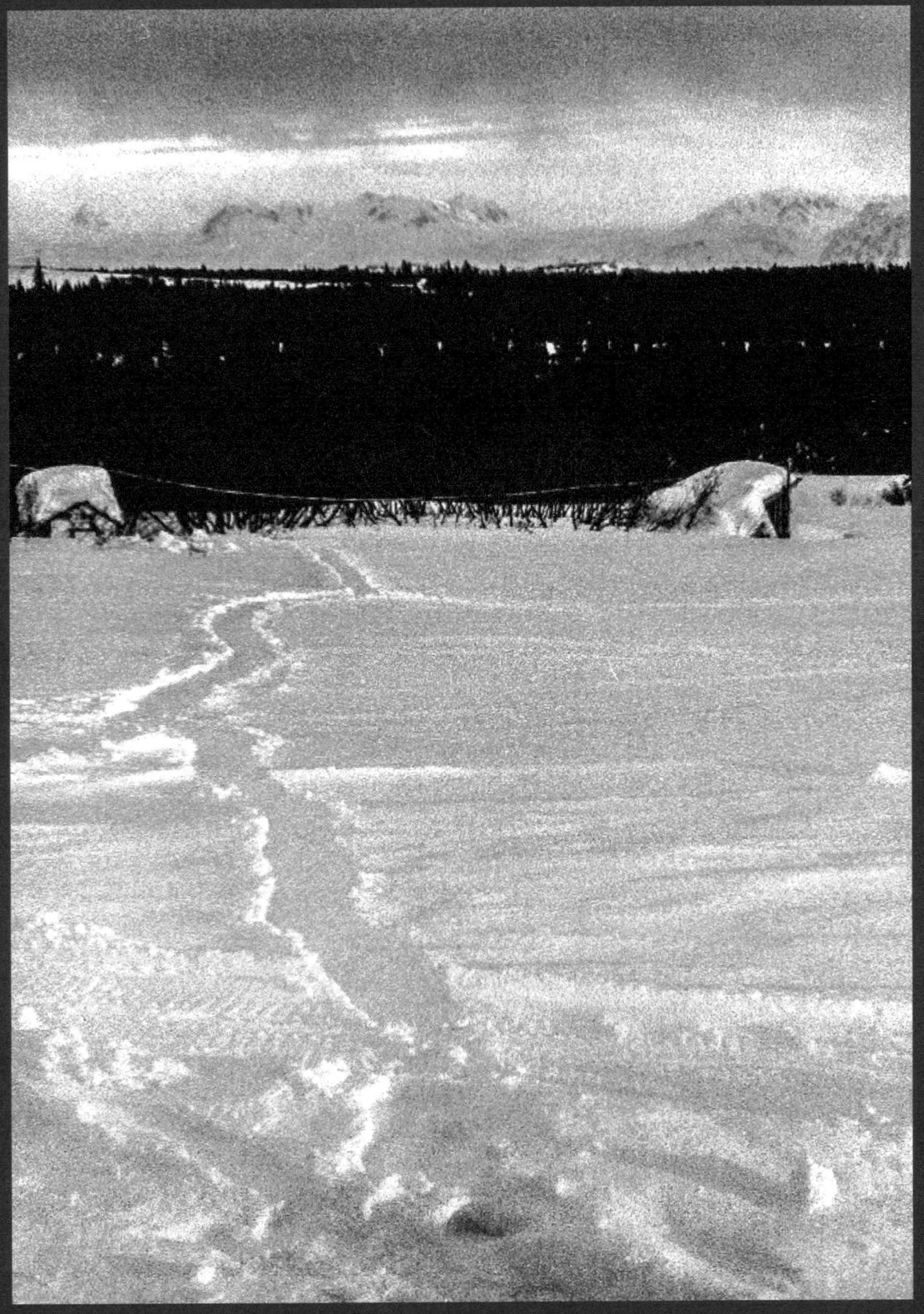

It was quite a hike down to the privy from the new housesite,
but I knew we'd have running water within the year, so no worries.

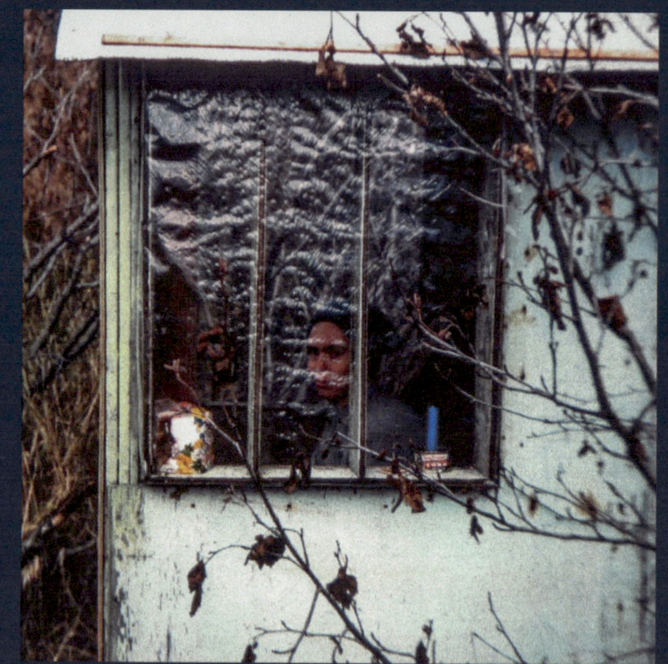

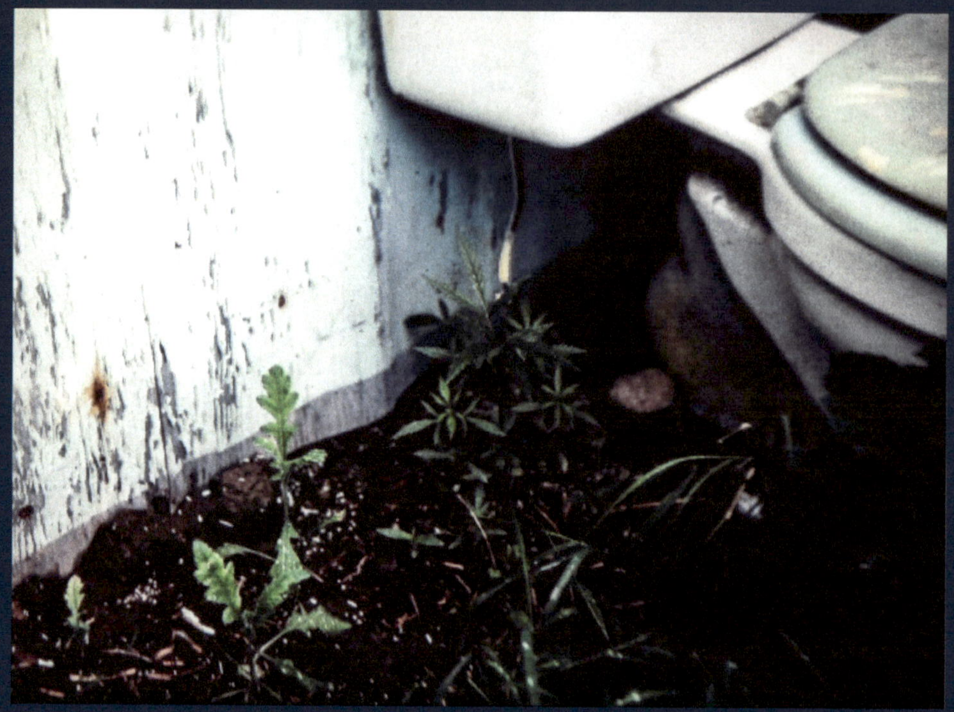

I even had a toilet standing by the privy, waiting for the big day.

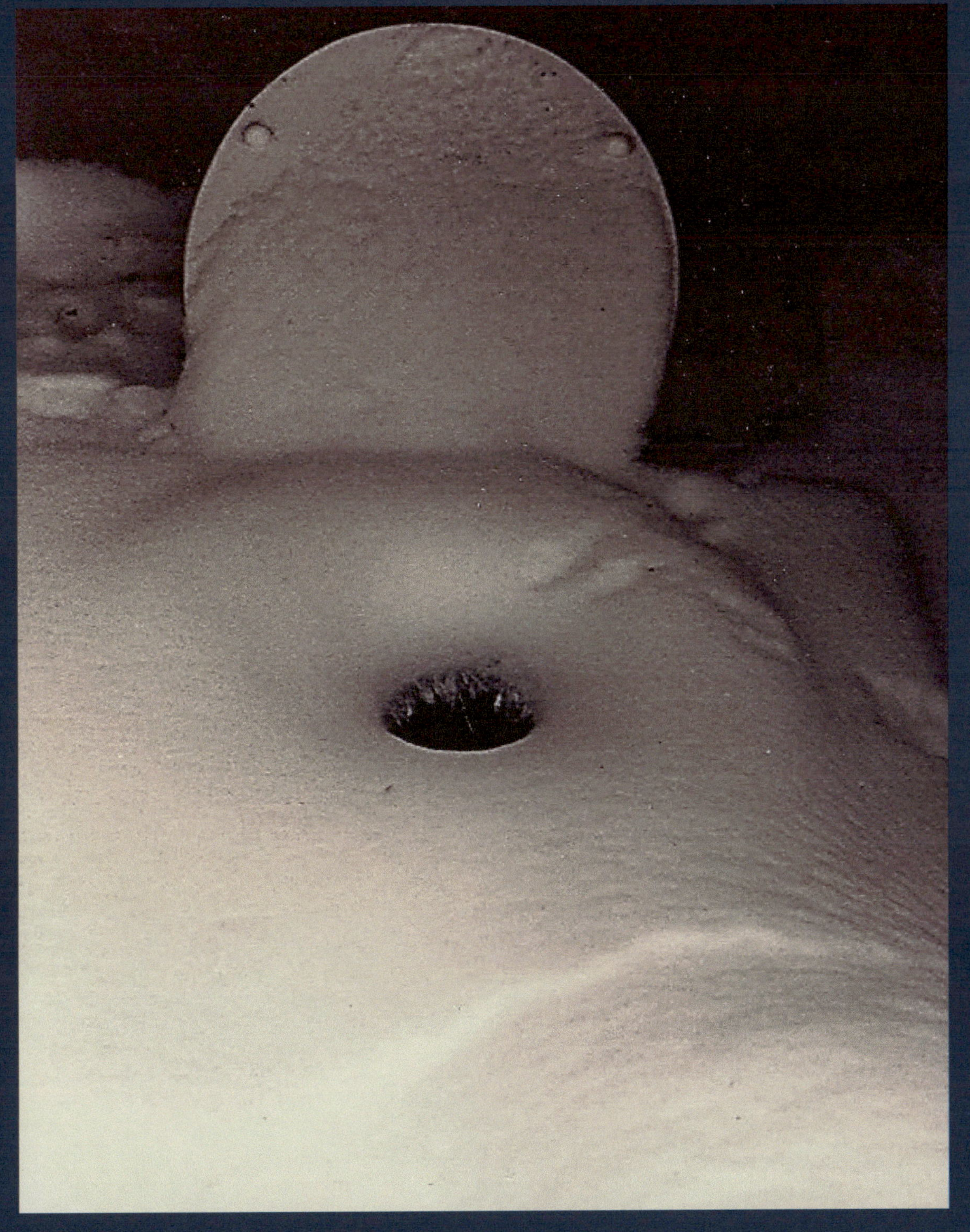

. . . which I figured would be a huge improvement, especially in winter.

But for now, it was five gallons in—five gallons out.

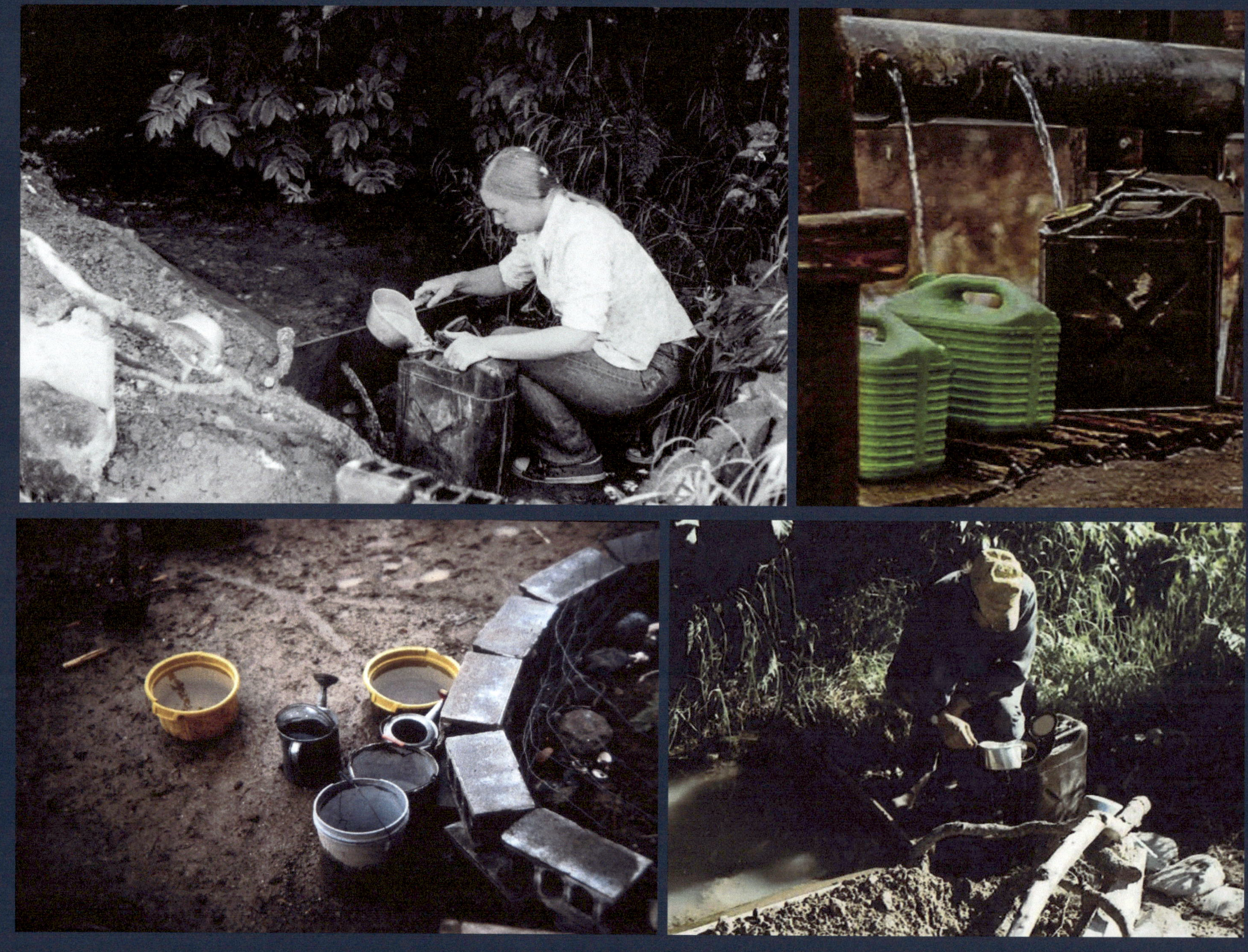

Meanwhile, it would take 200 peeled logs to build our "real" house on top of the basement.

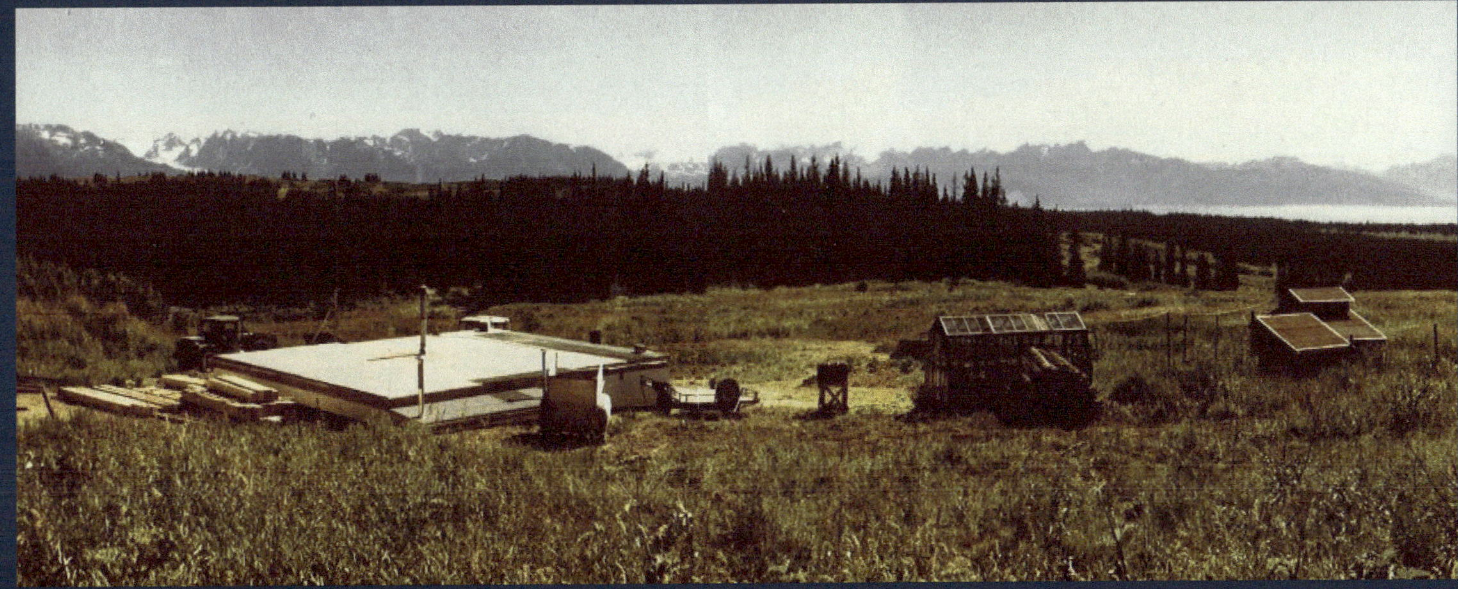

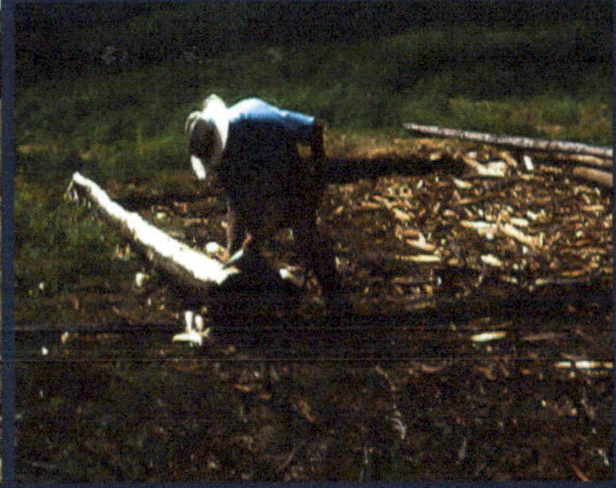

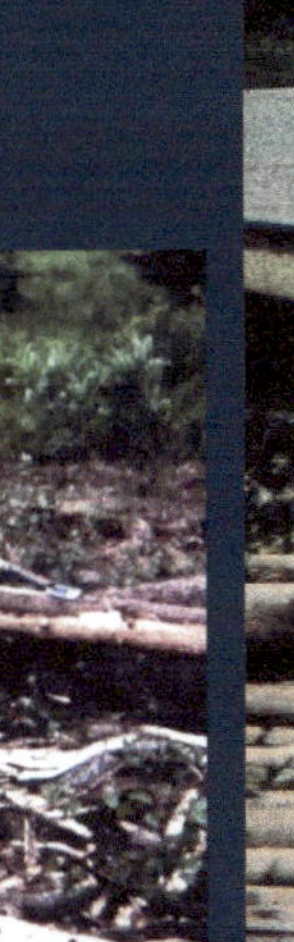

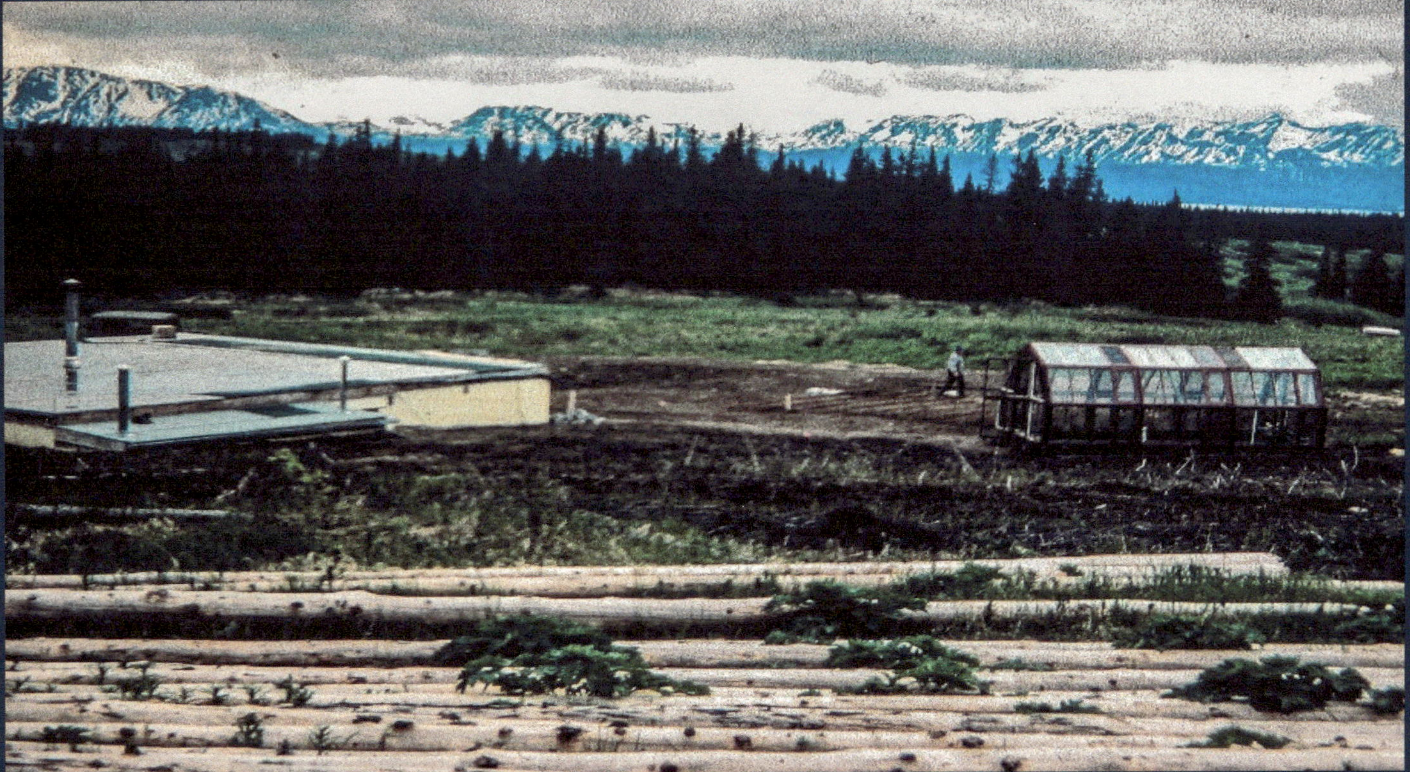

Done!

News of our pending first-born
convinced us to shelf the log cabin plans
and pursue a less (?) labor-intensive post-and-beam dream, instead.

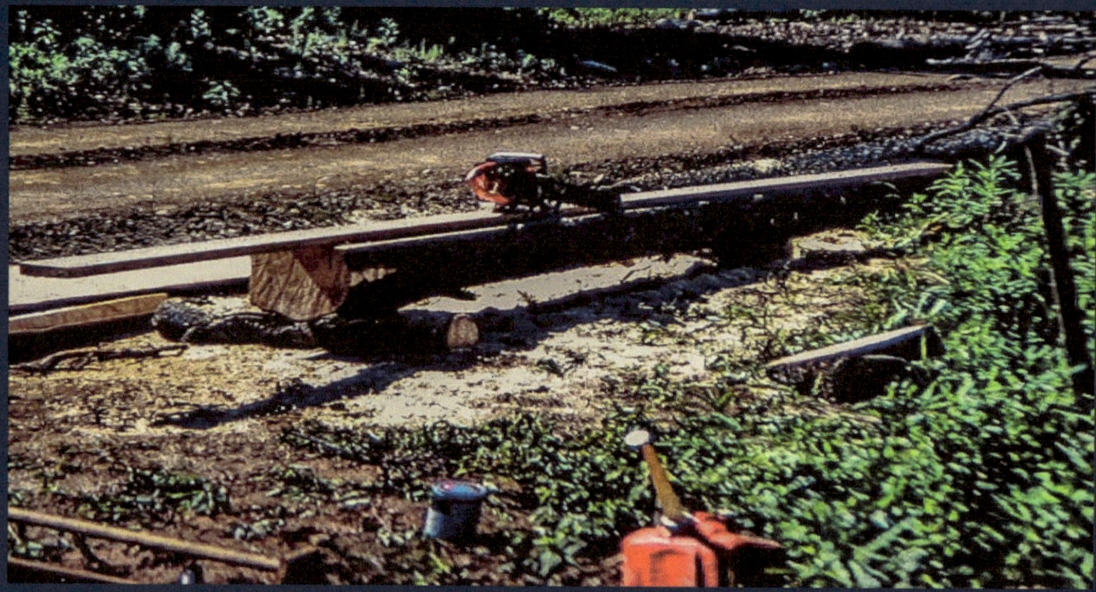

Hewing and hauling 55 beams out of the woods was sort of fun.

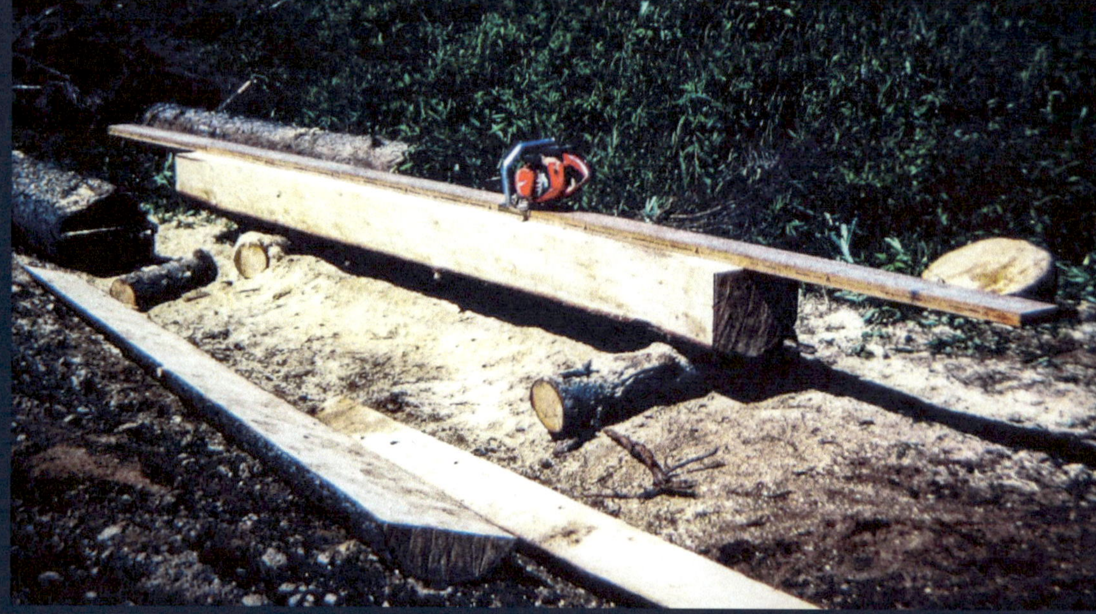

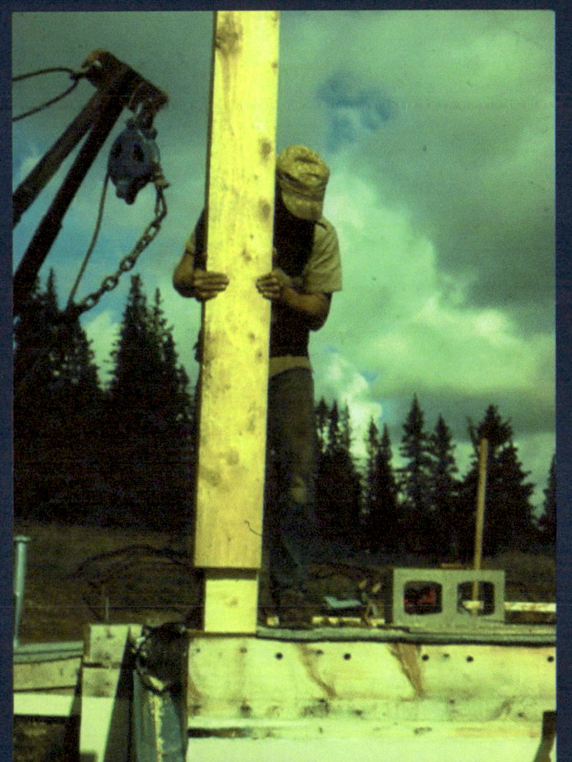
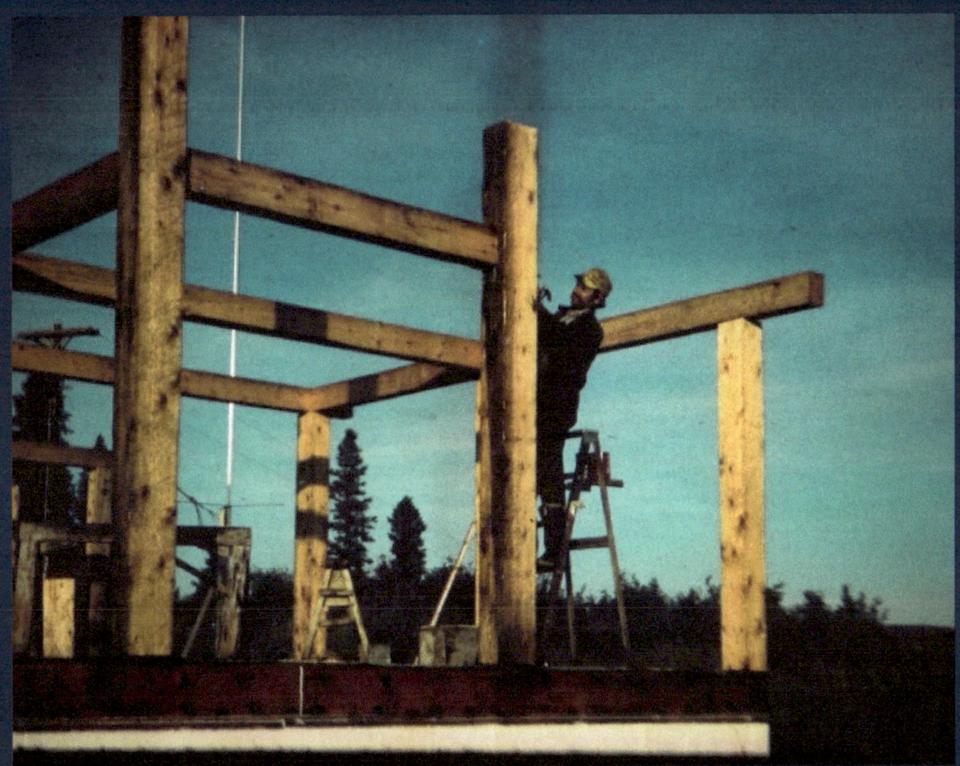
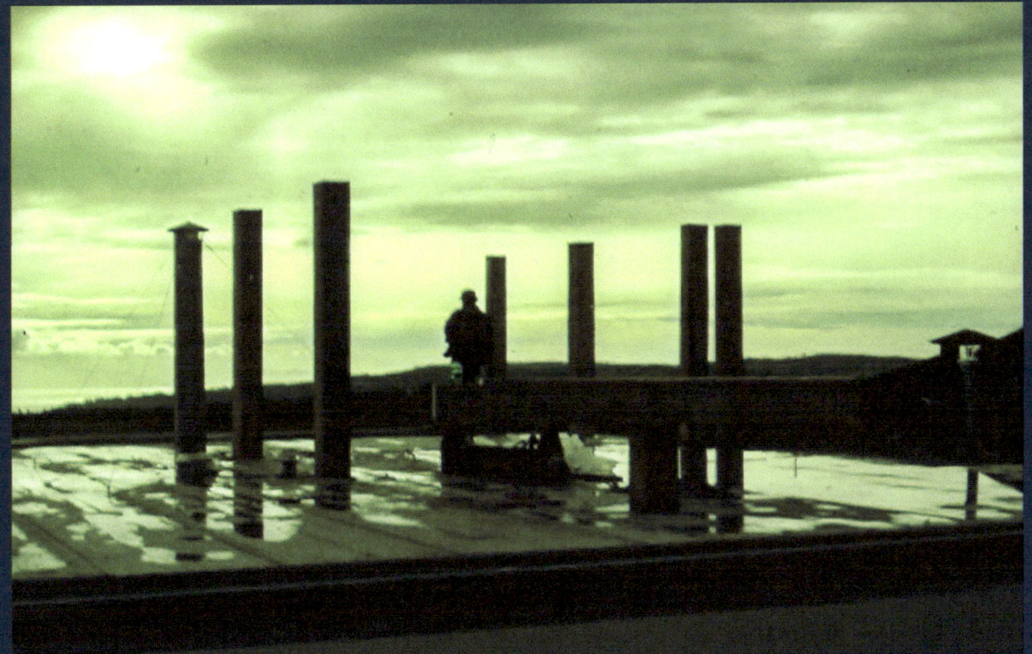

Tim looked exceedingly happy to be living his dream.

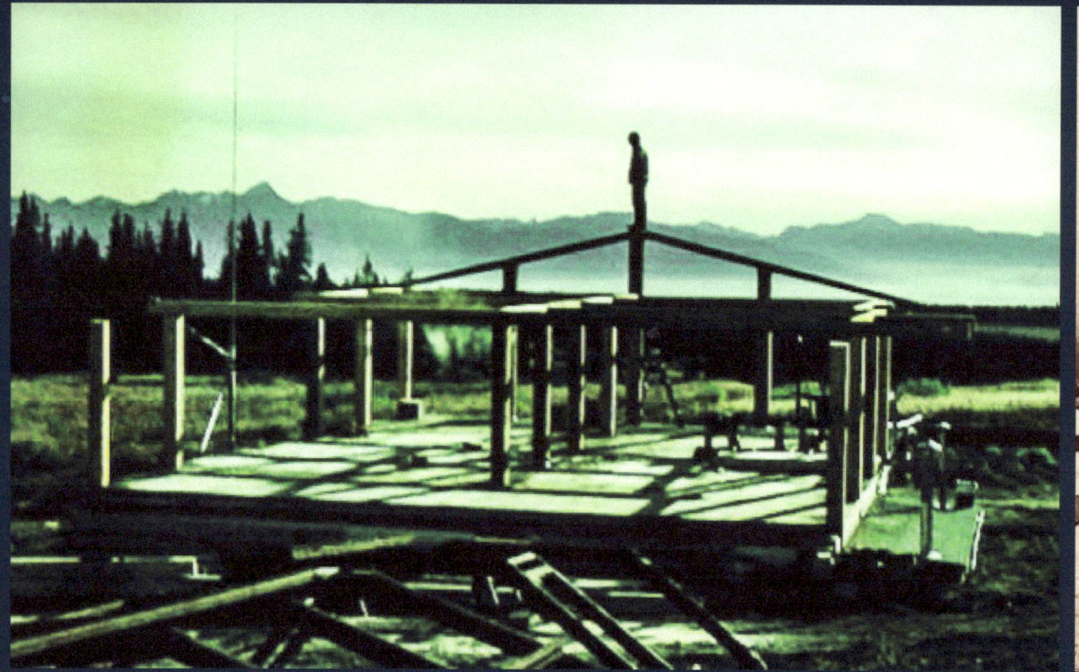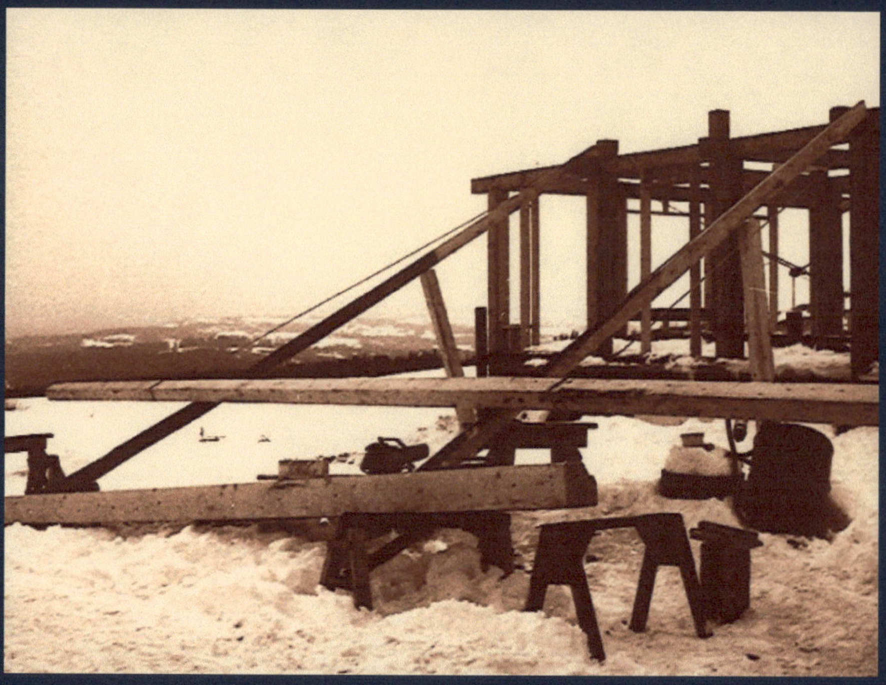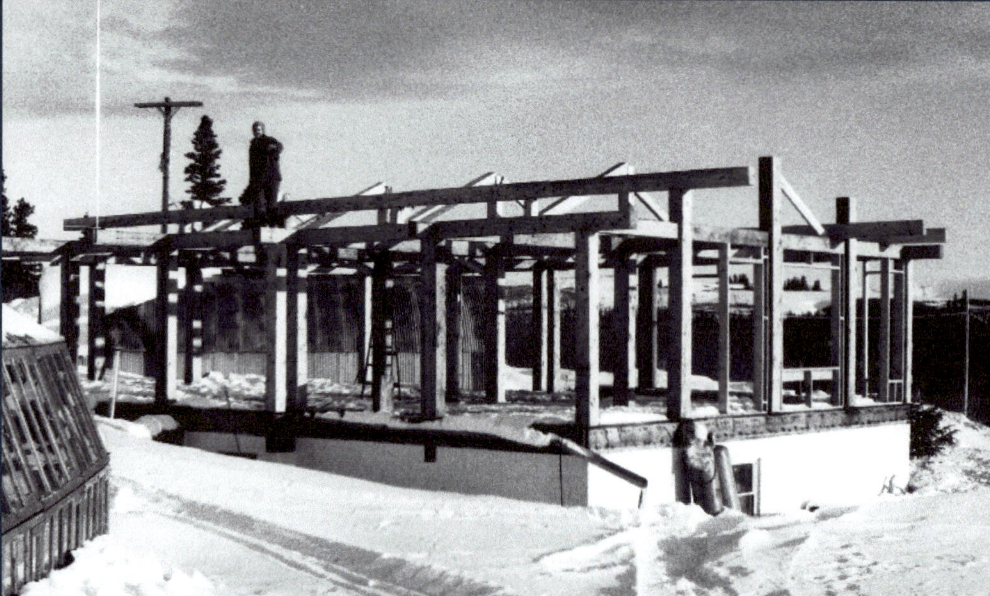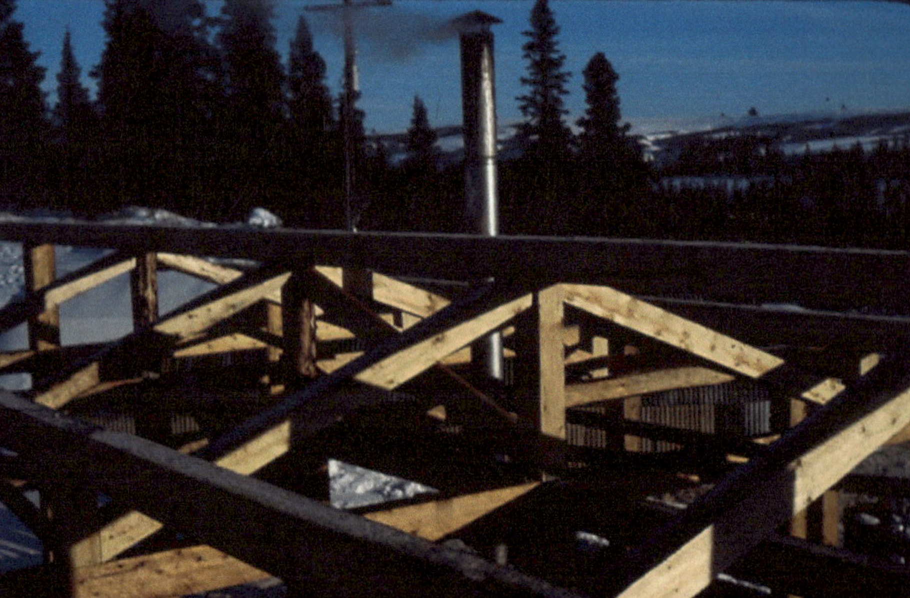

When the beamwork frame was completed
I was so proud of us that I thought I'd burst my buttons.

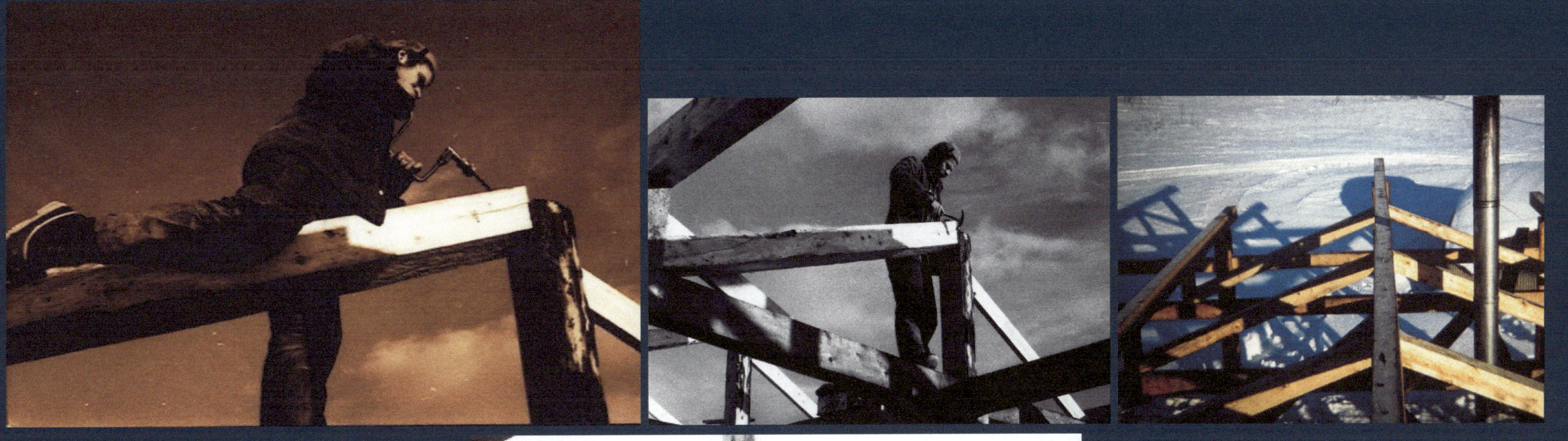

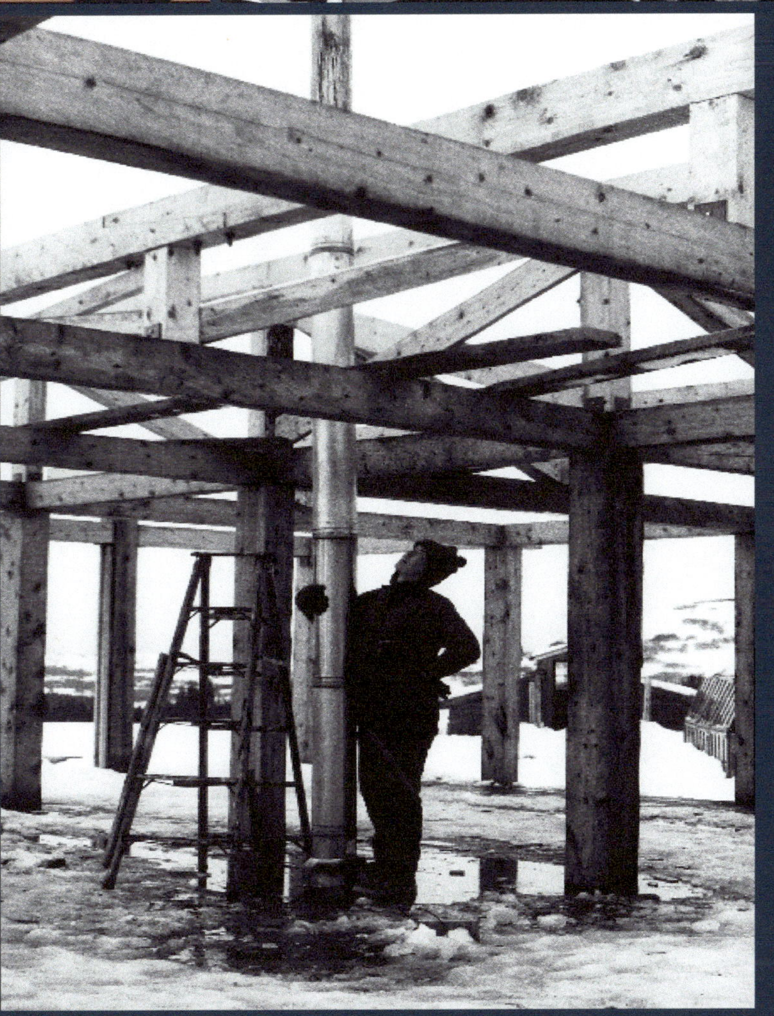

By this time,
I was nearly
nine months
pregnant.

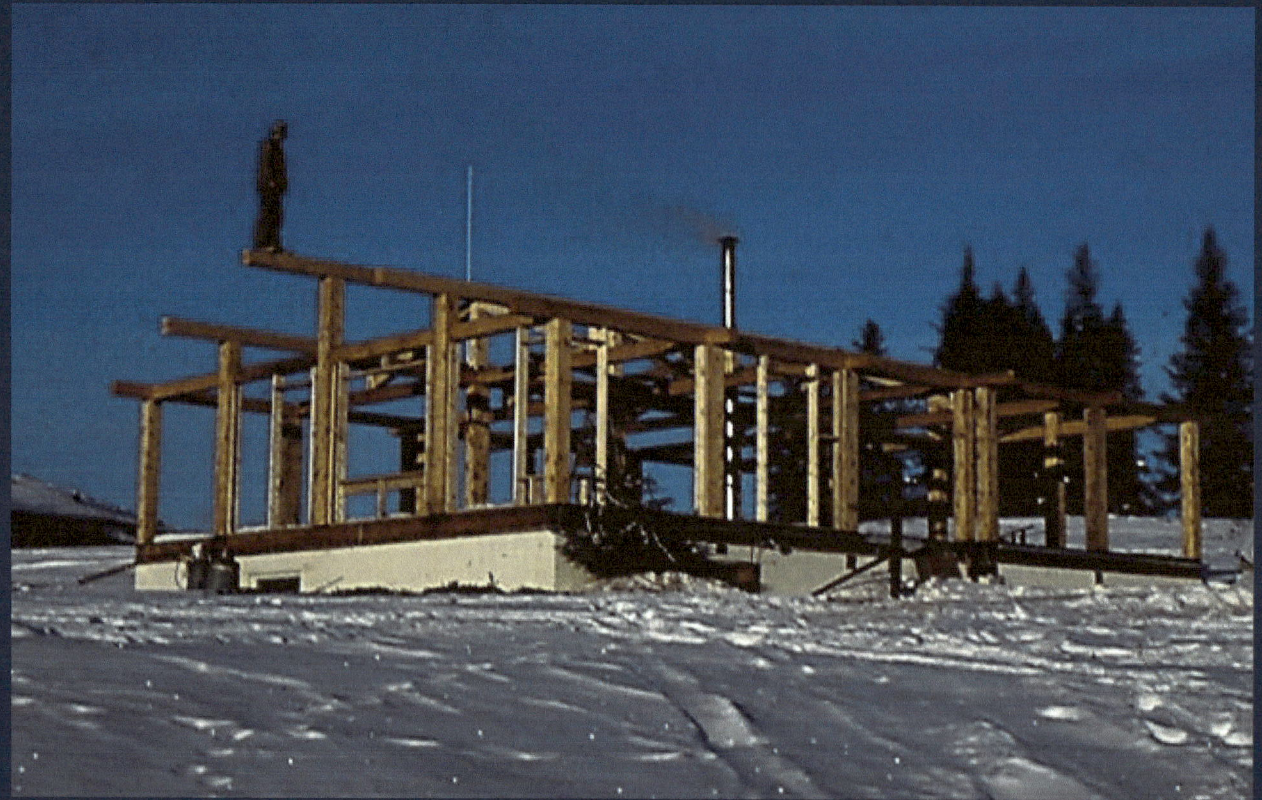

Now we raced to get the roof on before baby arrived.

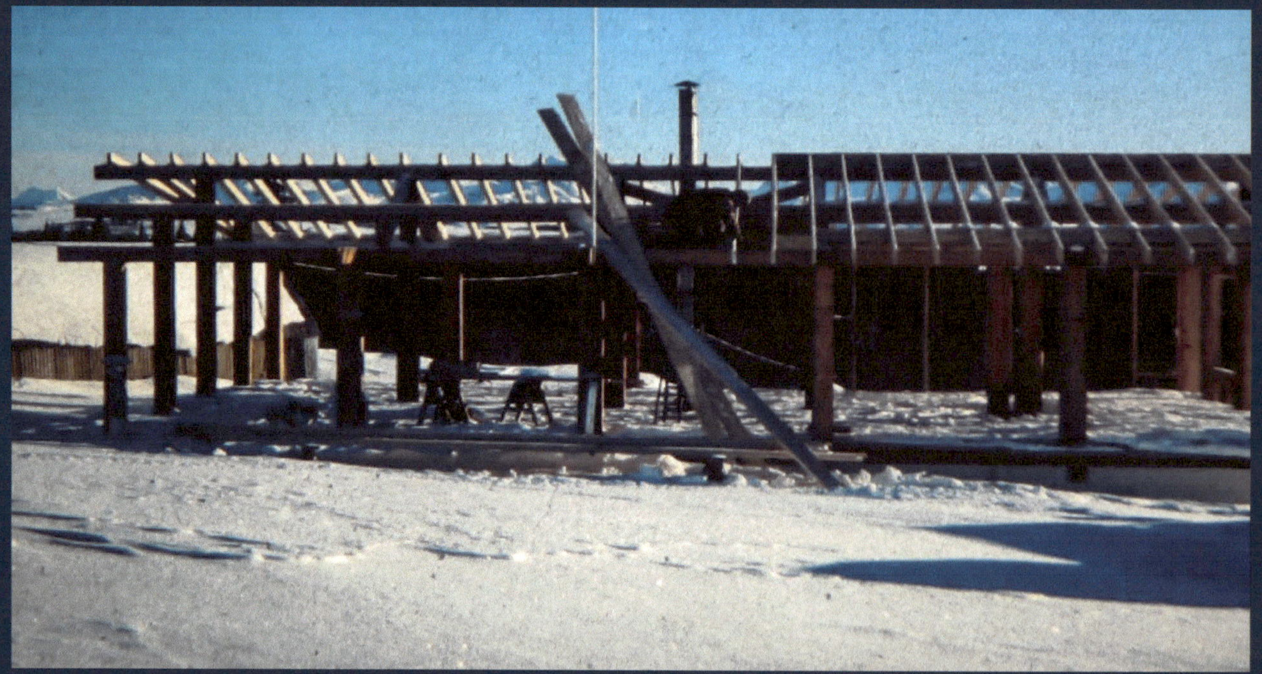

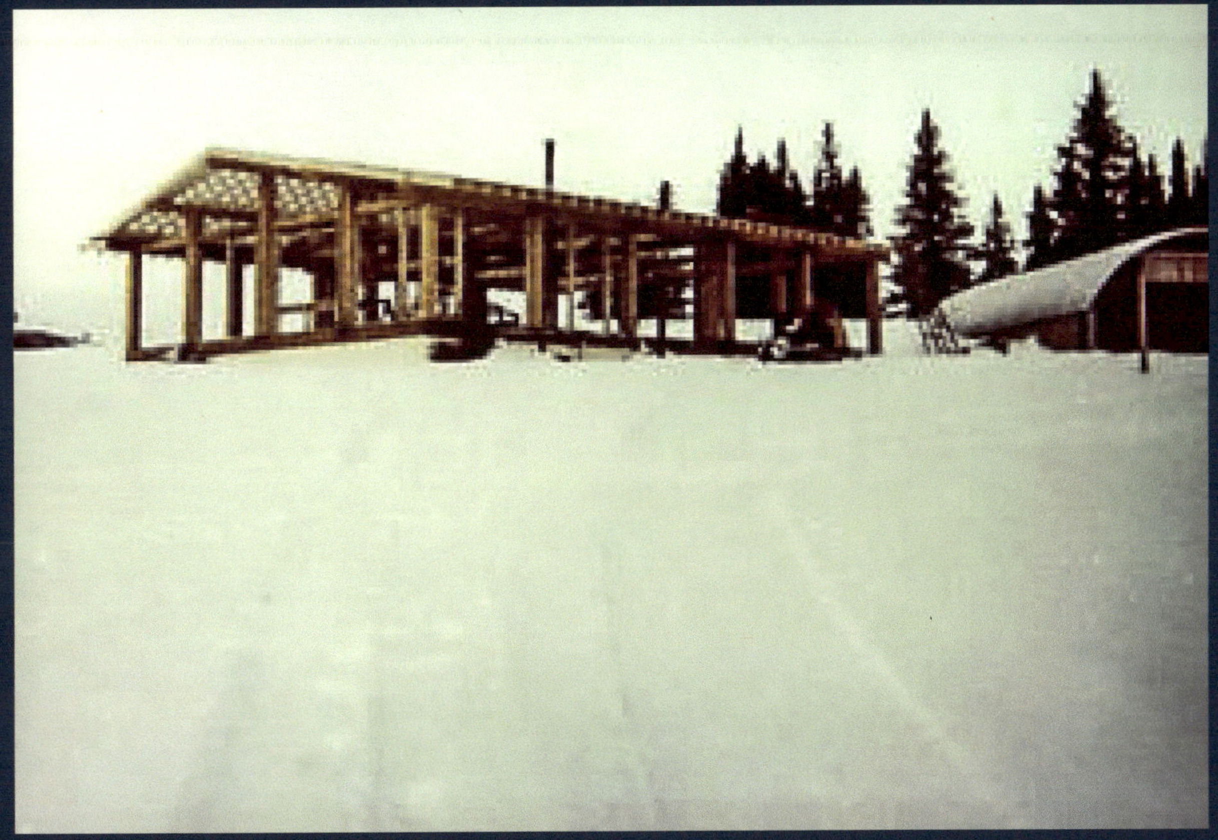

Bringing baby home (still without a roof) brought Grandma Tutu up to Alaska again.

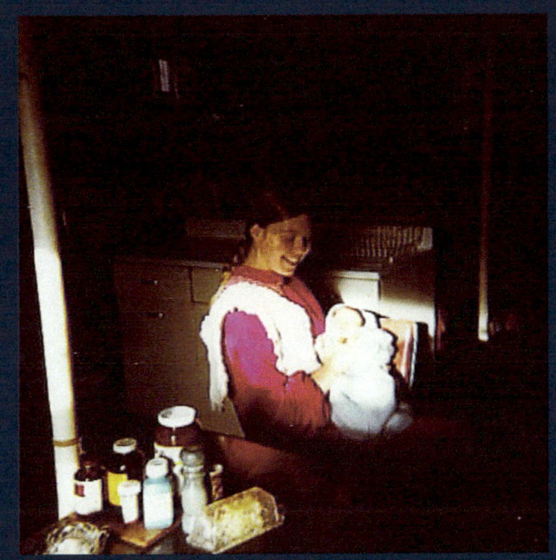

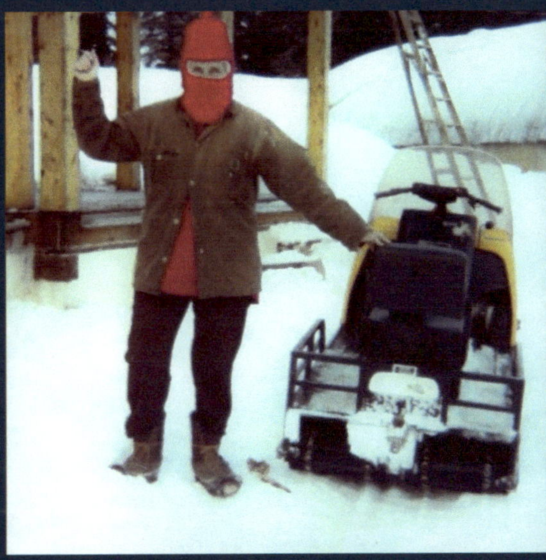

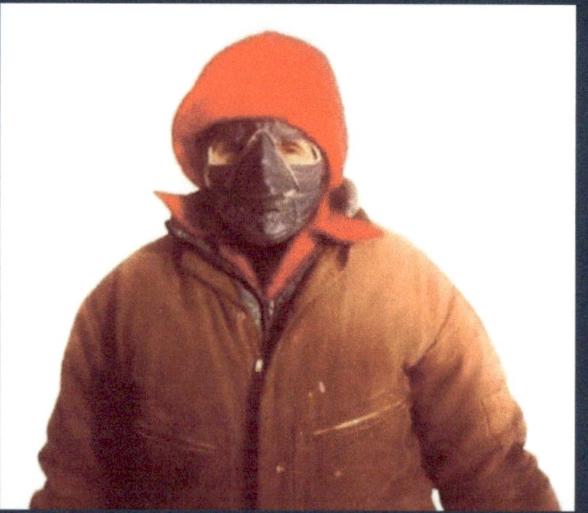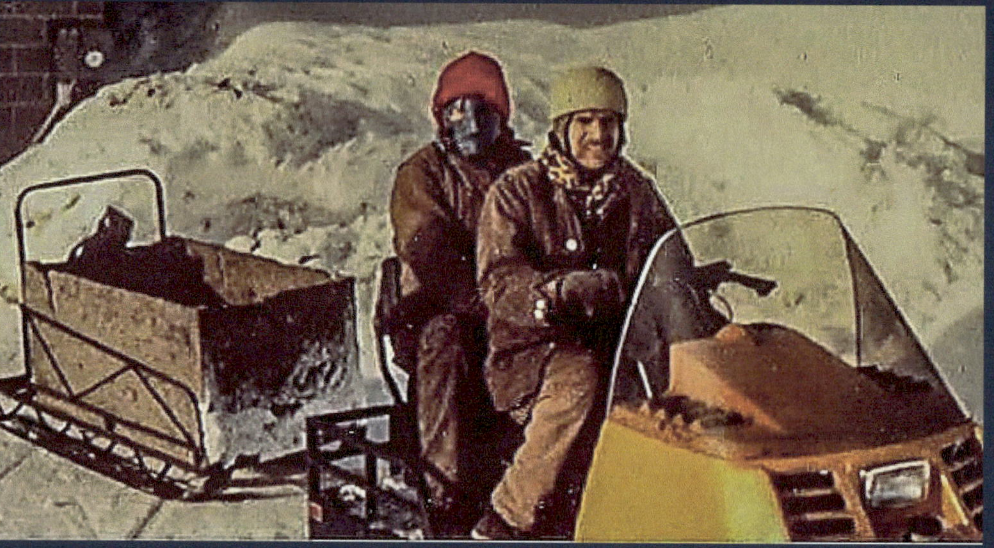

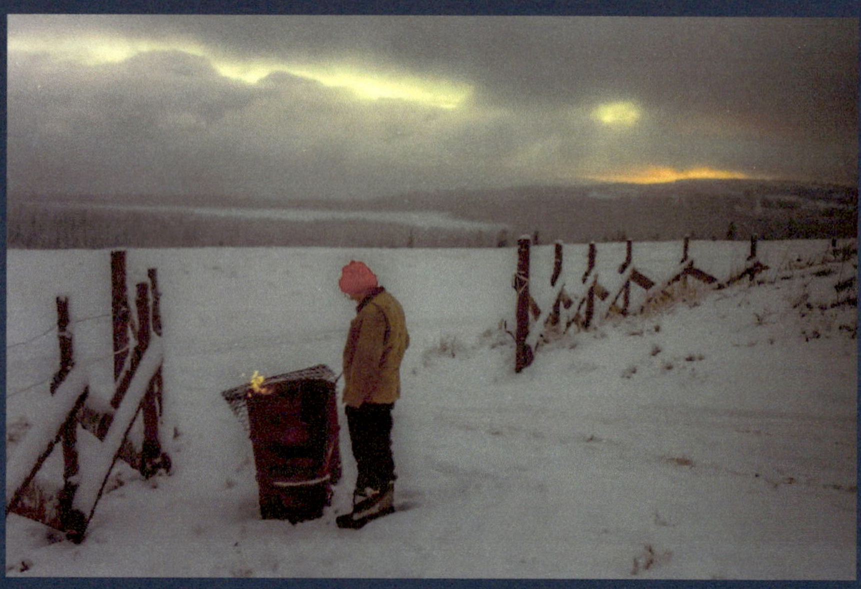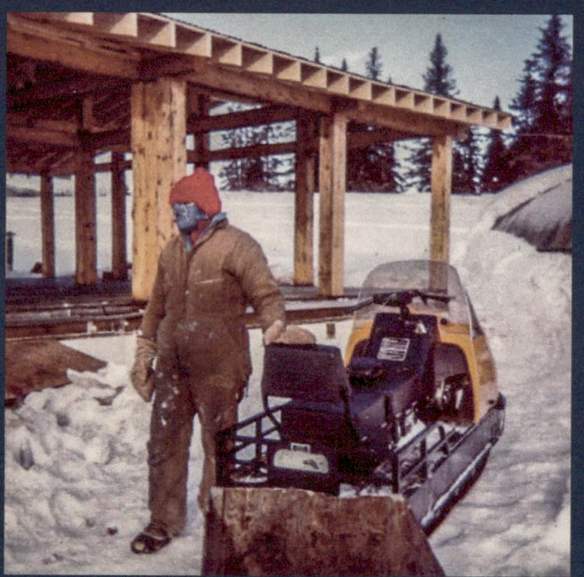

Even at 10 below zero, Mamasan really loved the place.
But after two weeks, she went home to Hawaii.

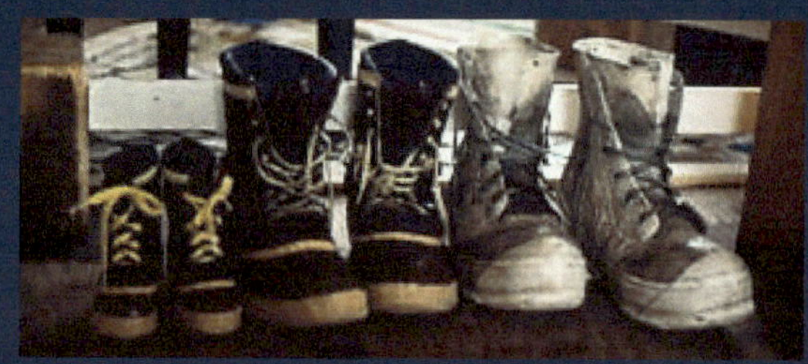

And now we were three.

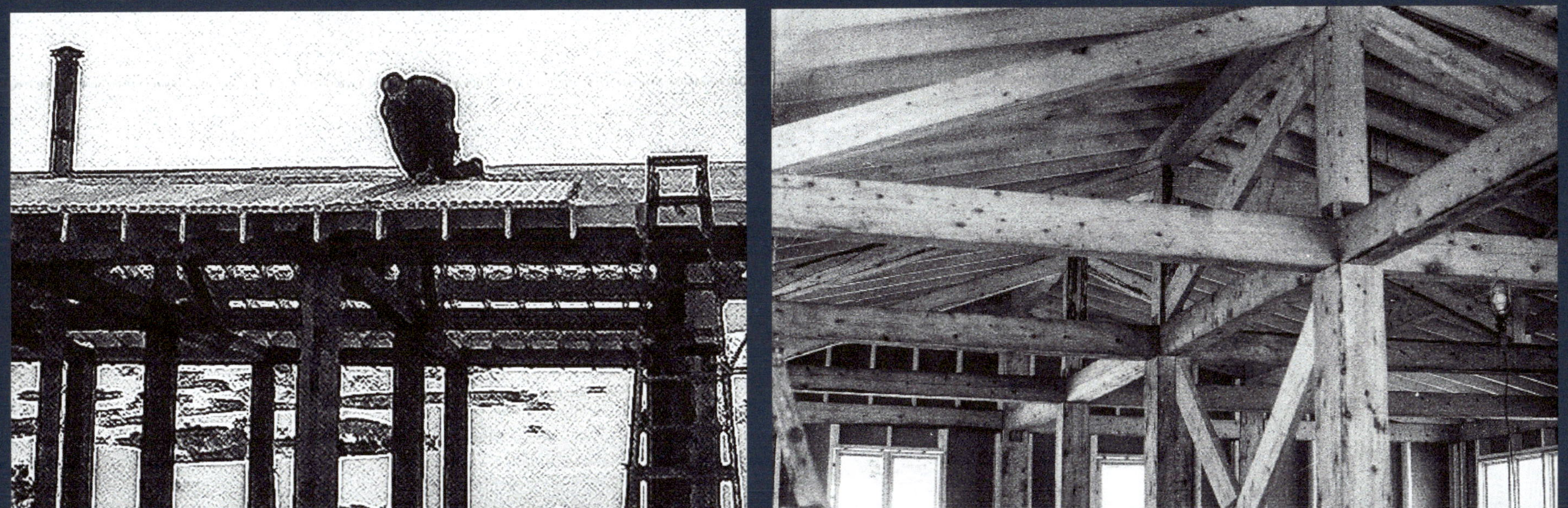

Tim finished the roof without much help from me. By May, we had the fiberboard shell completed. We took a plane ride to view the fruit of our labors from overhead.

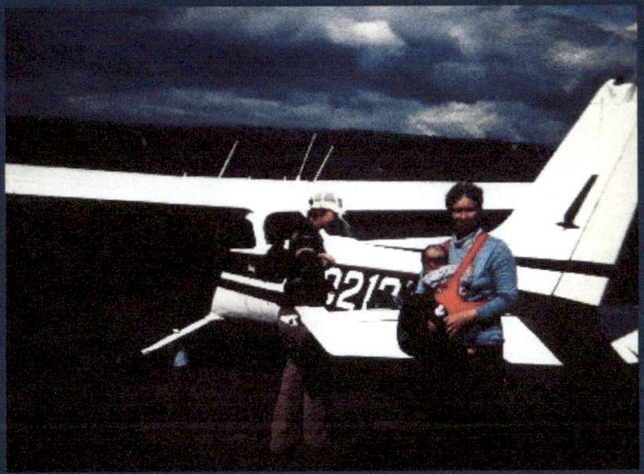

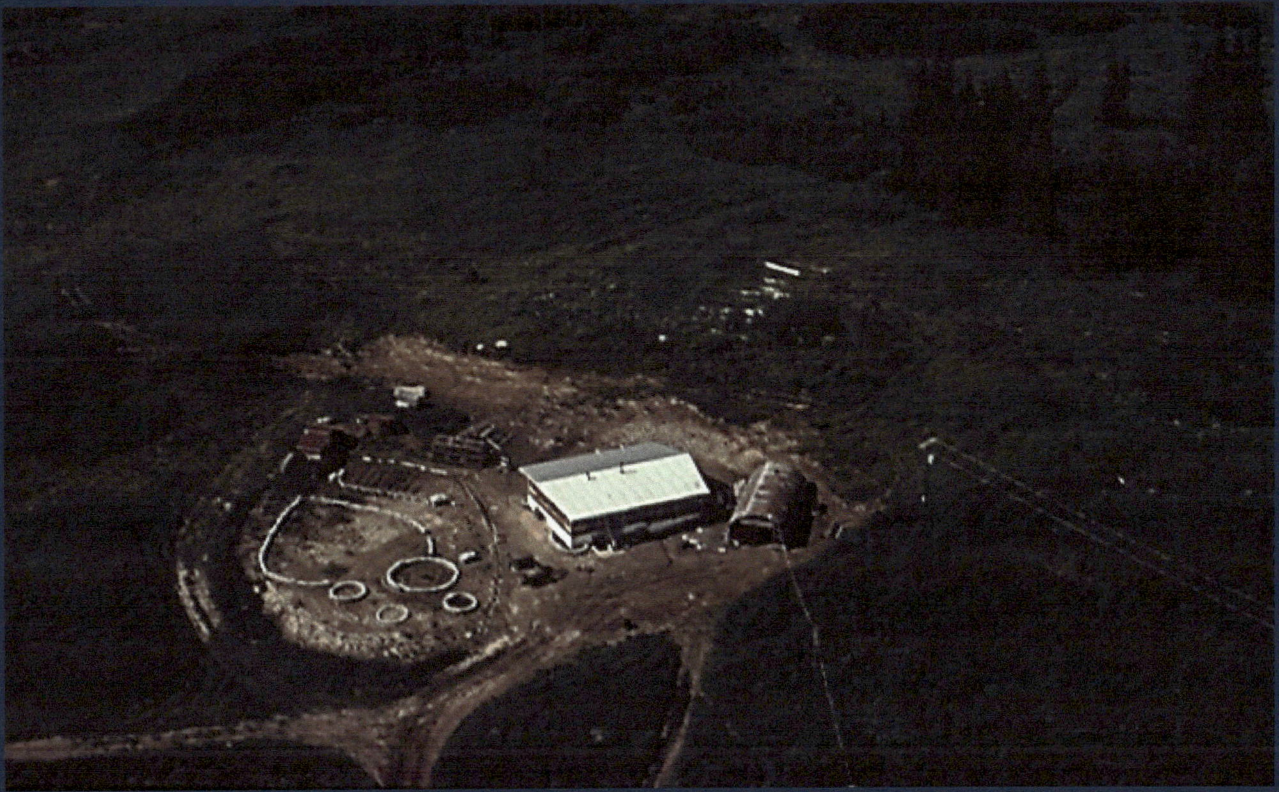

But from the air, my garden didn't look nearly as lush as I'd been envisioning.

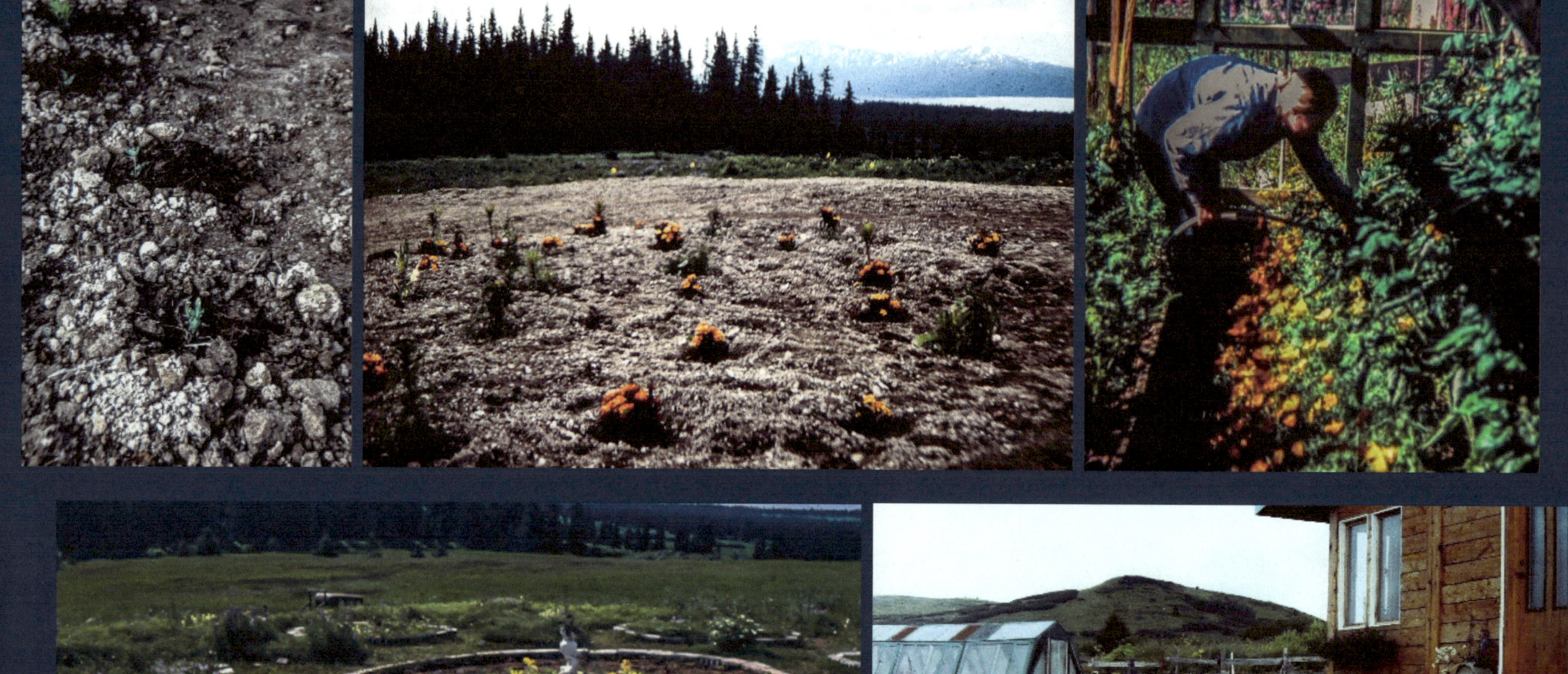

After that flight, greening-up the yard became a passionate labor of love for me.

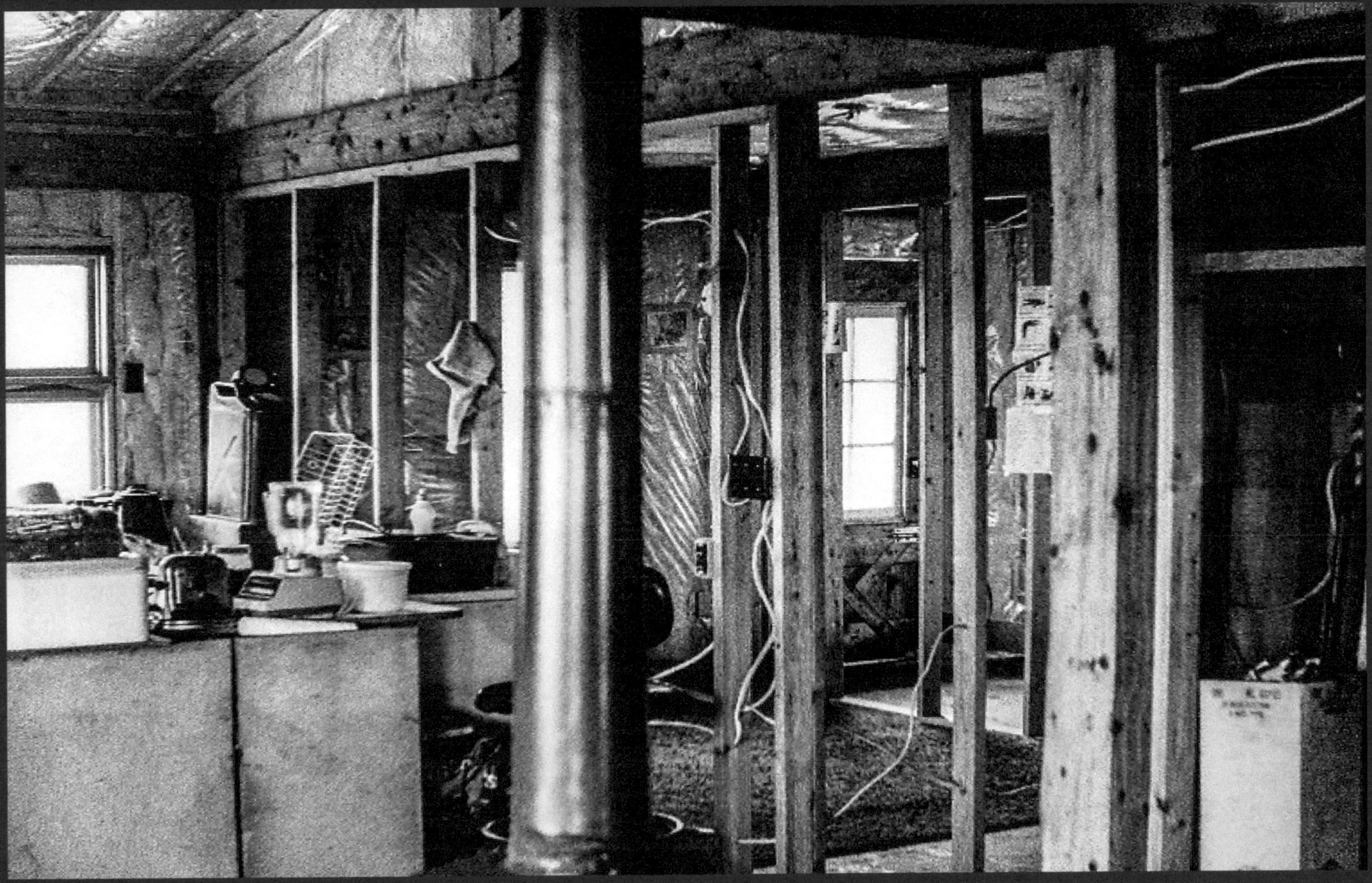

With only a little bit of finish work left to do, we moved in upstairs.

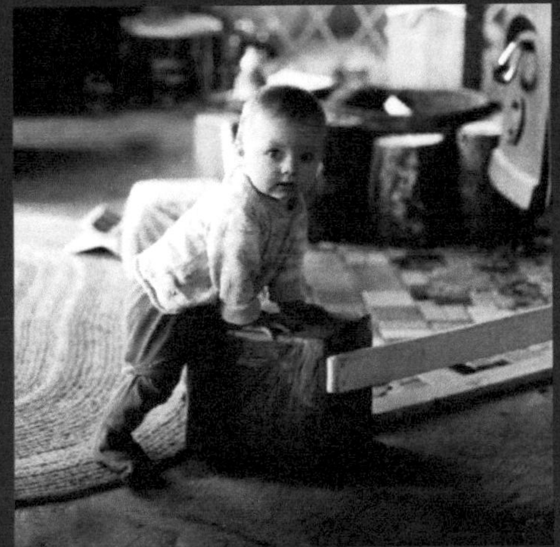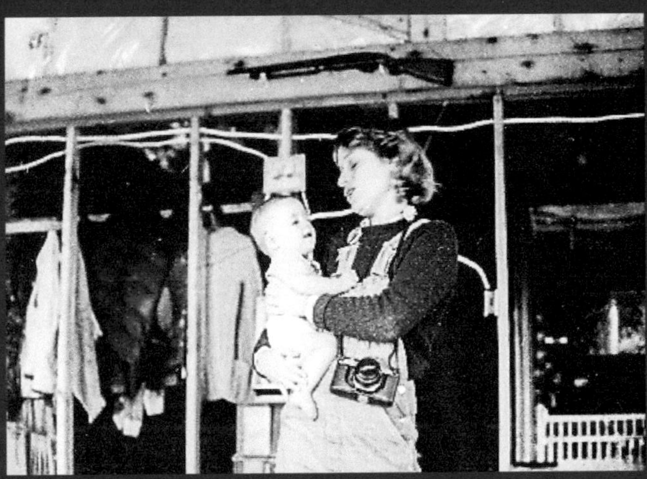

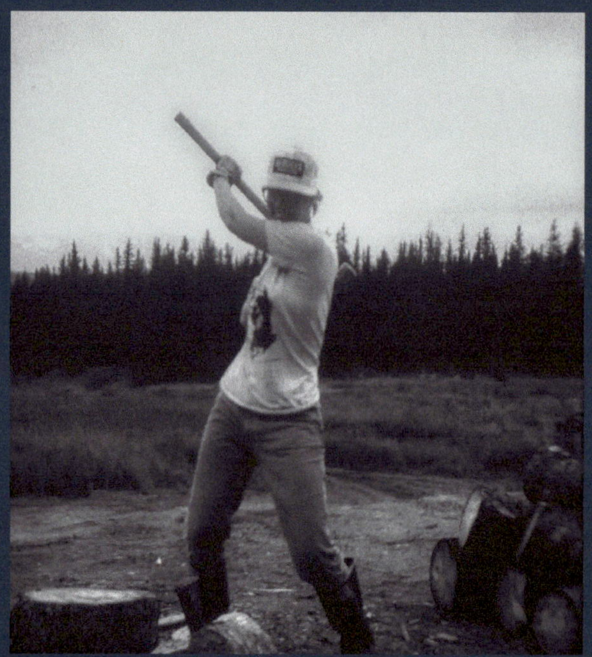

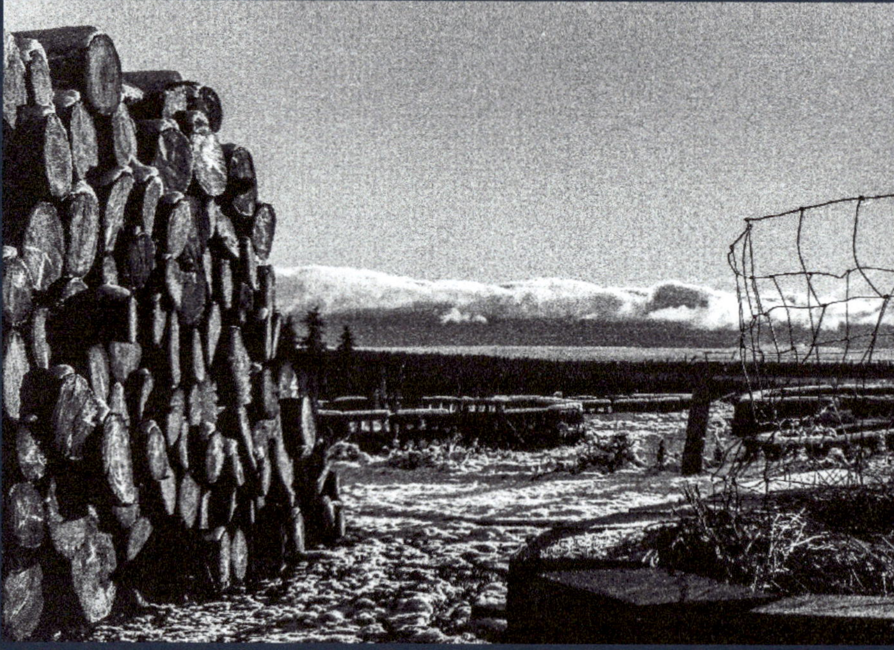

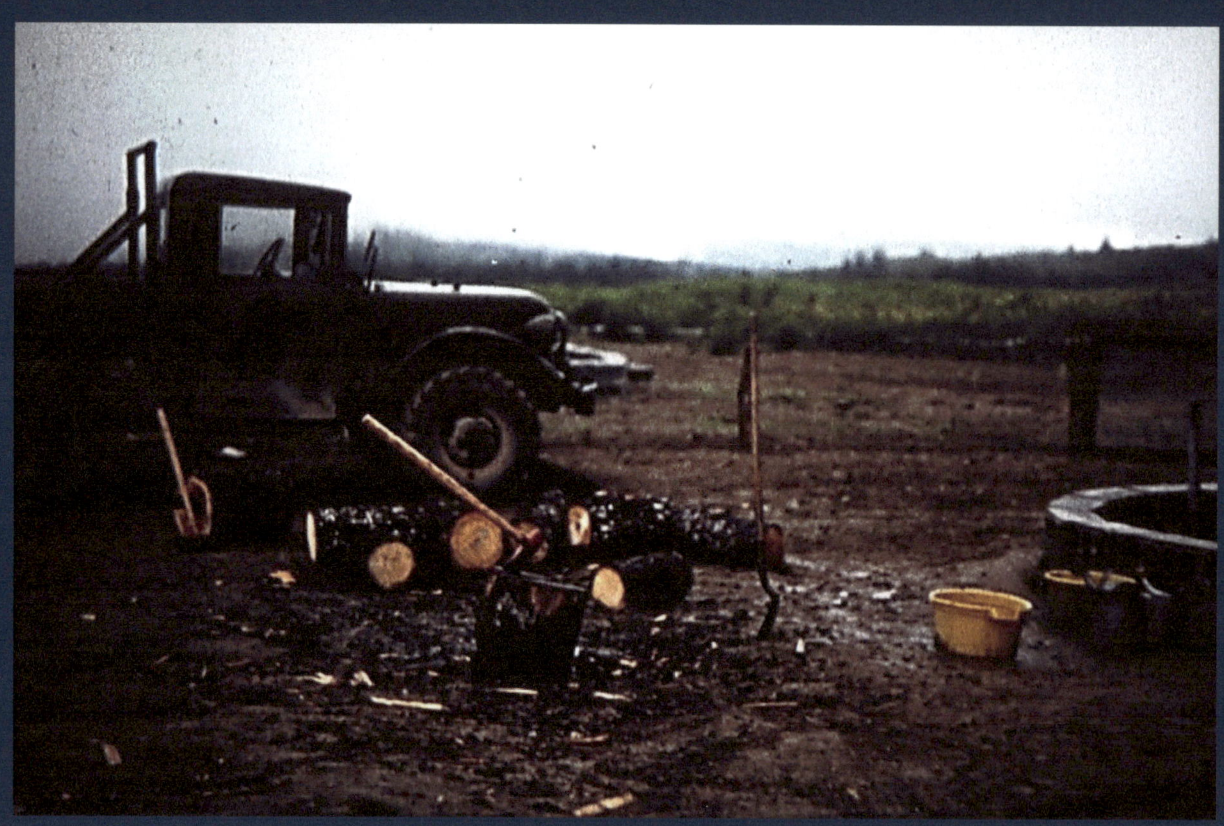

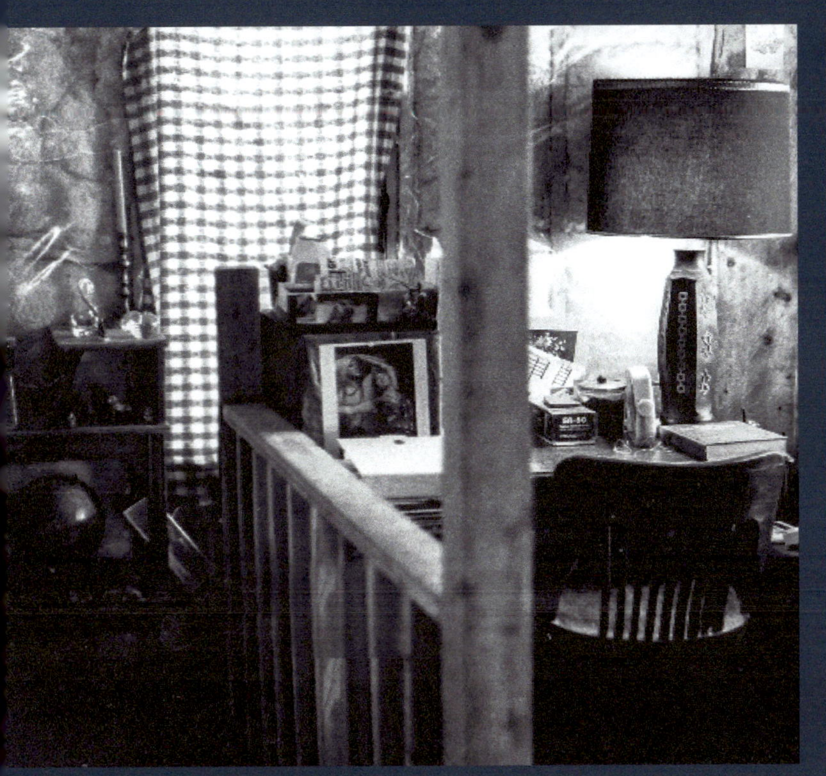
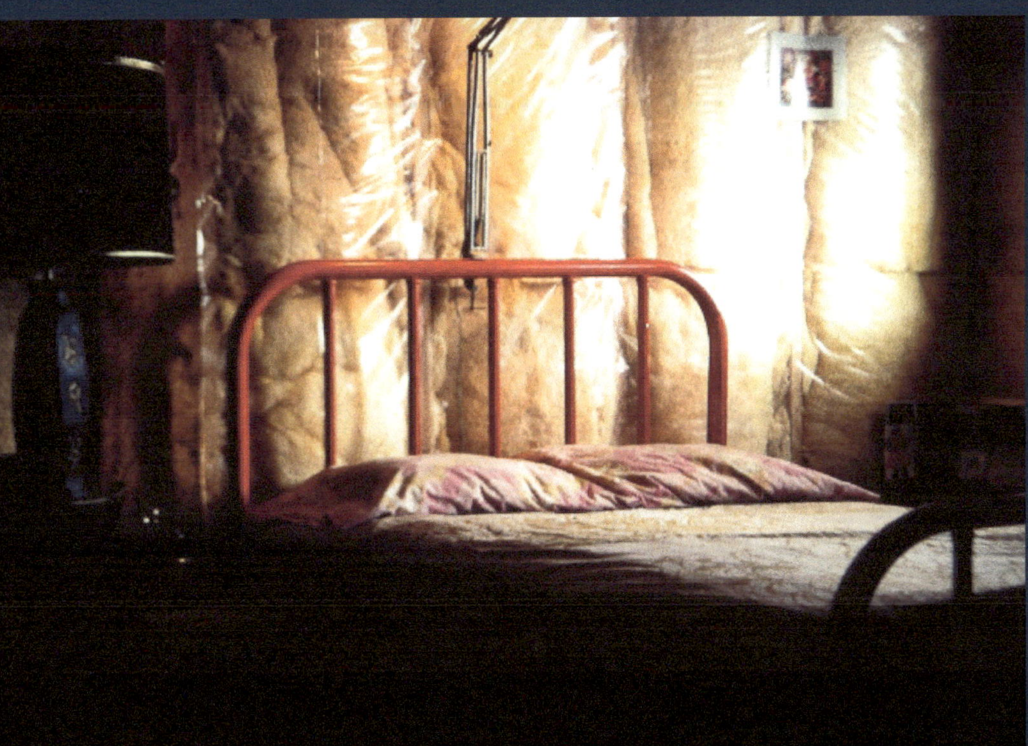
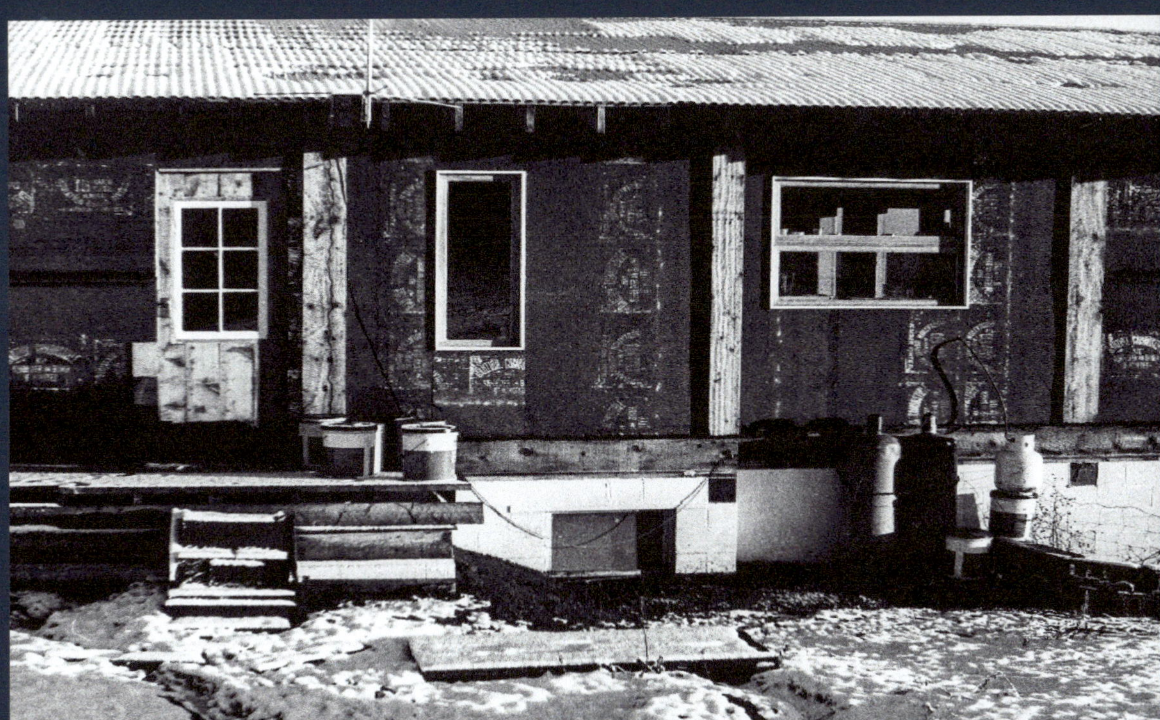

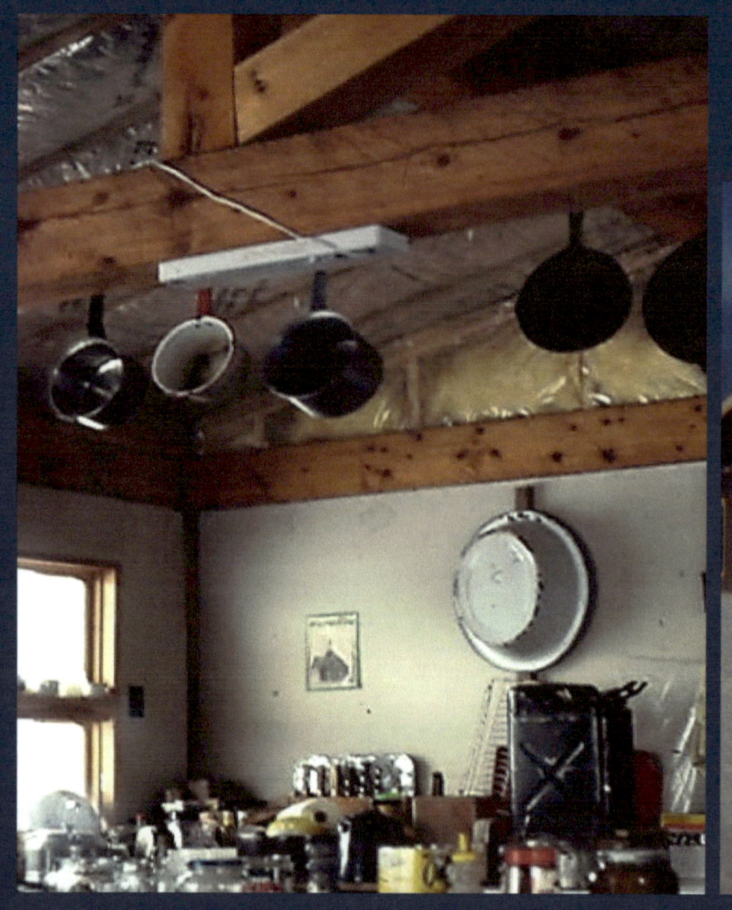

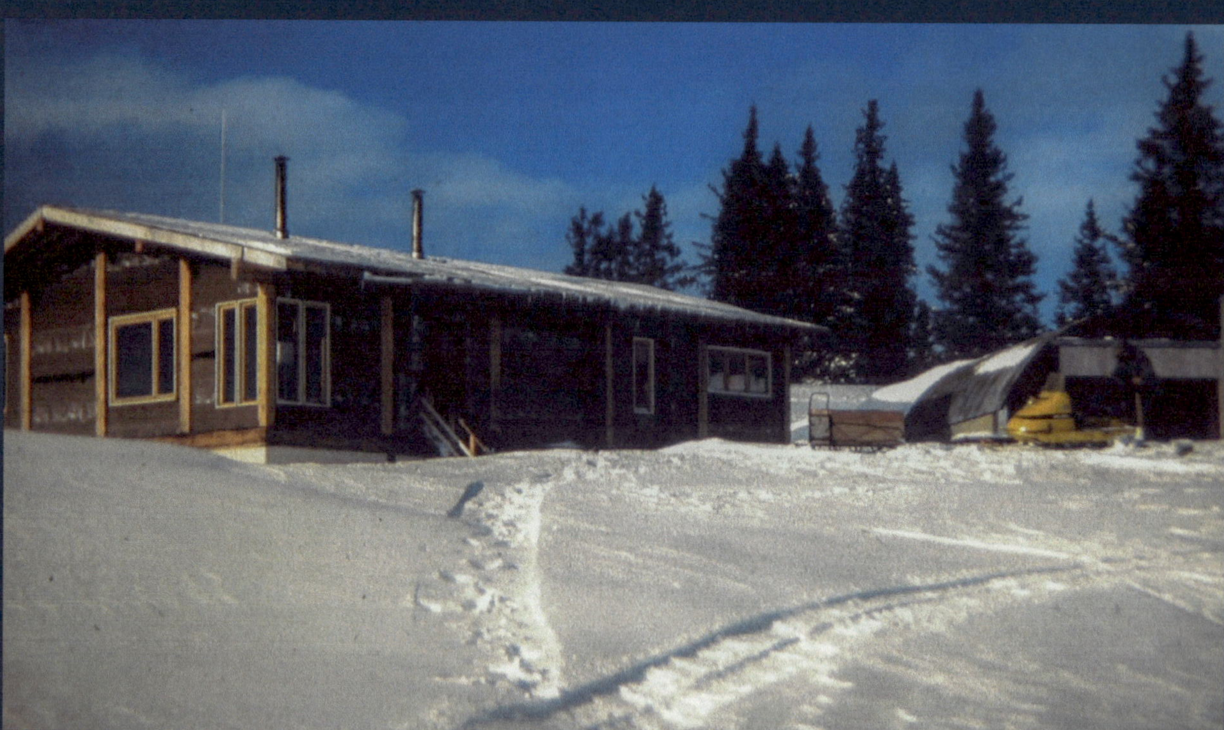

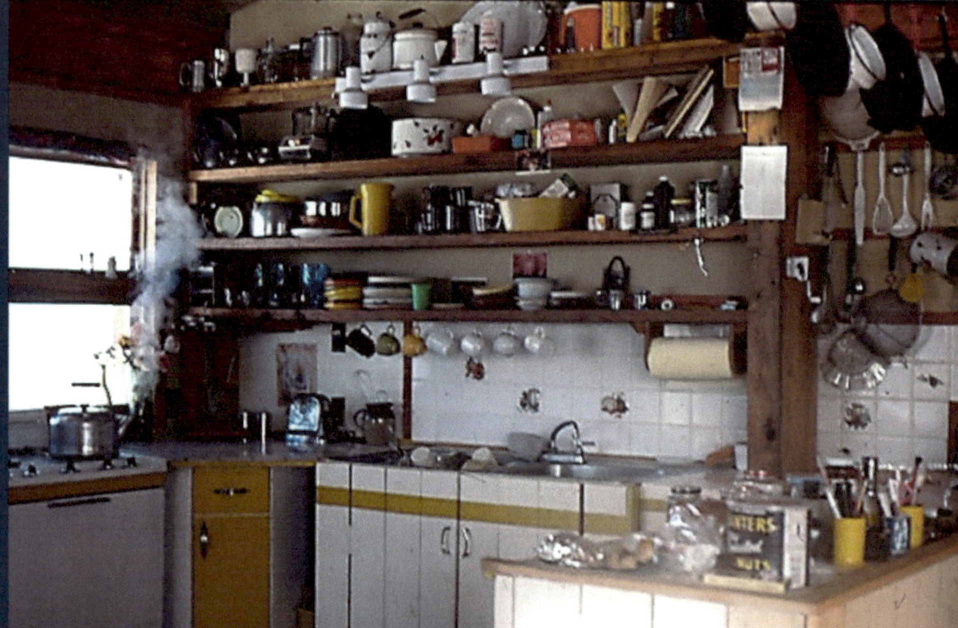

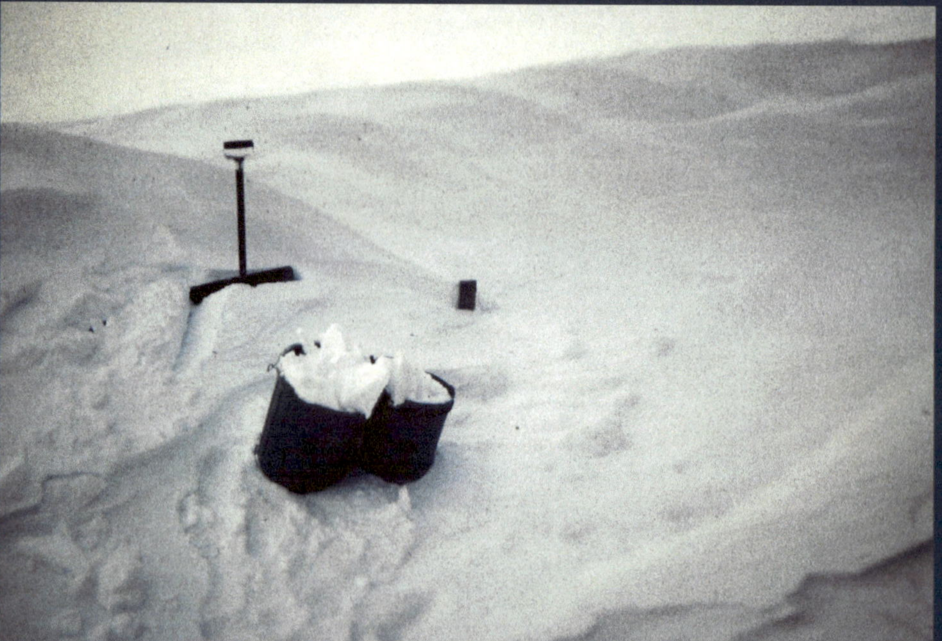

The winters of '79 and '80 tossed a lot of bad weather our way.

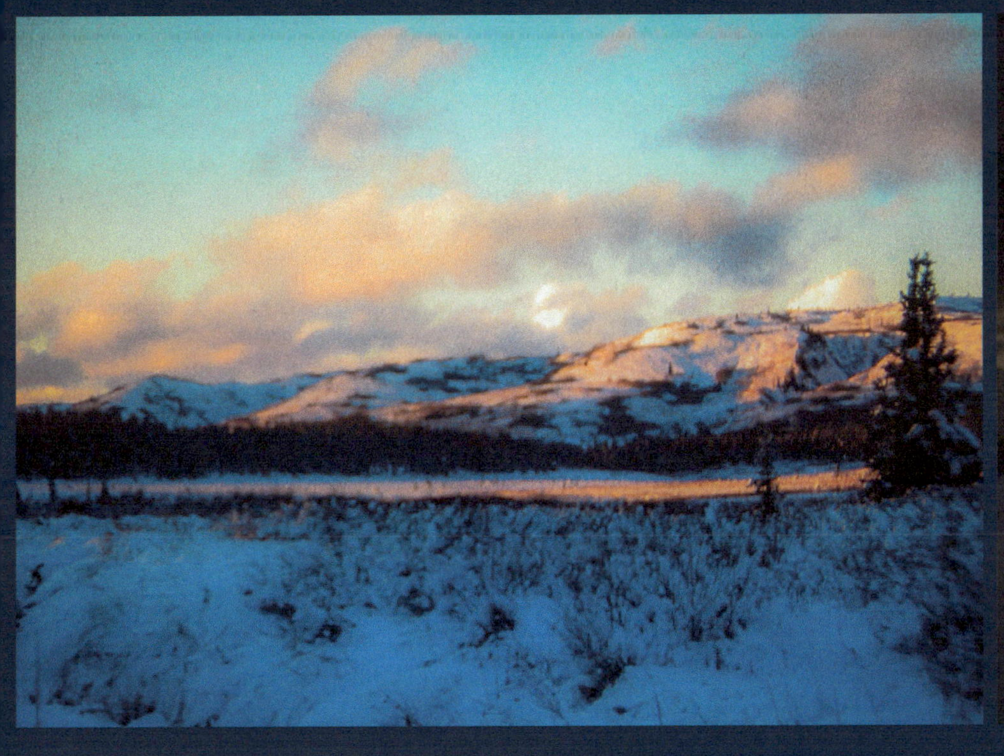

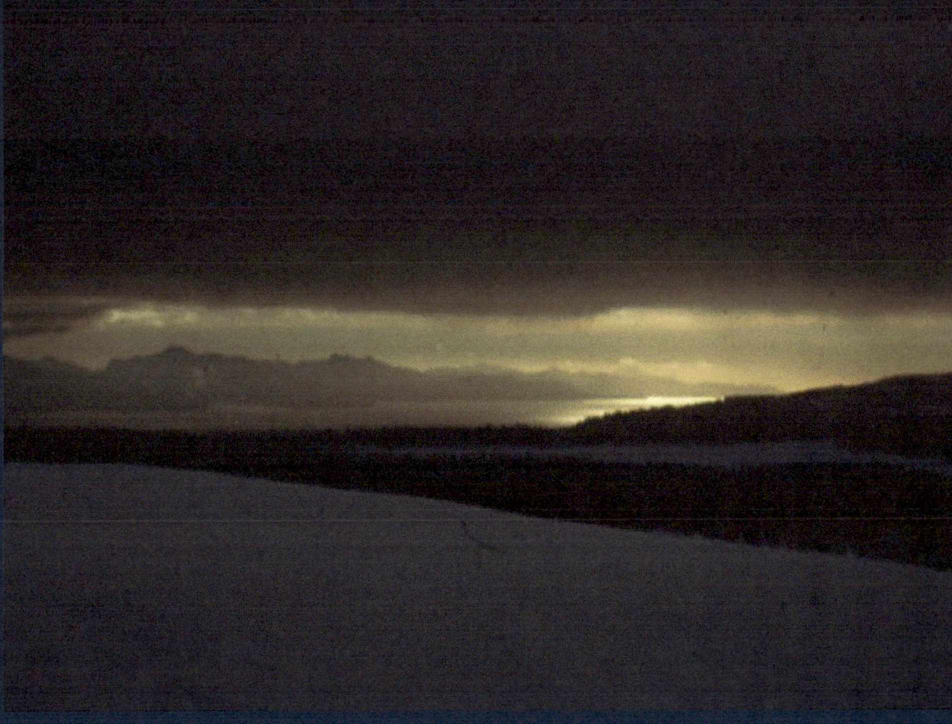

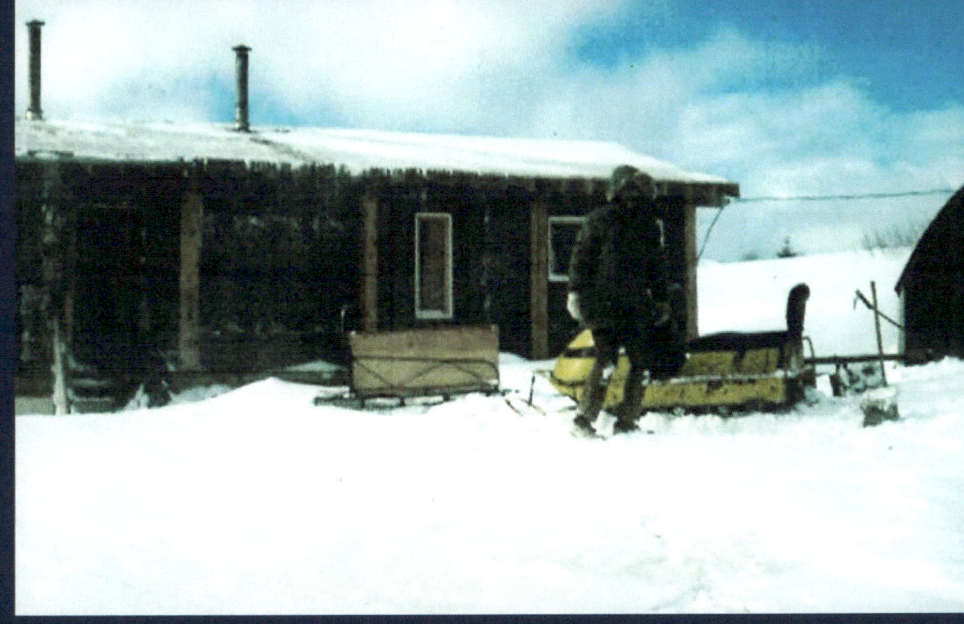

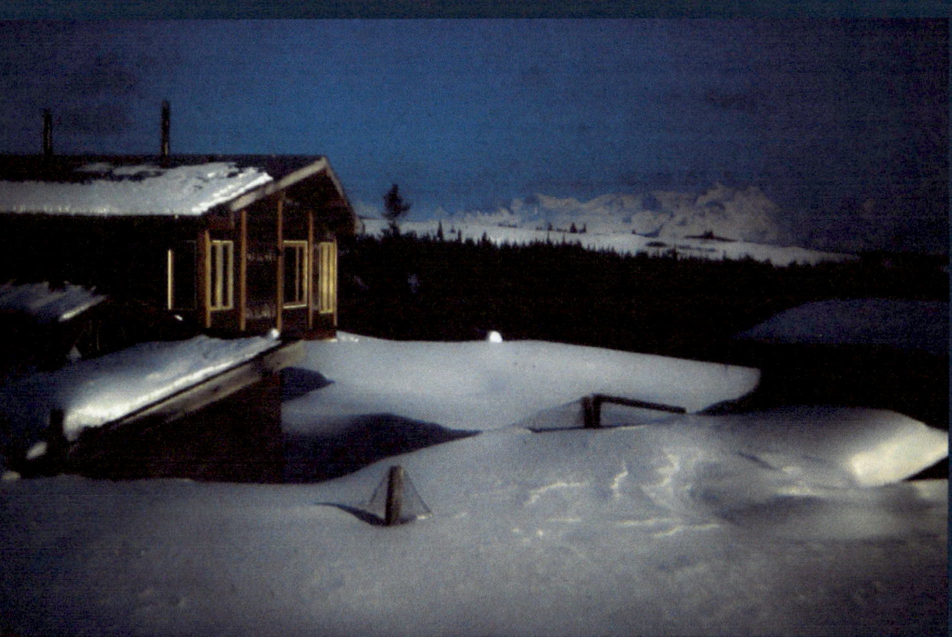

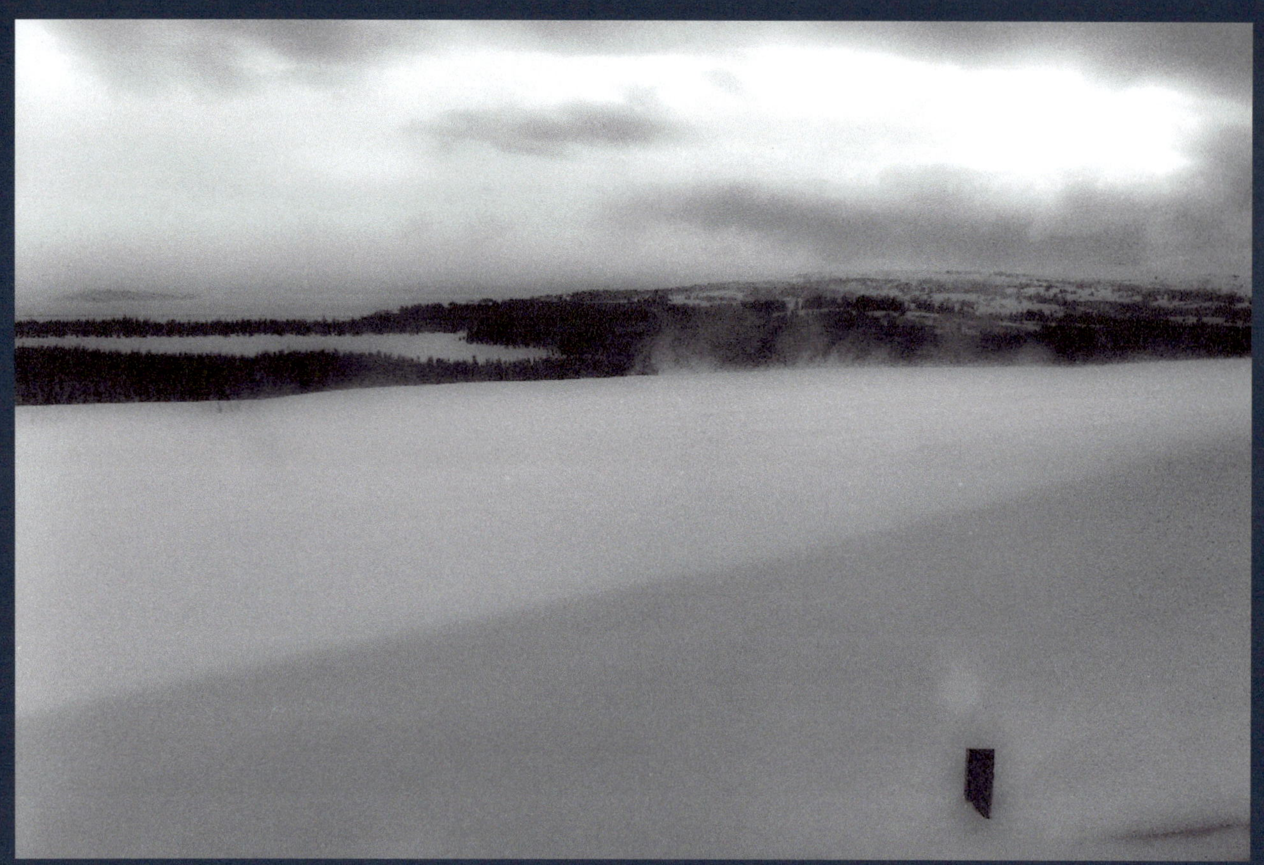

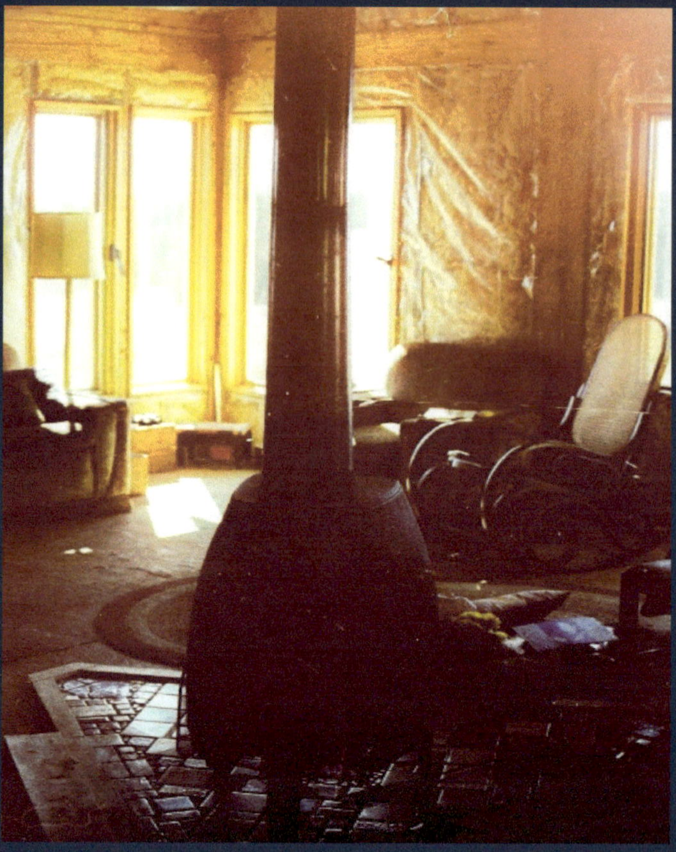

During blizzards, the breathing walls were unnerving, and fire tending was a full time job.

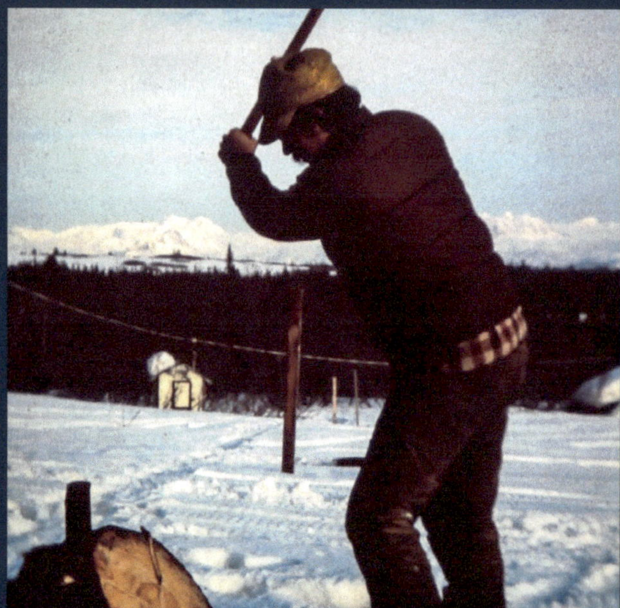

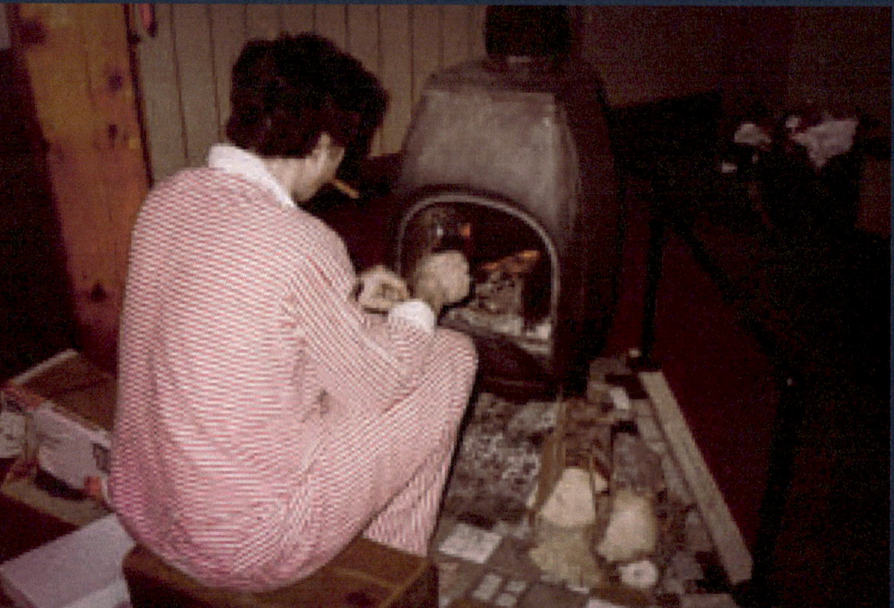

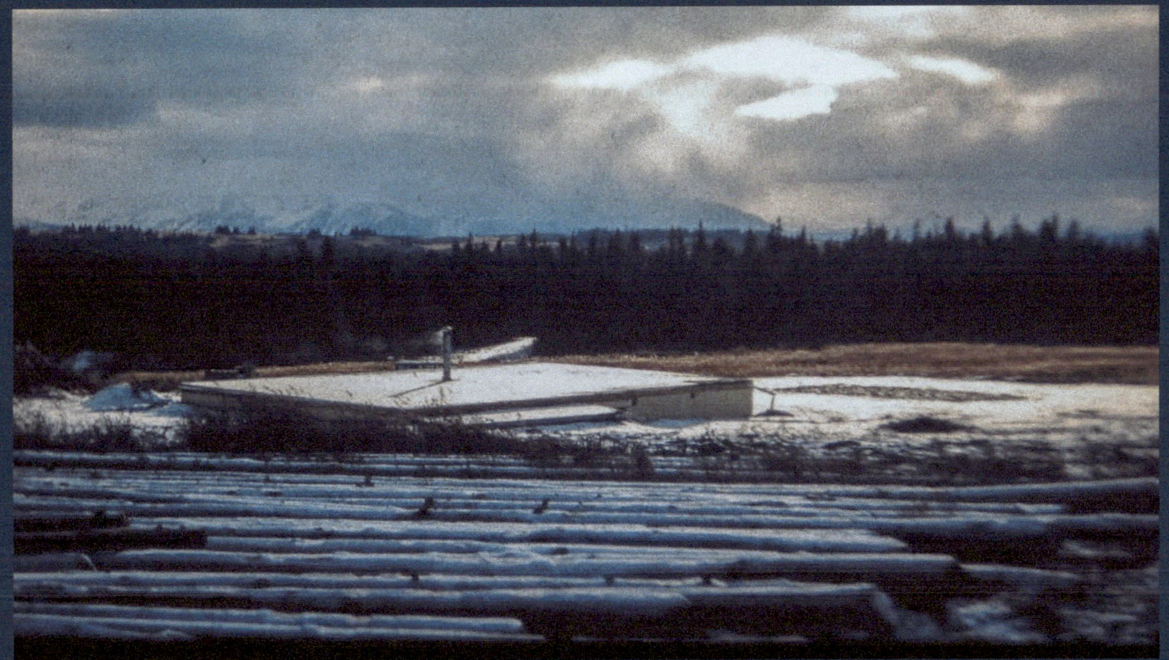

Were those peeled logs destined to end up as victims of our constant quest for firewood?

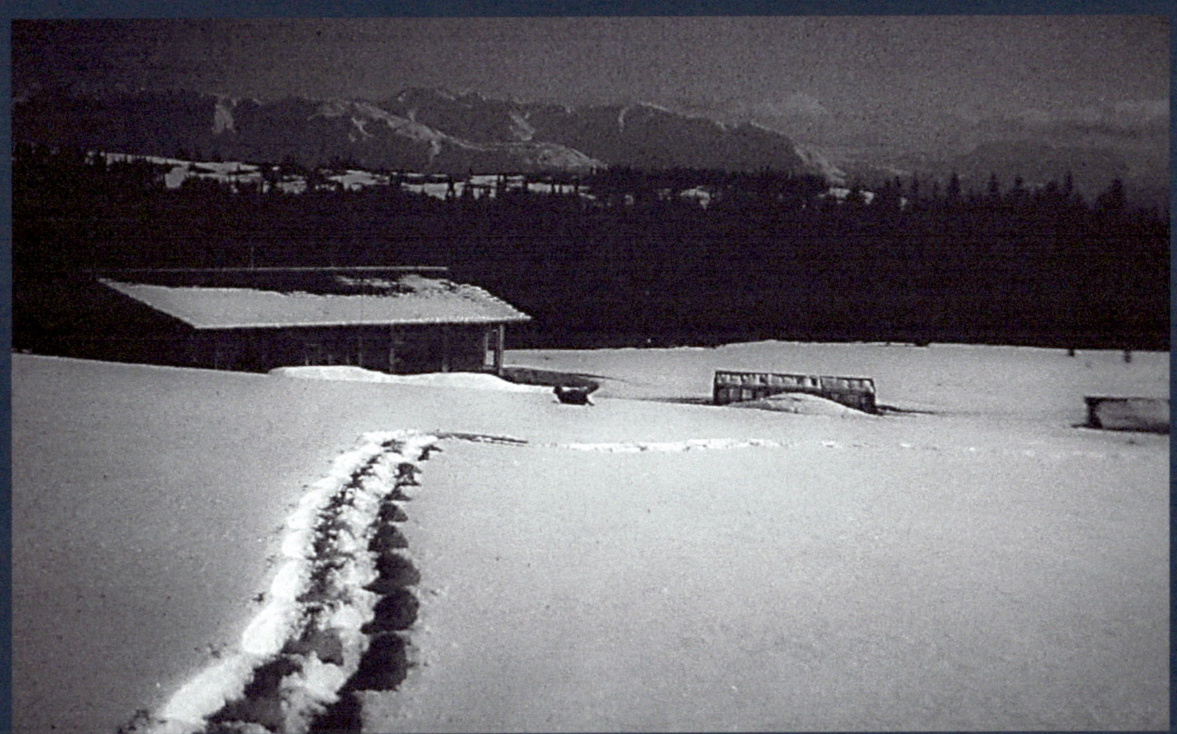

Once, we tried a condo in Anchorage,
but new construction plunged us into perpetual shade.

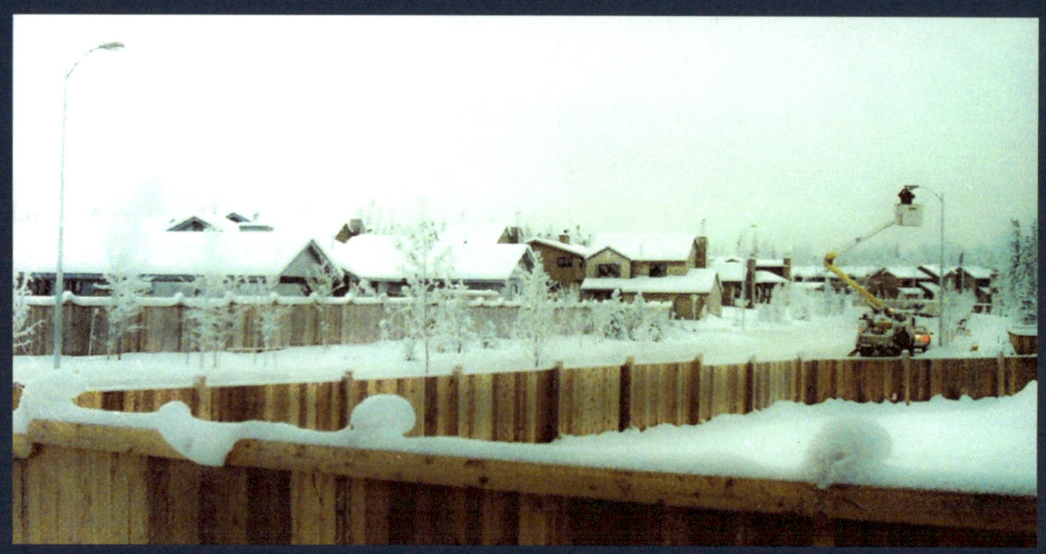

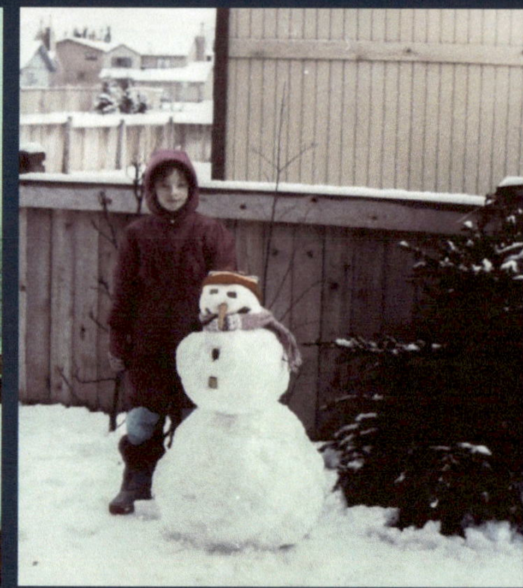

Note to self: Buy your view.

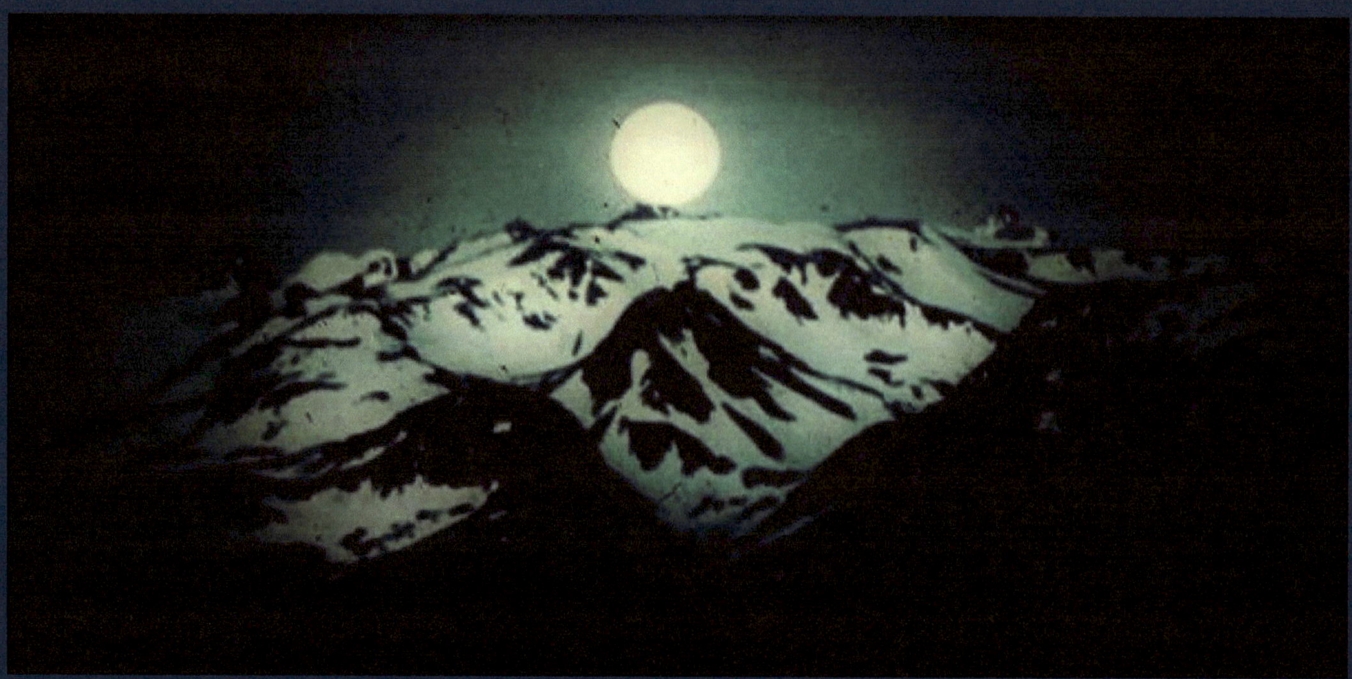

For several summers, we enjoyed cherished times on the mountain.

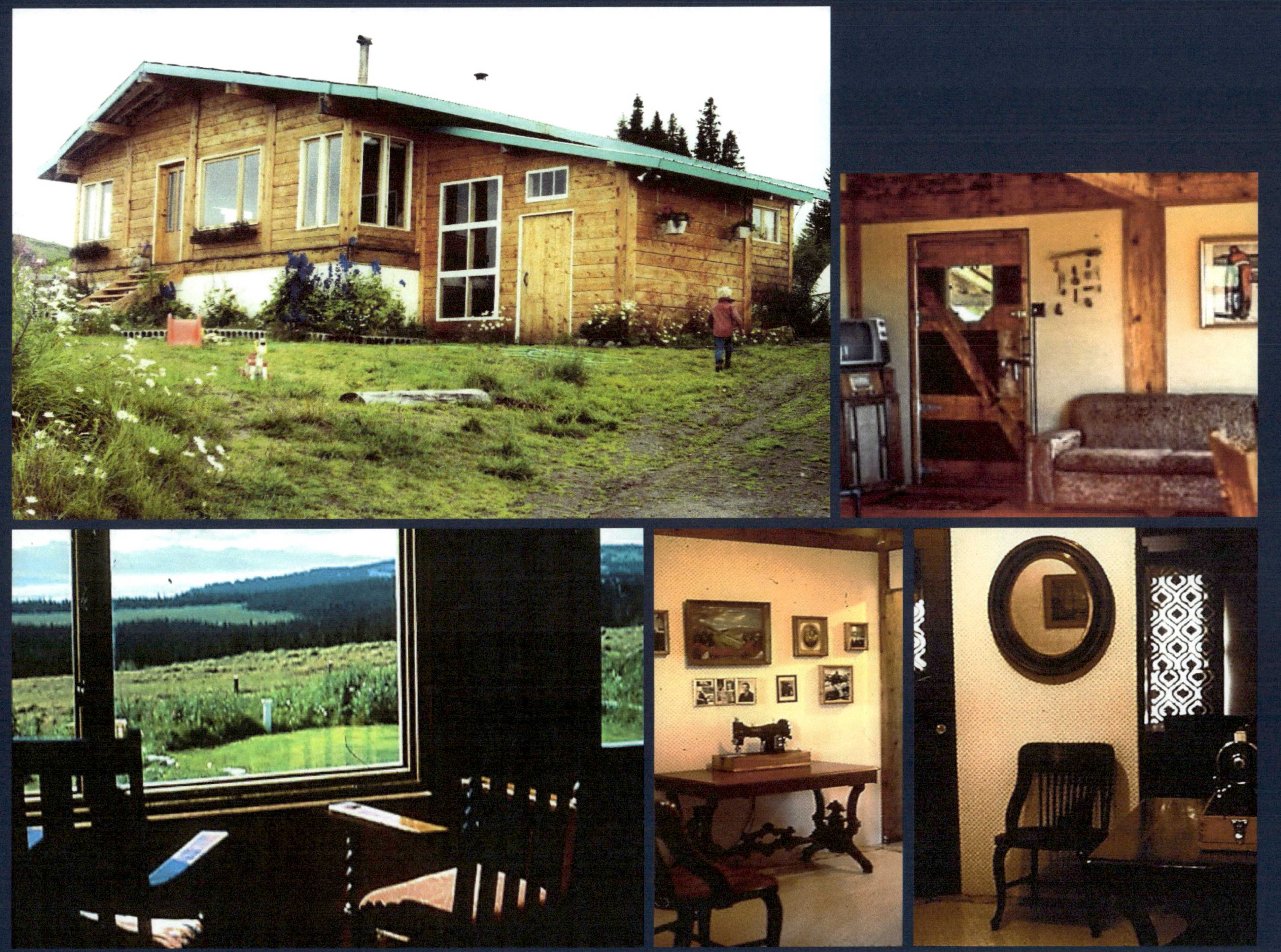

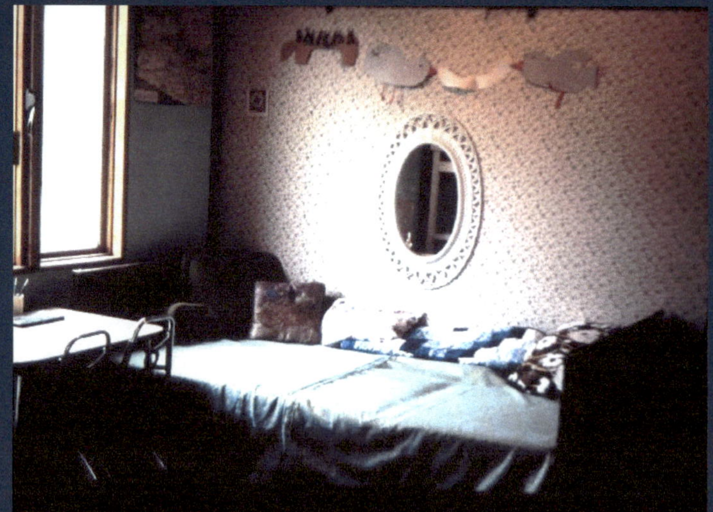

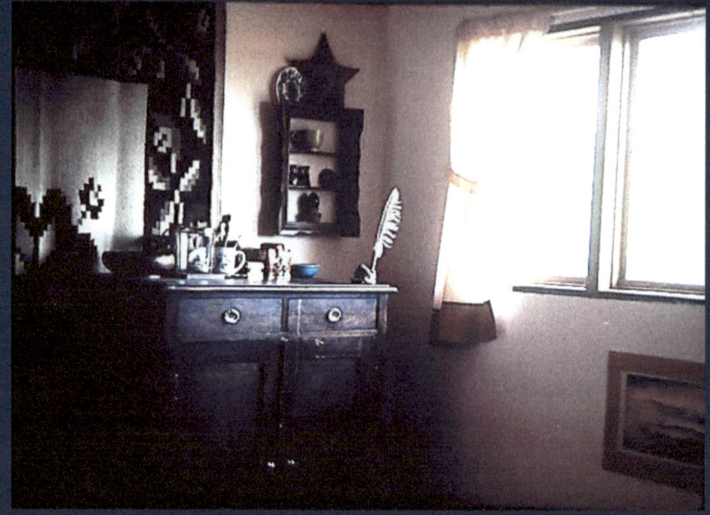

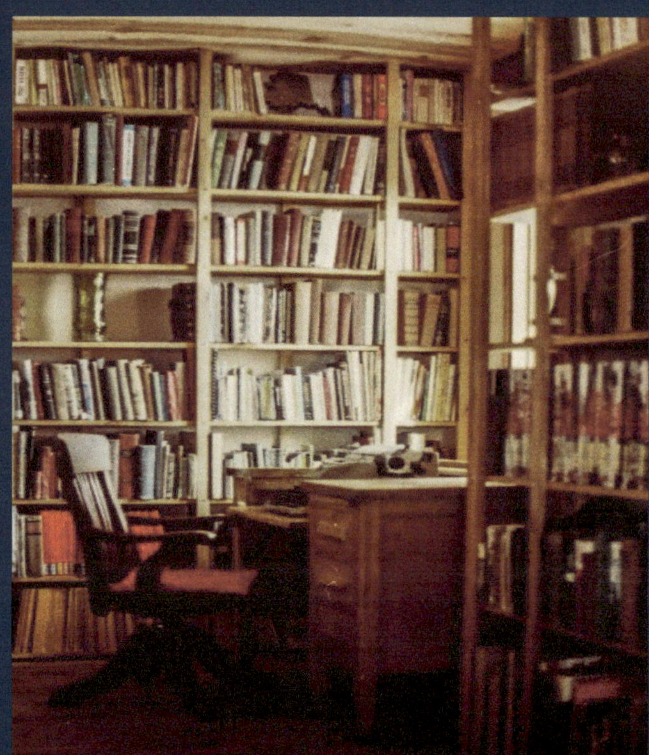

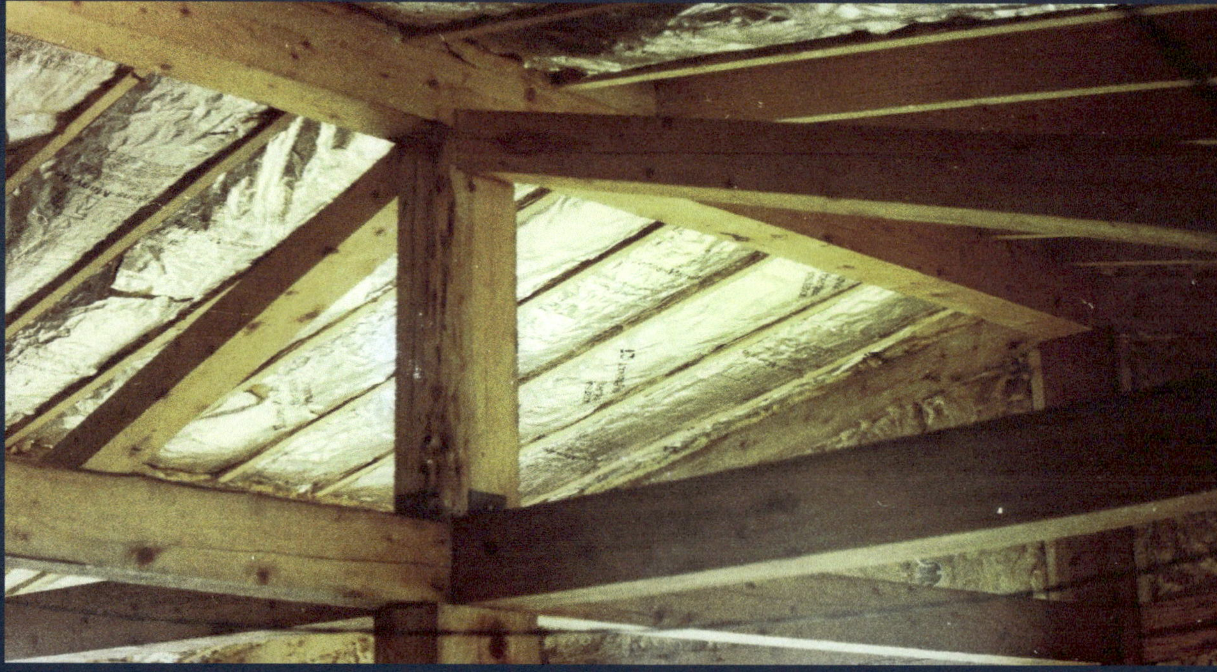

Happy to have both a library
and our beloved hand-hewn beams.

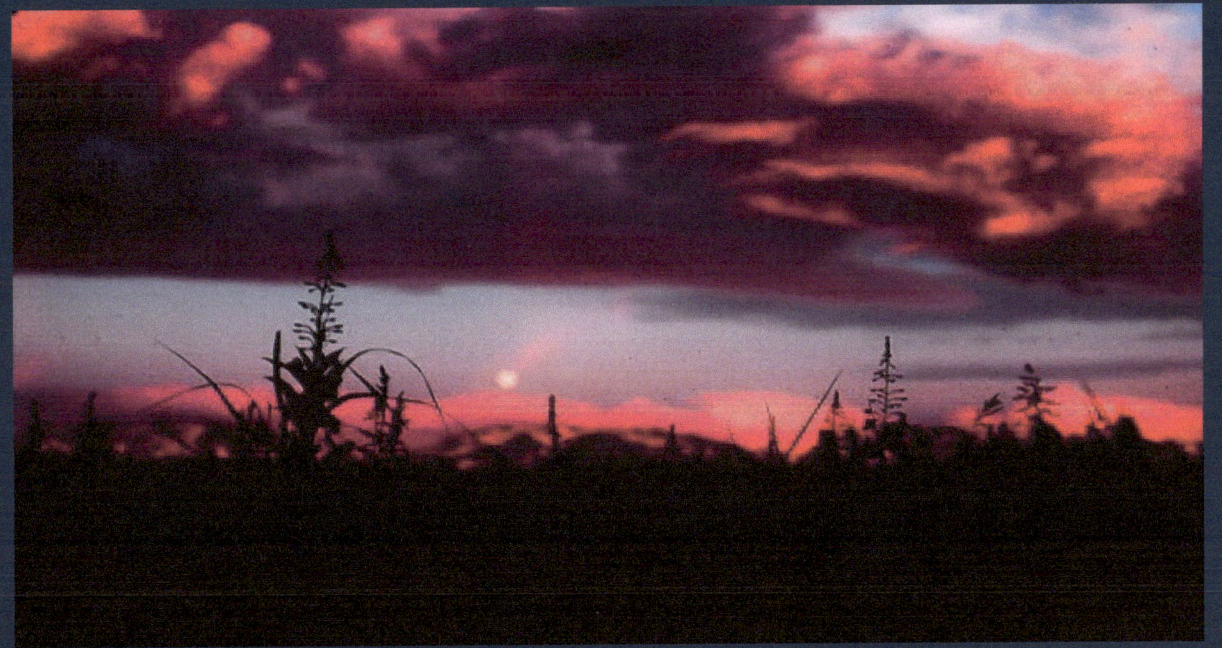

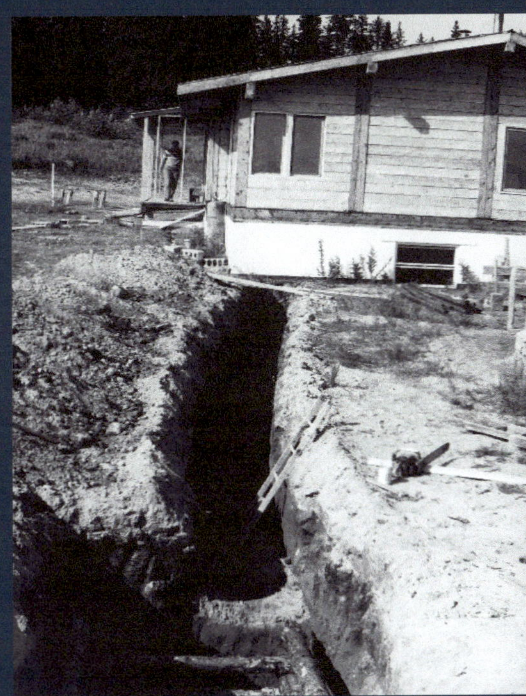

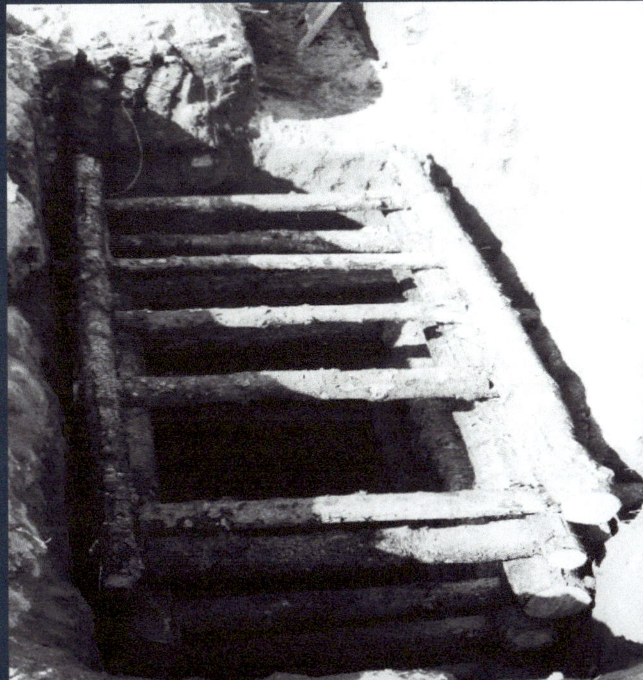

One summer we dug our cesspool.
Now, there would be no more slop buckets overflowing in the kitchen.
I saw this as a sign that we would have running water soon!

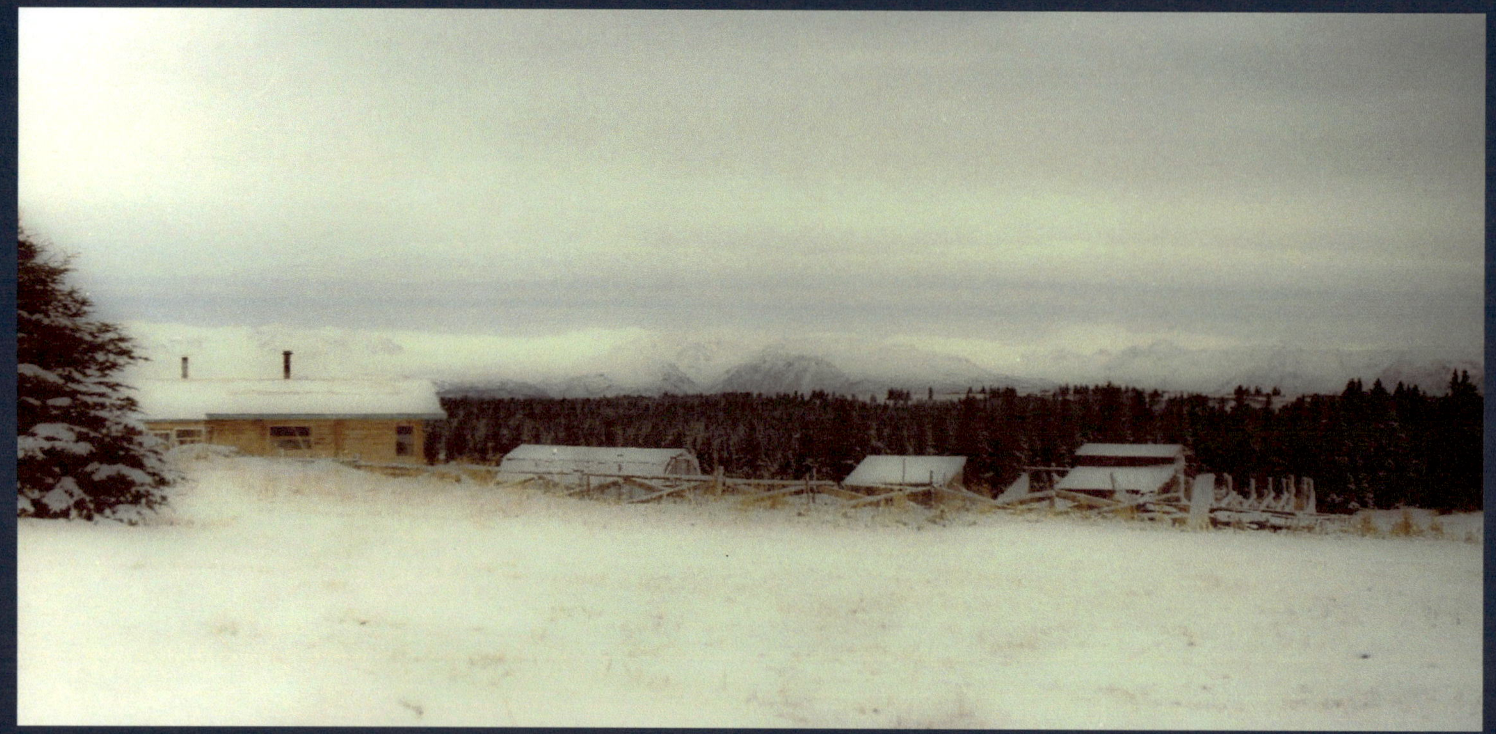

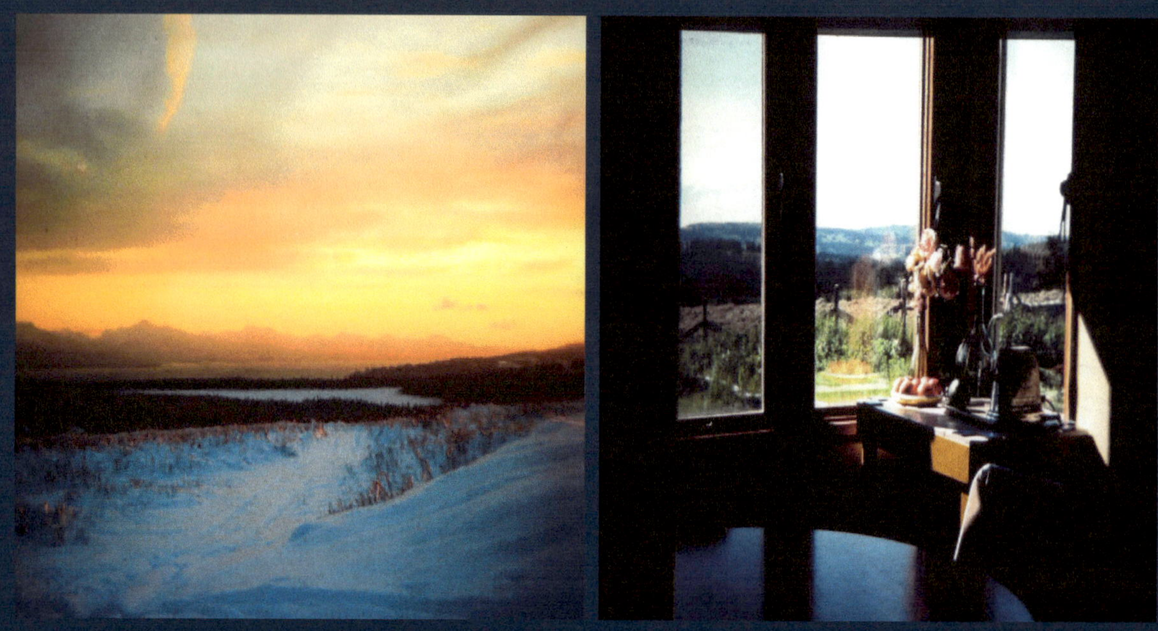

Two more years passed.

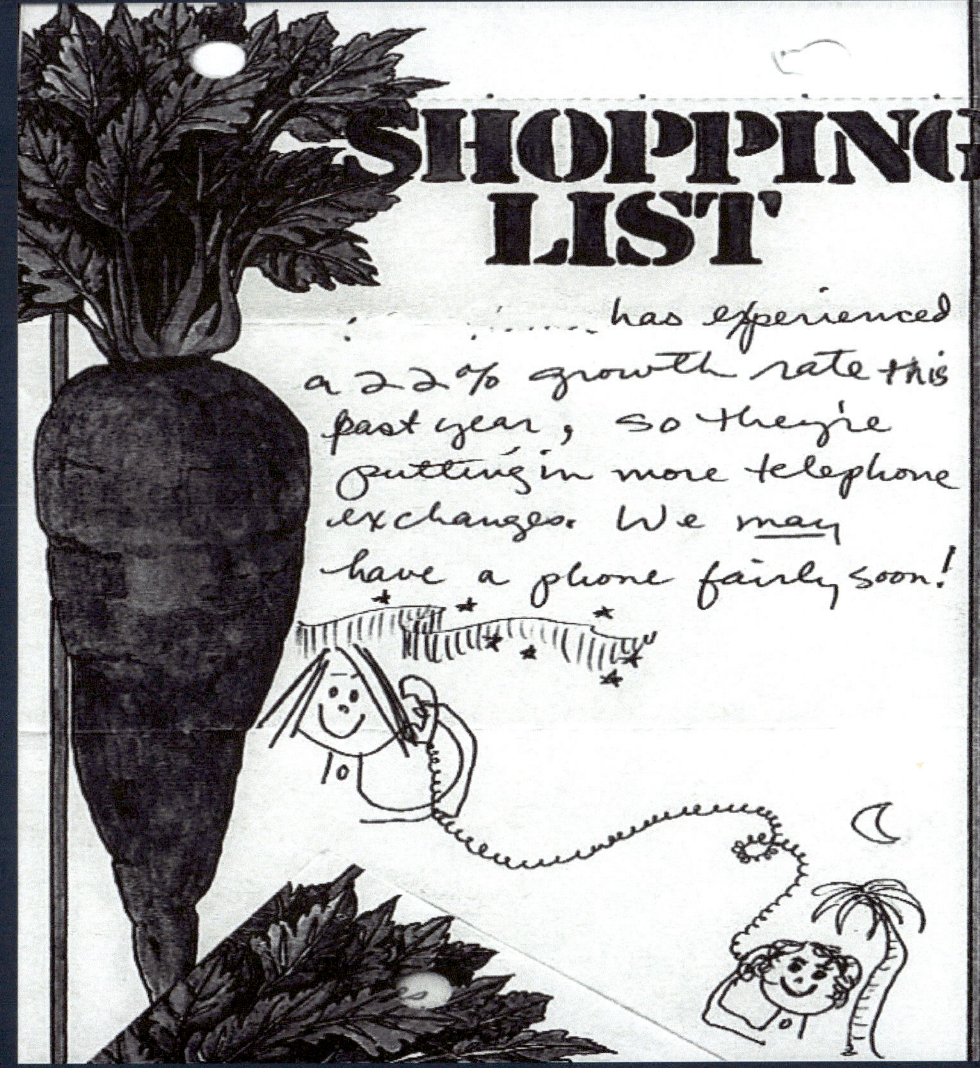

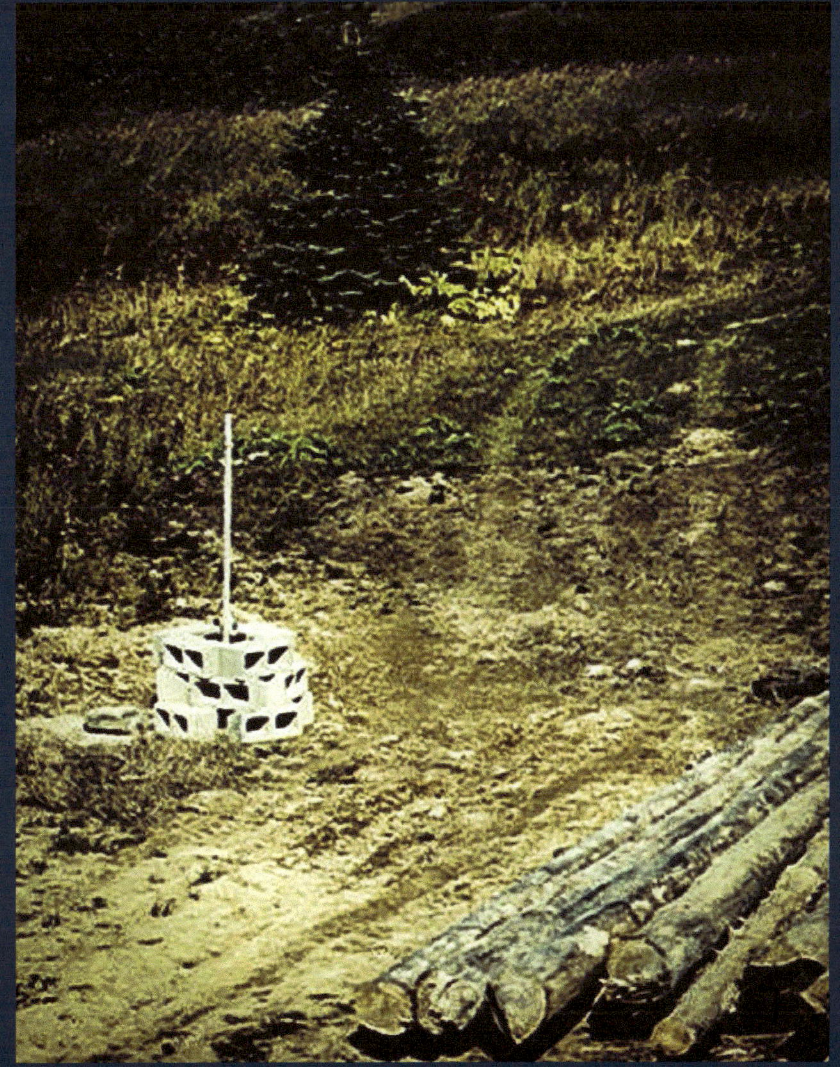

Finally, we got a phone. And soon after that, a well.
Tim worked on the water project whenever he was home from the Slope.
One day he called out, "Kate, turn on the hot water faucet."
I did as the man under the sink had asked.
. . . Ta-da!
Clearly, I had married a *very* handy man.

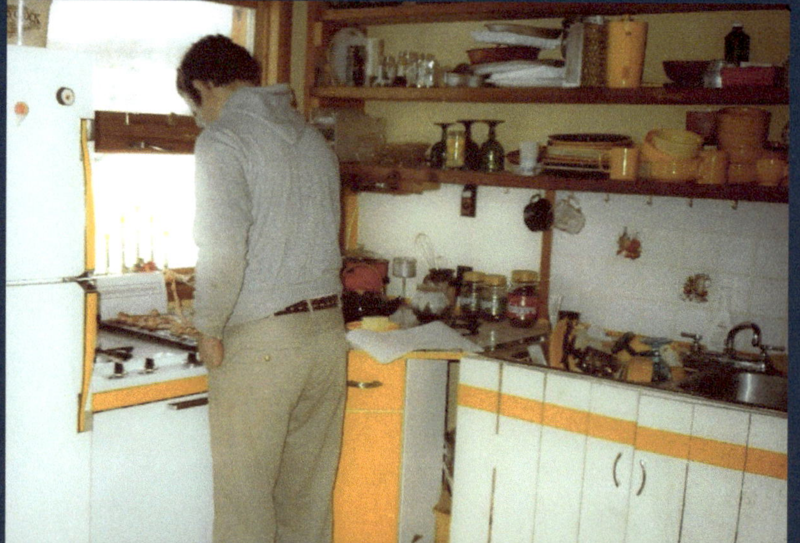
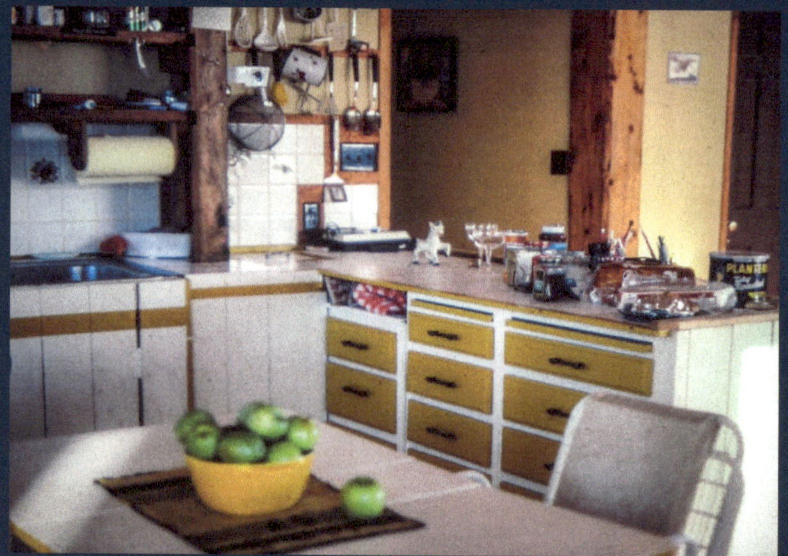

Now, with water running freely to and fro, the new kitchen functioned fully.

—1983—

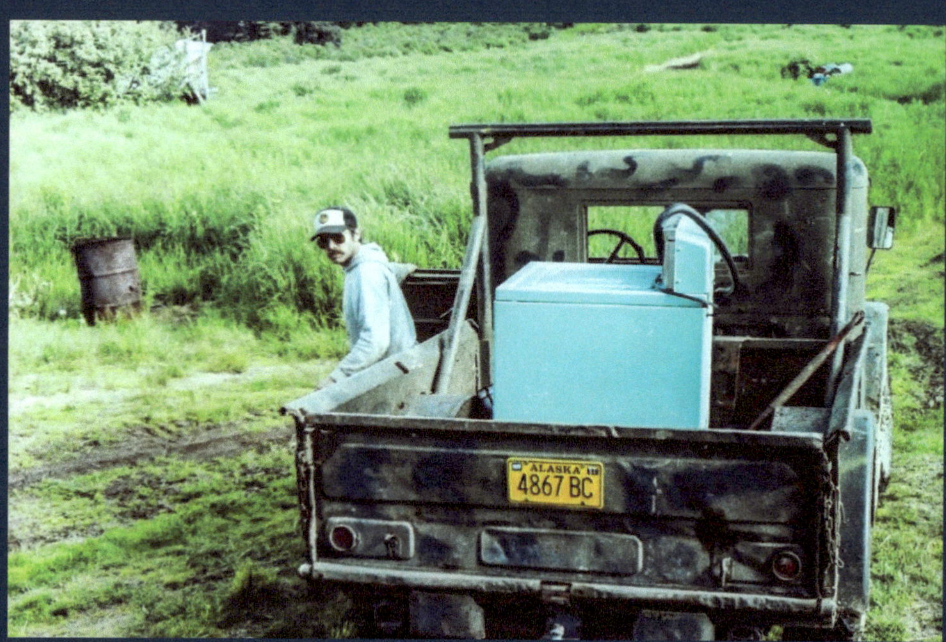
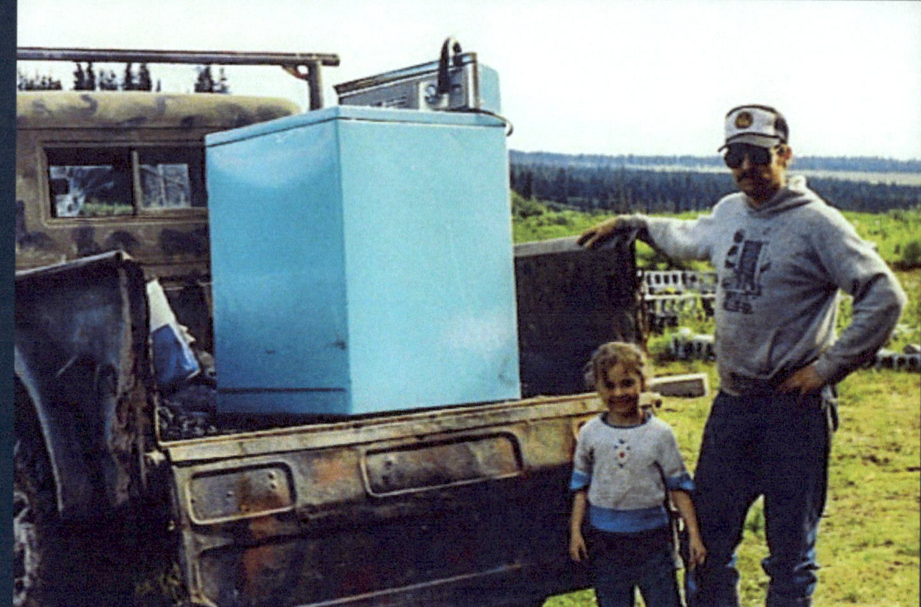

One day a washer arrived. "I picked blue for you, Momma."

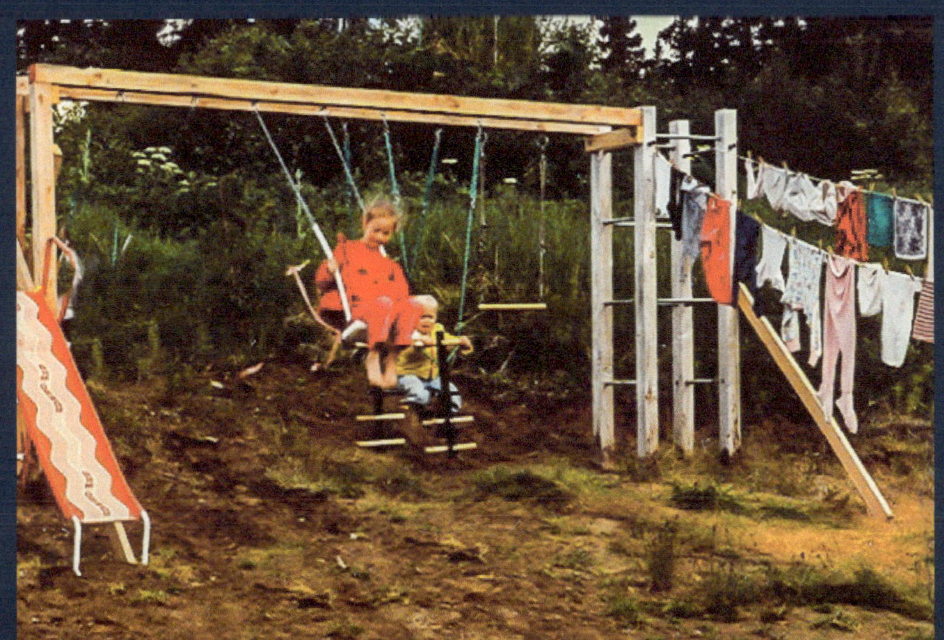

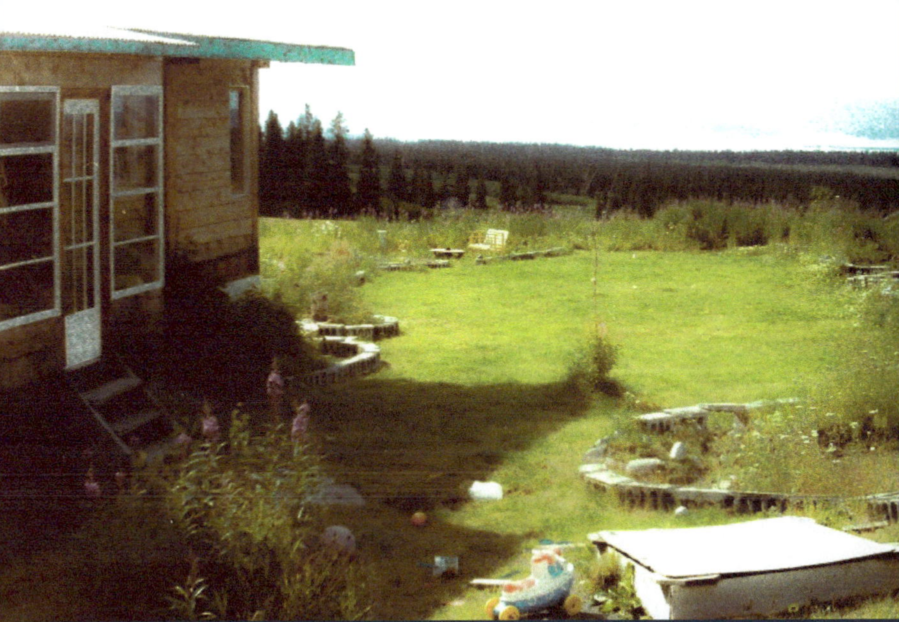

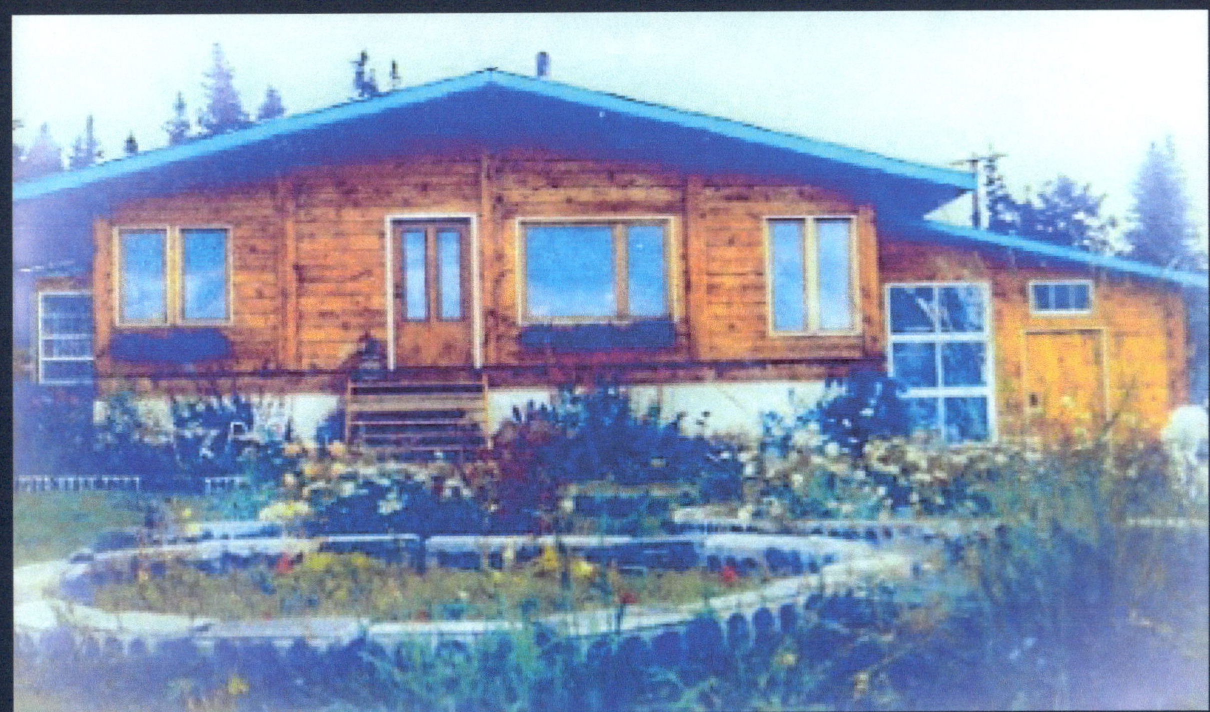

We were nearly to Camelot.

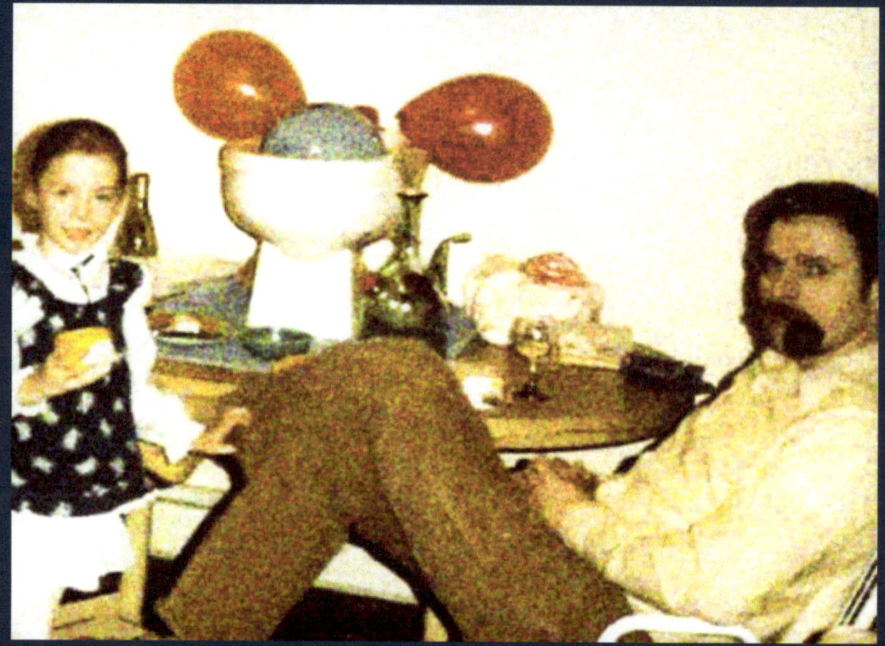

I received the best birthday present, ever!

"Go, toilet on the mountain!"
(Less than a year and a half later, we were celebrating the first flush.)

That summer I created an art deco masterpiece,
working through those quiet hours of long summer daylight while the children slept.

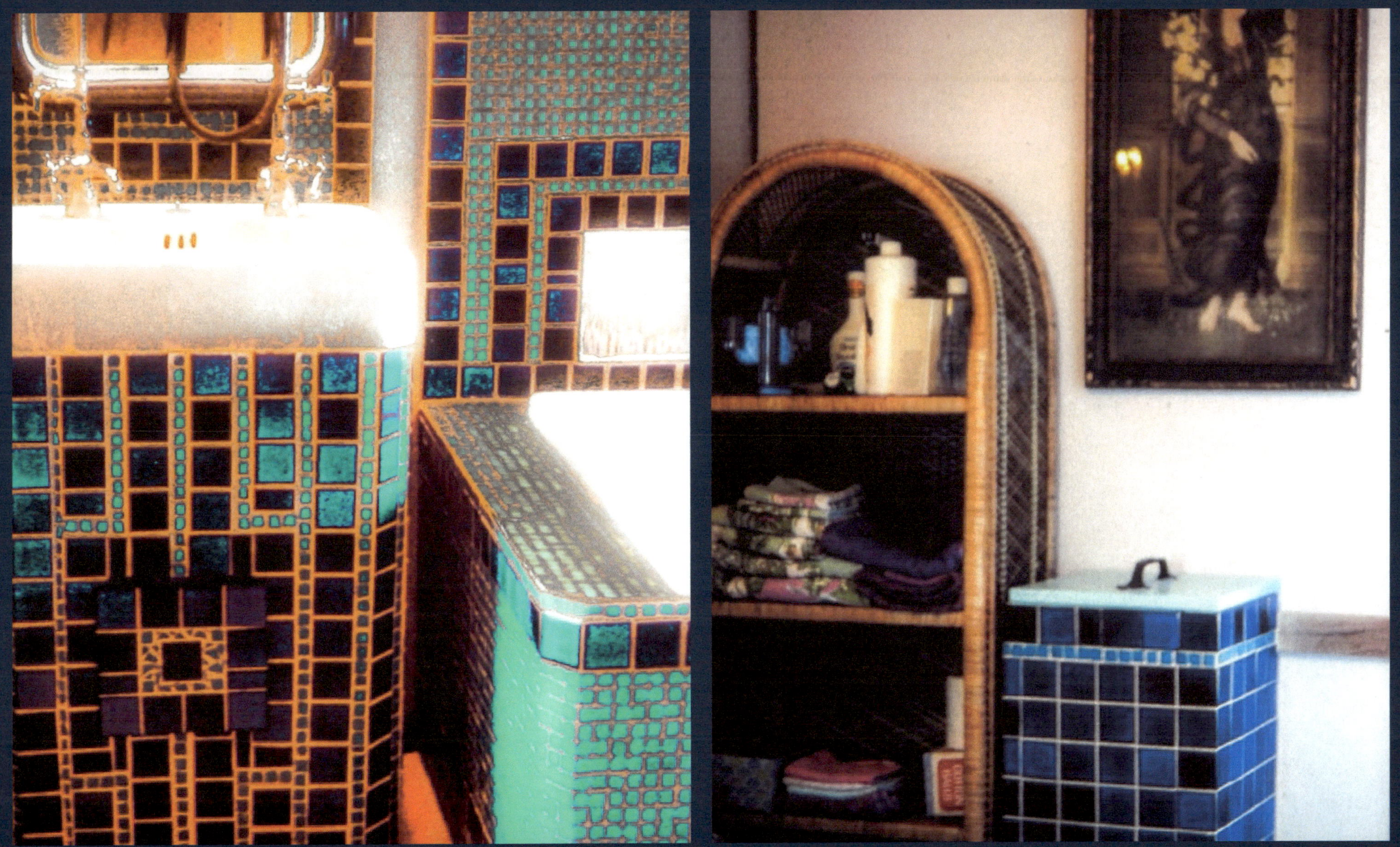

"My Shrine of Running Water."

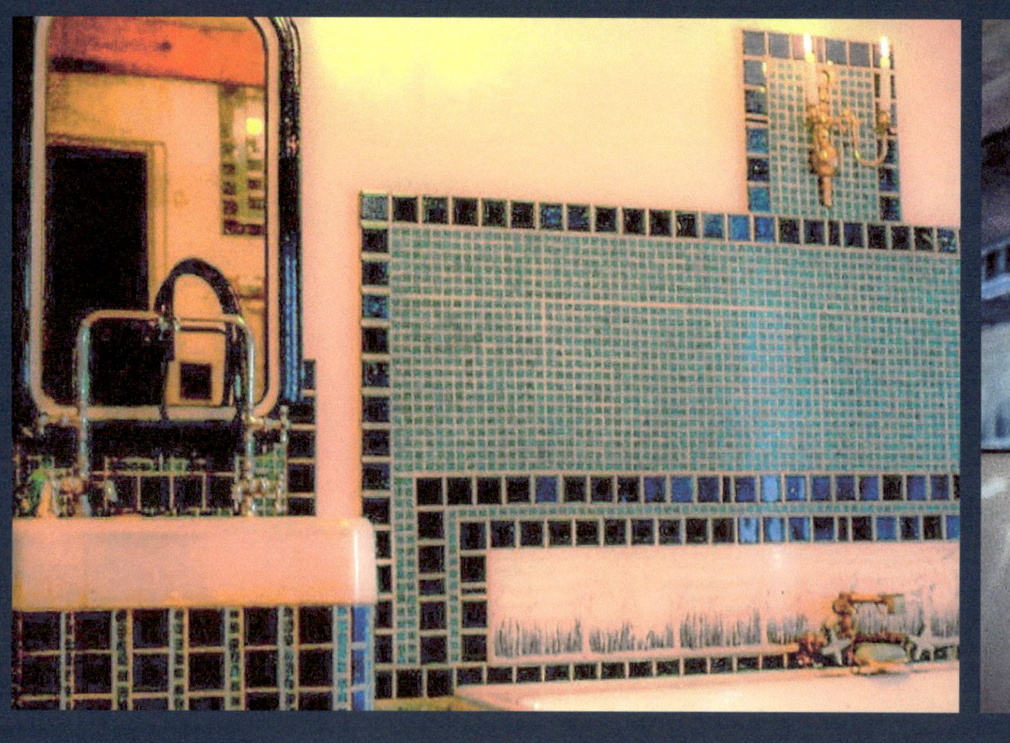
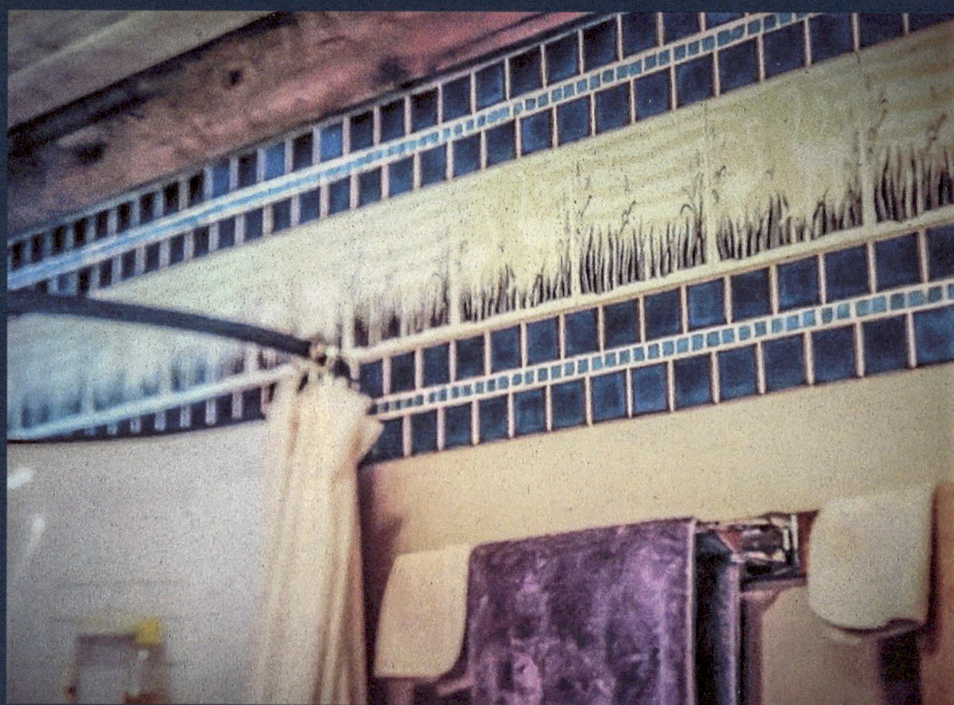

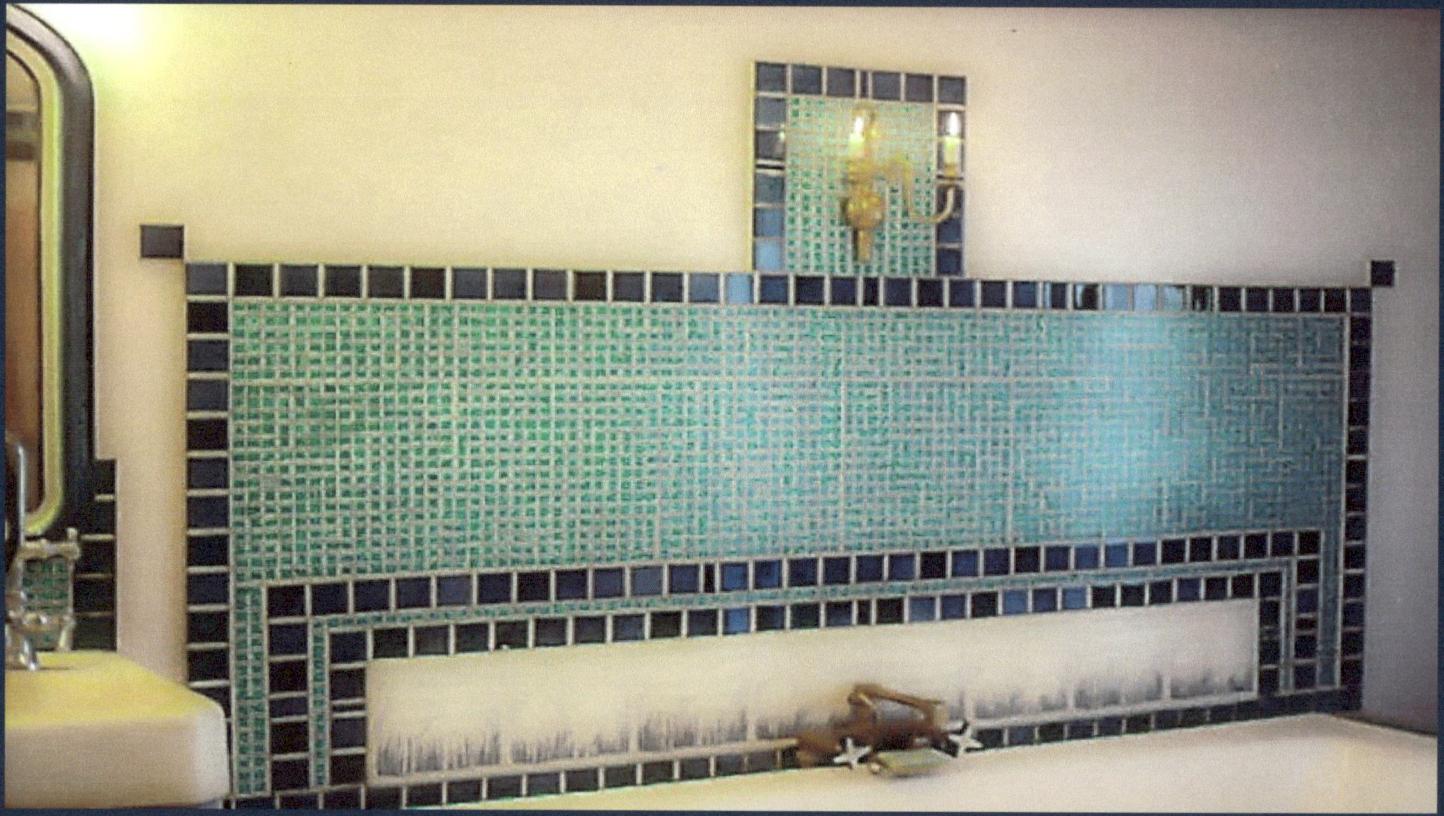

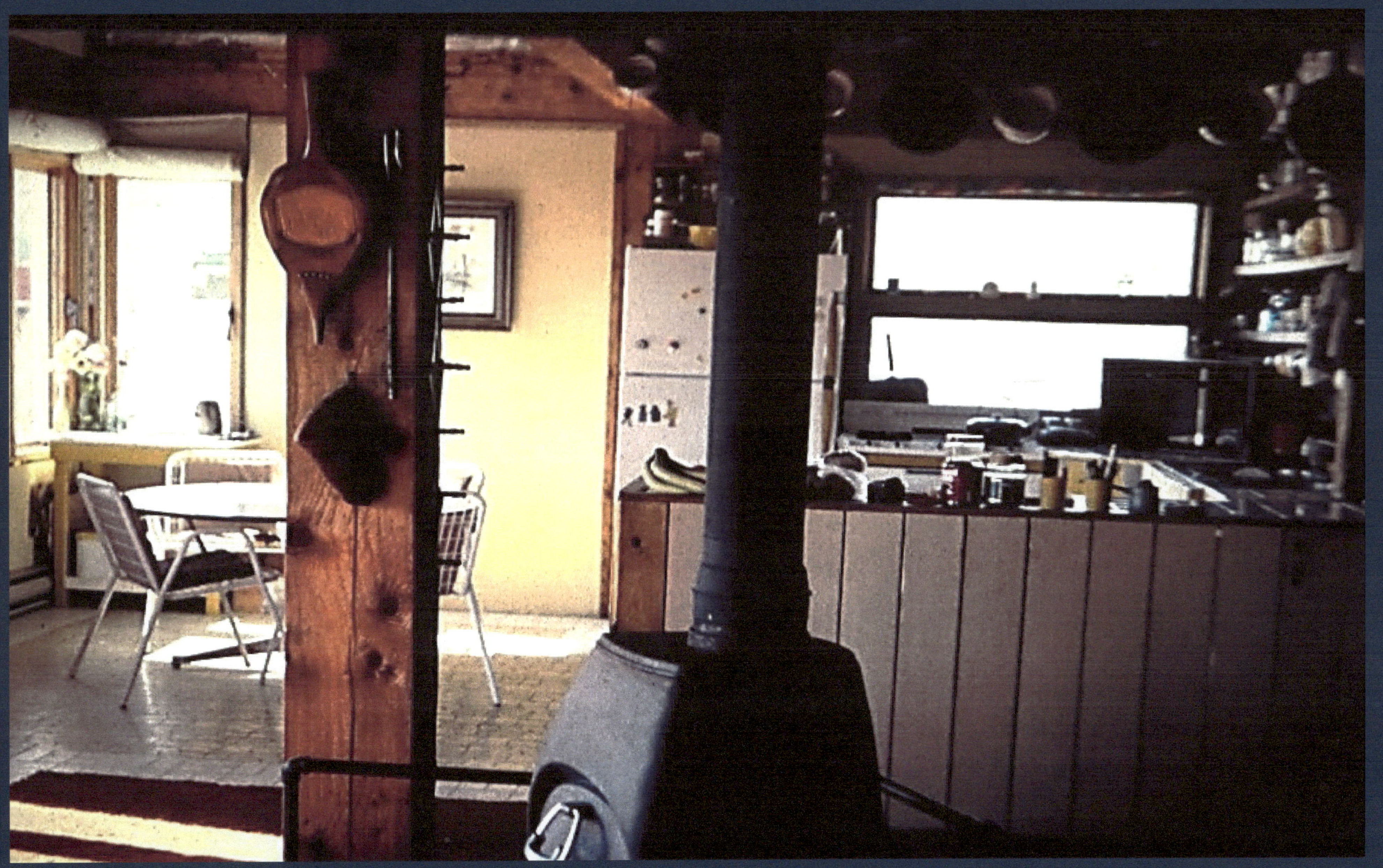

Et, voilà!

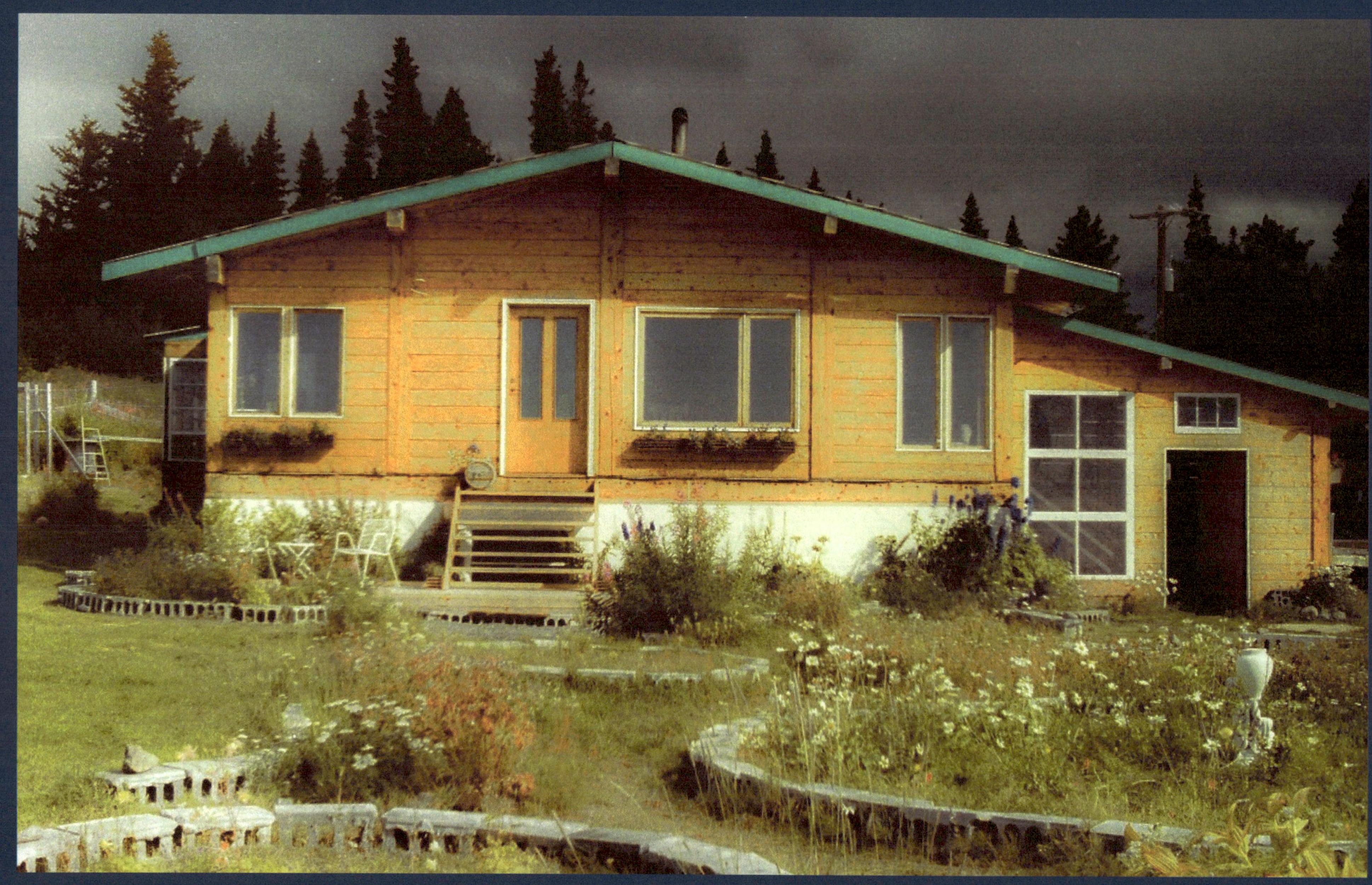

After a mere **decade**, our beautiful dream had blossomed into reality.

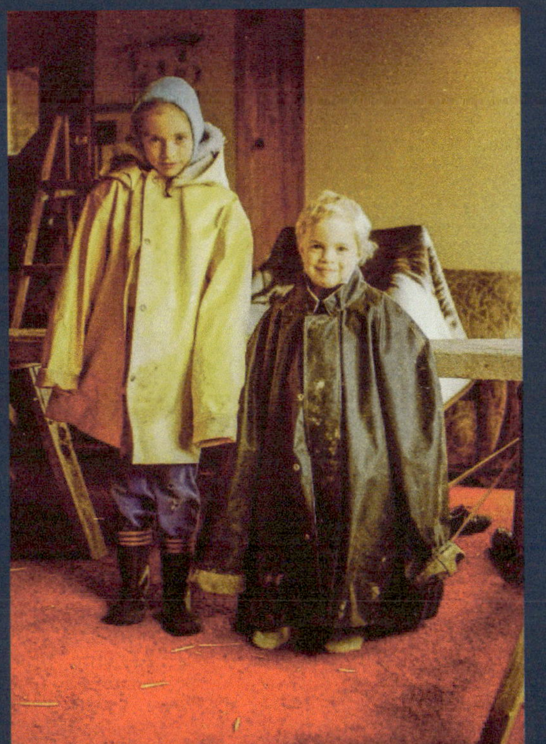 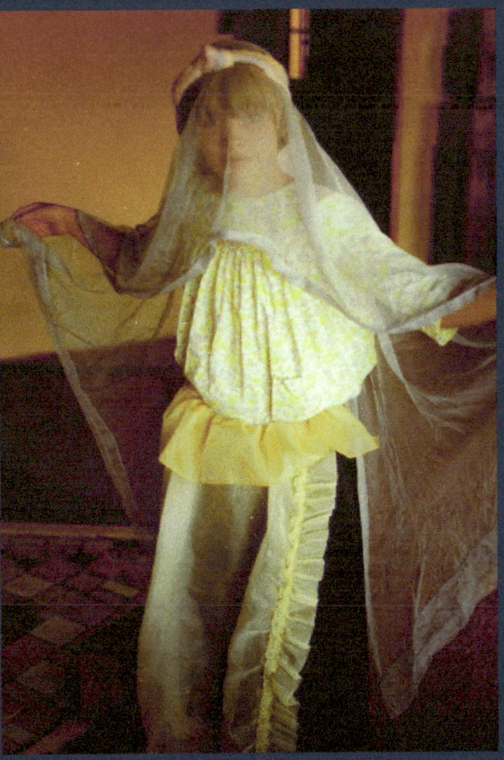

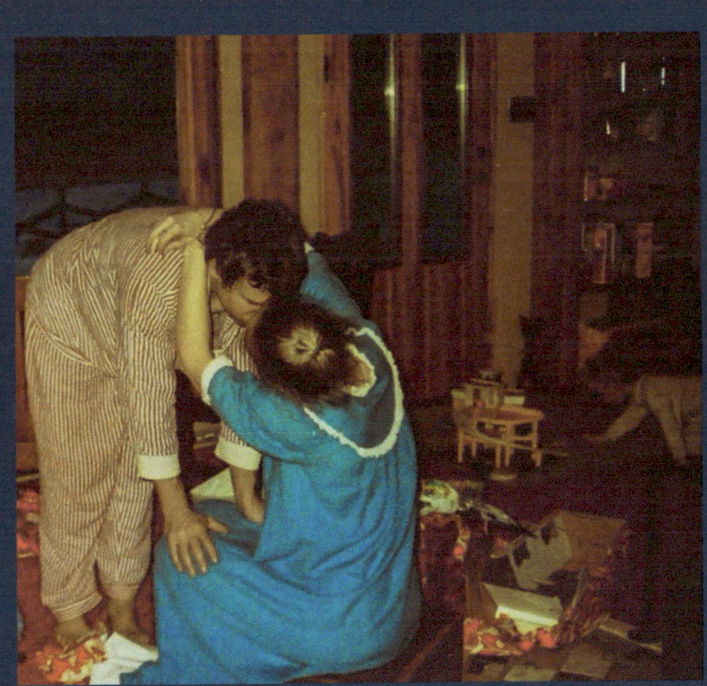

The End.

www.ingramcontent.com/pod-product-compliance
Lightning Source LLC
Chambersburg PA
CBHW042028050726

47599CB00005B/832